D0416209

ORIGINS OF MODERNITY

Social and Political Theory from Polity Press

Barry Barnes, *The Nature of Power*
Zygmunt Bauman, *Max Weber and the Theory of Modern Politics*
Richard Bellamy, *Modern Italian Social Theory*
Seyla Benhabib and Drucilla Cornell, eds, *Feminism as Critique*
Richard Bernstein, ed., *Habermas and Modernity*
Norberto Bobbio, *The Future of Democracy*
Norberto Bobbio, *Which Socialism?*
Raymond Boudon, *Theories of Social Change*
Pierre Bourdieu, *Homo Academicus*
John Burnheim, *Is Democracy Possible?*
Alex Callinicos, *Making History*
Antonio Cassese, *Violence and Law in the Modern Age*
Bob Connell, *Gender and Power*
Robert A. Dahl, *A Preface to Economic Democracy*
Brian Fay, *Critical Social Science*
Ferenc Fehér and Agnes Heller, *Eastern Left, Western Left*
David Frisby, *Fragments of Modernity*
Harold Garfinkel, *Studies in Ethnomethodology*
Anthony Giddens, *The Constitution of Society*
Anthony Giddens, *The Nation-State and Violence*
Anthony Giddens and Jonathan Turner, eds, *Social Theory Today*
Jürgen Habermas, *The Philosophical Discourse of Modernity*
Jürgen Habermas, *The Theory of Communicative Action*, vols 1 and 2
W. F. Haug, *Critique of Commodity Aesthetics*
Susan Hekman, *Hermeneutics and the Sociology of Knowledge*
David Held, *Models of Democracy*
John Heritage, *Garfinkel and Ethnomethodology*
J. N. Isbister, *Freud: An Introduction to his Life and Work*
Martin Jay, *Marxism and Totality*
Hans Joas, *G. H. Mead: A Contemporary Re-examination of his Thought*
Scott Lash and John Urry, *The End of Organized Capitalism*
Claude Lefort, *Democracy and Political Theory*
Claude Lefort, *The Political Forms of Modern Society*
Thomas McCarthy, *The Critical Theory of Jürgen Habermas*
Claus Offe, *Disorganized Capitalism*
Carole Pateman, *The Problem of Political Obligation*
Carole Pateman, *The Sexual Contract*
Mark Poster, *Foucault, Marxism and History*
Mark Poster, ed., *Jean Baudrillard: Selected Writings*
Shawn W. Rosenberg, *Reason, Ideology and Politics*
Barbara Sichtermann, *Femininity: the Politics of the Personal*
John B. Thompson, *Studies in the Theory of Ideology*
James Tully, ed., *Meaning and Context: Quentin Skinner and his Critics*
Jonathan Turner, *The Structure of Social Interaction*
Sylvia Walby, *Patriarchy at Work*
Georgia Warnke, *Gadamer*

JOHN F RUNDELL

Origins of Modernity

The Origins of Modern Social Theory
From Kant to Hegel to Marx

Polity Press

Copyright © John F. Rundell, 1987

First published 1987 by Polity Press in association with Basil Blackwell
Reprinted 1989

Editorial office:
Polity Press, Dales Brewery, Gwydir Street,
Cambridge CB1 2LJ, UK

Marketing and production:
Basil Blackwell Ltd
108 Cowley Road, Oxford OX4 1JF, UK

British Library Cataloguing in Publication Data
Rundell, John F.
  Origins of modernity : classical
  German philosophy and the origins of
  modern social theory.
  1. Sociology—History   2. Philosophy, German
  I. Title
  301'.01   HM26
ISBN 0 7456 0346 7
ISBN 0 7456 0703 9 (pbk)

Typeset in 11 on 12pt Garamond
by DMB (Typesetting), Oxford
Printed in Great Britain by
TJ Press Padstow

Contents

Acknowledgements

This book is a shortened and in part rewritten version of my Ph.D. Thesis 'Reason, Labour and Capital : an anthropological critique of Hegel's and Marx's constructions of a social theory of, and for, the modern epoch'. I would like to thank the following people who contributed much to the interpretation and ideas developed in this work: my Ph.D. supervisor Johann Arnason, for his discussion and critical comments, encouragement and patience; Agnes Heller and Ferenc Fehér, for their discussion, commentary and support; my friends and colleagues associated with the journal *Thesis Eleven*, in particular Paul Harrison, Julian Triado and Peter Beilharz, who all read sections of the work. I also thank Suzanne Fairbanks for being my most trenchant critic and ardent friend. I also warmly and gratefully thank Karen Burrows, the secretarial staff of the Anthropology and Sociology Department, Monash University and especially my Ph.D. typist Gai Dunn, for their help in the final preparation of this manuscript.

The author and publishers are grateful to Penguin Books Ltd, Harmondsworth, and Random House, Inc., for permission to quote from the following:

Karl Marx, *Early Writings*, introduced by Lucio Colletti, translated by Rodney Livingstone and Gregor Benton (Pelican Marx Library, 1975), selection copyright © New Left Review, 1974, translation copyright © Rodney Livingstone and Gregor Benton, 1974;

Karl Marx, *Grundrisse*, translated by Martin Nicolaus (Pelican Marx Library, 1973), translation copyright © Martin Nicolaus, 1973;

Karl Marx, *Surveys from Exile*, edited and introduced by David Fernbach (Pelican Marx Library, 1973), selection copyright © New Left Review, 1973, translation copyright © Ben Fowkes and Paul Jackson, 1973;

Karl Marx, *Capital Volume 1*, introduced by Ernest Mandel, translated by Ben Fowkes (Pelican Marx Library, 1976), edition copyright © New Left Review, 1976, translation copyright © Ben Fowkes, 1976.

Introduction

This book is an essay in the decomposition of manifest forms of theorizing in the works of Kant, Hegel and in particular Marx. It is also a thematization of their latent and lingering insights concerning the self-constitution of modernity; insights that were either constrained by the formal nature of their theories, remained visible and explicit despite it, or were circumvented and suppressed. In this sense, the work is not a series of intellectual biographies or a genealogy of basic, and at times competing, concepts. It is different from these types of approaches because the work both reconstructs and deconstructs Kant's, Hegel's and Marx's work not only from within the structure of their own theorizing, but also from the vantage point of the cultural self-understanding of the modern epoch. Each takes the modern epoch as his vantage point, his critical object and weaves its preoccupations into his internal philosophical and theoretical-investigations and constructions. Because of this we are able to establish similarities and differences between and within each of these writers. Kant and Hegel are, however, located on the periphery of this work. They are preliminary, yet important and constituting stages for our analysis of Marx's radicalization and departure from their formulations. Kant and Hegel, as well as the problematic of modernity, are approached to illuminate our major task – to uncover in Marx's *oeuvre* the patterns of continuity and congruence, discontinuity and dissonance which result in both totalizing one-sidedness and a suppression of insights.

Our approach, as outlined already, suggests that modernity is not merely a historical and geographical entity or object that provides a historicistically conceived backdrop to a history of ideas. Rather, it is constitutive of social relations in a double sense. On the one hand, the category of modernity refers to the historically specific series of complex social forms and institutions that social actors themselves create and inhabit; on the other it is simultaneously a practicointerpretative nexus through which these social forms themselves are constituted. In other words, the first conceptualization of modernity is irrevocably linked to a second, the paradigms of the human condition. These paradigms address the nature of human or social action and develop through the Enlightenment's specific reformulations of rationality and freedom. They presuppose that human beings act freely and rationally in any of the differentiated spheres that constitute the institutional terrain of modern life. This is the double dialectic of this work – theorizing/formulating modernity belongs as much to modernity's self-constitution as do the historical actions of classes, groups and institutions.

In this work, therefore, Kant, Hegel and Marx are approached through a series of conceptions concerning the nature and constitution of modernity and the human condition, or more specifically, formulations concerning philosophical anthropology. These approaches draw from, and have a bearing on, their recasting in contemporary social theory. Given this multilayered approach it is appropriate to outline briefly the nature of each layer in order to illuminate the path ahead.

Modernity can be conceptualized as a process of societal and cultural differentiation and pluralization propelled by and revolving around a series of developmental logics or dynamics which may be located within each of the differentiating spheres. These developmental logics or dynamics include the general capitalization of social life; industrialization; the autonomization of art; and democratization or the debates and conflicts concerning the sovereignty of civil society and persons as autonomous beings. This last logic, associated with the emergence of the public sphere, interacts and clashes with the developmental logic of the state and its tendency to absorb society. Kant, Hegel and Marx see modernity in this light and address it as a problematic. Moreover, this formulation of modernity connects them to contemporary approaches, in particular those of Cornelius Castoriadis, The Budapest School and Jürgen Habermas.[1] All of these contemporary writers, in their own ways, view modernity as a field of multiple tensions between combinations of these logics rather than seeing one logic as coextensive with modernity. Either together or separately these logics create crises and tensions between and among societal differentiation and societal integration. This may not only result in a pluralization but also in a privileging of one logic against others and a tendency towards systemic or societal reunification and totalization.

This first conceptualization of modernity is linked to the more general, but no less important, problem of philosophical anthropology, that is the way in which humankind is interpreted and conceptualized. Often imbedded only implicitly in formal theoretical structures, philosophical anthropology can either spill over to problematicize the formal structures, or can be absorbed and paralysed by them. In the context of a broad intellectual and cultural current that encompasses the Renaissance, the Reformation and their inheritor or successor the Enlightenment, philosophical anthropology is recast to mean the modern relation of the human subject to his or her own world. It establishes humankind – as both a genus and a composite of social actors, although the position of women remained a latent feature – as fundamentally autonomous, and can be seen, as Taylor notes, to constitute a fundamental shift in the core problematic of human self-definition: 'The modern subject is self-defining, where on previous views the subject is defined in relation to the cosmic order'.[2] This problematic develops through the Enlightenment's specific reformulations of rationality and freedom and presupposes that human beings act freely and rationally in any of the differentiated spheres.

Up to and including Hegel the notion of the self-defining subject is developed through the category of reason which orientates the investigation and reconstruction of the world according to the principals or processes of subjectification and objectification. The former refers to humankind's self-declared patterns and structures of meaning, whilst the latter refers to humankind's finite process of observation and measurement through which the natural and empirical worlds are studied and objectified.[3]

There are two ways in which this double-sided nature of self-definition developed. Implicitly, and like the institutional or systemic development of modernity, it can be argued that the anthropological one also followed a pattern of differentiation according to three images: *homo cogitans*, *homo politicus* and *homo economicus*. Each is apparently confined to its own object domain: epistemology and the reconceptualization of the foundations of knowledge; civil society and debates and conflicts concerning the sovereignty of the state; the sphere of needs and the restructuring of the nature of work. Moreover, these anthropological images themselves can be seen to become the not uncontested expressions of the logics themselves; a homology develops between the developmental dynamics of modernity and the anthropologically located principles through which the spheres could be structured. In other words, under the auspices of the self-defining subject the epistemological and cognitive reorientation of humankind is tied to industrialization; capitalization is seen to be expressive of *homo economicus* and *homo politicus* expressed through democratization.

This structuring of homologies, however, is also matched by another development of the problematic of the self-defining subject – the investigation of the principles from which humankind is to express and articulate itself. It is in this context specifically that Kant, Hegel and Marx are crucial. By simultaneously drawing on, stepping outside and abstracting from the three images, they problematize, systematize and radicalize the notion of self-definition and its processes of subjectification and objectification on either transcendental, ontological or anthropological grounds, respectively. Moreover, this systematization and radicalization goes hand in hand with their critiques of modernity, in particular its formulation of reason as an implicit philosophical anthropology. The Enlightenment *philosophes* had, in fact, rendered the notion of reason crisis ridden. Through their interrogation, use and expansion of the two-fold formulation of reason they extended the conception of objectivity to the world of humankind itself. Humankind and its anthropological images and spheres of action fell more and more under the jurisdiction of the new regime of rational objectivity. The newly won freedom of the subject from externally imposed regimes of meaning was gradually eroded. The Enlightenment becomes increasingly a freedom to codify, to observe. In other words, in objectifying the domain of nature, it also problematizes the domain of society, but in a negative way. The objectifying practices of 'pure reason' construe the anthropological images, in instrumentalist terms, and thus construct models of society based on externalized principles and present no ethical guidelines for human life in a demagified world. This undermines an essential ingredient of the paradigm of the self-defining subject – freedom to act. This is the problem-complex that Kant, Hegel and Marx confront. Each in his own way addresses the problematic of the self-defining subject and its capacity for, and relation to, freedom. Their enquiries occur either at the level of a critique of institutions or processes or at the level of the formal investigation of the *notion* of freedom itself. For Kant and Hegel the notion of freedom is first problematicized and then constructed in either transcendental or ontological terms. Each of these formulations contains an implicit philosophical anthropology which Marx locates and reconstructs in order to both develop a systematic critical theory of modernity and recentre the self-defining subject in its own terms. We shall introduce each of these theorists in turn.

Without relinquishing the precious modern insight of the notion of self-definition, and sharing the assumption that an objectified reason presents no ethical guide-lines, Kant paradigmatically constructs two worlds of reason – the pure and the practical. The actor, no longer confined to an externally imposed order of meaning, confronts the natural and social worlds on his or her terms, but not from a position of either a rationalist or sceptical empiricism or a philosophy of virtue. The central notion of Kant's ethics – a moral freedom to act – is grounded transcendentally. Kant traces the free determination of the will back to two universal transcendental principles of human reason; one pertaining to the world of nature, the other to the world of the social.

The Kantian version of the social actor, having confronted the de-naturalized social world, discovers the domain of the 'other'. This is Kant's great achievement, for it not only reintroduces *homo politicus* as a central problematic, but does so under the auspices of the question of moral autonomy in the context of an intersubjectively formed society. Kant views moral autonomy as the core ethical claim of the Enlightenment which can only be fulfilled under conditions of civil society's sovereignty over the state, a sovereignty which is necessarily posited by a notion of a critical public sphere, which minimally em-bodies the free space available for all those who wish to learn to be political actors. This notion is grounded transcendentally and estab-lishes a three-tiered conception of civil society – as the sphere of needs, as the formal basis of sovereignty and as the realm of public discourse. In other words, Kant resolves the problematic of modern (self-defining) *homo politicus* by giving primacy to practical reason and thus the social against the theoretical. *Homo politicus* encompasses both dimensions of sovereignty and autonomy. Moreover, in resolving the problematic in this way, Kant locates practical reason publicly. According to Kant, practical reason exists simultaneously in a publicly created and orientated republican constitution, and in a public sphere that is driven by a notion of critical judgement which belongs to and can be initiated by all social actors. While this dual formulation of public and critical judgement is an important background to Hegel's and Marx's social/theoretical formulations, it is circumvented and undermined by them.

Despite Kant's own transcendental formulations he is seen – at least by Hegel – to sit too close to the current of Enlightenment ration-alism. As far as Hegel is concerned Kant's transcendentalism leaves the self-defining subject disembodied – a fate similar to that which it suffers at the hands of the Enlightenment *homo cogitans*. In accusing Kant of not overcoming the antinomy of the Enlightenment but rather of reconstructing it at a higher level through the paradigmatic separa-tion of noumena and phenomena, Hegal draws on another current that criticizes the Enlightenment (termed by Taylor 'the expressivist current').[4] It is to this that we turn briefly to enable us to grasp Hegel's (and Marx's) reformulations of the Enlightenment – reformulations that centre the notion of the self-defining subject and its various images within specific anthropological determinants.

The central notion of the expressivist current that develops out of the German response to the Enlightenment, is that human life and activity are a realization by the subject of an intrinsic potential. The current involves two lines of thought; on the one hand, that in realizing itself, the human form necessarily imposes or strives to maintain and realize an inner force or inner shape on or against an external reality. On the other hand, this inner-propelled realization and imposition 'clarifies or makes determinate what that form is'.[5] Through both self-realization and self-clarification the subject gains the autonomy which was thwarted by an objectifying rationalism. Under the so-called expressivist interpretation of autonomy, the subject's freedom is only made fully determinate in being fulfilled. The anthropological image of self-definition under expressivism posits, as Taylor points out, that 'at his fullest man is realized not only as life but also as a being capable of expressive activity and therefore of achieving self-clarity and freedom'.[6]

A further interesting aspect of the notion of expressivism is its emphasis on language as a determining feature of humankind's self-defining capacity. Through this interest in the self-realization of the subject, expressivism originates and develops a current that not only implicitly unifies at least two of the images of humankind that emerge in the modern epoch, but also achieves this from neither an objectifying nor transcendental perspective. Rather, the implicit unification is brought about through language. Language is the basic determination of human autonomy and freedom. In this context, *homo cogitans* and *homo politicus* now have an anthropologically determining source or focus. Moreover, this source (language) does not present them as isolated, objectivistically construed atoms. Following Kant's 'discovery', these two images of the self-defining subject require other subjects through which to be fully constituted and realized. In other words, expressivism can be read as connecting up two images of the human condition to a notion of a self-actualizing and inter-subjectively constituted anthropological determinant. The expressivist formulation of self-actualization and self-clarification sets the scene, so to speak, for Hegel's and Marx's significant, if not unproblematic, transformations of the theoretico-philosophical terrain of the modern epoch.

Hegel's philosophical enquiries concerning the nature of reason depart explicitly from the expressivist current. From this perspective he is able to charge Kant with separating the self-defining subject from the structures of reason that are transcendentally given to it. In the context of our interpretation (as well as Hegel's work as a whole) it is Hegel's relation to Kant which is most important. In Hegel's view, Kant cannot, from within his transcendental philosophy, resolve the problem of *how* the actor is to act in accord with the principle of autonomy, that is, in accord with the universality of freedom, when she or he is driven by many inclinations. For Hegel, Kant's formulation ultimately lacks both philosophical and institutional foundation. It cannot address the question which is the central one in Hegel's mind: how does the self-defining subject live a total life of freedom? This is the question from which Hegel's philosophical enterprises depart, and to which they constantly return.

In order to answer this question Hegel both joins the expressivist and Kantian premisses together – the subject embodies reason and through activity actualizes and clarifies it – and systematically introduces and problematizes the notion of society. The notion of society enables Hegel to argue that the subject/reason actualizes itself as a totality in all spheres of life. The self-defining subject is conceived of not only in generic/active terms but also in terms of objectified social structures and configurations. The self-defining subject constitutes the centralization and self-clarification of freedom and autonomy simultaneously through the use of reason and in the objective domains in which human needs are met and political institutions formed. In this context Hegel integrates all three images with which the self-defining subject was introduced. They are no longer disparate or isolated but form a complete whole through which the actor works, engages in politics and thinks.

The so-called dialectical relation between reason, subject and society generates a particular problem throughout Hegel's work: does the self-defining subject comprise and constitute reason, or does reason comprise and constitute the self-defining subject?

This question goes to the heart of the particular interpretation of Hegel contained in this book, which, in turn, owes much to Taylor. Hegel's attempts to resolve the modern problematic of autonomy results in two competing formulations of his dialectical philosophy. The first requires the self-defining subject for the actualization of reason. The self-defining subject is portrayed as a self-objectivation that reflects upon itself through the social and cultural forms that it develops. This formulation is termed a historico-interpretative dialectic in which the norm of freedom is rooted in the anthropological determinants of politics, labour and language. It is these that give it expressivity. Hegel's other formulation systematically minimizes this implicit anthropology and more forcefully articulates reason as an ontology.

The ontological formulation of reason, or Hegel's ontological dialectic, subsumes each of the images of self-definition under its own principles. Humankind is part of reason, but does not itself exhaust the structure and framework of reason and its activity. This entails that the anthropological determinants are subsumed under reason's externalizing purpose. Each determinant is posited, by Hegel, as pertaining to a sphere of human life which ultimately leads to reason's self-consciousness. Reason is structured as a system into which each of the determinants is integrated. Analogously Hegel posits society in the same way. Civil society becomes the sphere of needs, the 'home' of *homo economicus*; the state, the 'home' of *homo politicus*. Together, they constitute the domain of Objective Spirit. The result (at least at the level of social structures) is the corporatization of the relation between state and civil society, thus annihilating the notion and possibility of the public sphere from within the structure of Hegel's ontologized theory. *Homo cogitans*, to be sure, resides in civil society and the state. But because *homo cogitans* is posited as the real embodiment of reason, its role is qualitatively transformed in two ways; one that points directly towards the centrality of language and the problematic of normativity in twentieth-century philosophy and social theory, while the second points back towards the Greek legacy and the notion of an ontological and rational priority of the (cosmic) world. On the first level, humankind as *homo cogitans* is capable of achieving full self-consciousness, not through politics or work as pure activity, but through language. On the second level though, *homo cogitans* does not exist in its own right as a self-defining subject. Through language, as well as the other determinants that are objectified as structures and configurations of humankind, *homo cogitans* is posited by Hegel only as a vehicle for reason's self-expression and self-clarification. Language is thus the most important determinant for Hegel, but in a specific way and for a specific purpose. It is the form that carries reason's self-reflexivity at its most actualized, and thus enables humankind to reflect on its relation to reason. This occurs in the realm of Absolute Spirit in which art, religion and philosophy provide the fullest and most complete externalized forms of self-actualization and self-clarification. These become, as an embodiment of a culture and only because they are the most adequate forms of reason's externalization, the constitutors and mediators of the human world. Through them, all instances of life are actualized, reflected upon and incorporated into a world made according to the principles of reason. The human world is totalized.

This long preamble now brings us to the heart of our interpretative enterprise – the reconstruction of Marx's work. Marx radically converts the more or less explicit yet systematically minimized anthropology of his predecessors. He not only recentres the self-defining subject, but does so in a manner that (purportedly) gives to it a full capacity for self-formation and self-activity.

Marx's basic objection to Hegel concerns the ontological primacy which is given to reason. As far as Marx is concerned Hegel revokes the relative primacies of intersubjectivity and practical reason in the name of self-positing spirit. Hegel places reason, that is humankind, beyond humankind itself, beyond the Enlightenment's claims to freedom and rationality.

Marx, though, does not undertake his critique of Hegel empty-handed. On the one hand, he relies on both Kantian and Hegelian preoccupations, problematics and formulations – the idea of the good, the nature of civil sovereignty and civil society, the grounding of practical reason in either transcendental or ontological terms. Marx also absorbs the objective institutional structure of Hegel's formulation of *Sittlichkeit* and in so doing removes from critical reflection not only the structure of Objective Spirit, but also the possibility that his own interpretation of freedom and rationality unreflectively absorbs echoes of Kantian transcendentalism and Hegelian ontological immanentism. On the other hand, Marx develops a series of critiques and critical theories that address both the shortcomings of these problem-complexes and new social forms of domination.[7] Initially his critiques are propelled by a defence of the category of freedom in analysing the systemic constraints against it. Subsequently they move to ones in which there is a materialist reworking of Hegel's implicit anthropology, one that emphasizes and privileges the category of labour. This pinpoints one of his departures from Hegel; however, it also provides a point of congruence. This suggests that the anthropological legacy implicit in the universalistic philosophies of Kant and Hegel is not solved unproblematically for Marx. In this light, the periods of his critical theory from the 1844 *Manuscripts* to *Capital* represent not only disjunctures and ruptures, but also a continuous project of definition and redefinition within the notion of labour itself. The notion of labour is the ground from which Marx radicalizes the Enlightenment's notion of self-activity and self-definition. Through labour he raises this as an explicit and generalizable claim: humankind makes its own history and society.[8] It is this claim, developed also into a series of theses, that lies at the heart of Marx's theoretical formulations and critiques of the modern world, and through which he reinterprets and transforms the problem of freedom from one dealing with 'civil sovereignty' to one concerning the 'free autonomy of the (labouring) subject'. This is done not un-problematically, though, and prompts one to ask: which Marx?

WHICH MARX?

Our lengthy and quite detailed interpretation of Marx's work proceeds from two basic and apparently opposed assumptions. Firstly, that the anthropological claim that he raises remains both a formative *and* structuring principle throughout his entire work. Because of this continuity, and its Kantian and Hegelian ancestry, an 'epistemological break' does not occur. Yet secondly, and in spite of this continuity, Marx's work can be described as containing competing approaches and paradigms. Marx approaches and constructs his critiques and critical theories through two problem-complexes which inform the whole of his work – class conflict and social production. Both become constant pivots for a materialist grounding and radicalization of the Enlightenment's implied anthropology. It should be pointed out even preliminarily that these two pivotal problem-complexes stand as separate and at times competing and mutually obstructing elements in Marx's theorizing.

Of course the competing approaches and paradigms tend to indicate an internal and at times assumed mutually excluding series of episodes within Marx's work, but this is not the aspect that is important or emphasized here. Rather the theoretical shifts and episodes that occur should be seen in the light of differing formulations of a *constant* project which permeates and constitutes all of Marx's works. Imbedded in the critical enterprises themselves are heterogeneous and alternative formulations which denote, as Markus argues, four basic concerns which revolve around the two core problem-complexes through which Marx's anthropological claim 'lives'.[9] The first of these concerns of critique, because of its practical component, is the identification of an empirical – practical addressee – the working class. The theory raises different arguments concerning the working class's revolutionary role and the alternative socio-political strategies which it can use to enact this role. This is related to the second and third concerns; the definition of the goal of emancipation which is formulated in terms of a future socialist society in response to the critique of capitalism, and the identification of the mechanisms of the self-transcendence of capitalism. The fourth concern (and certainly for our purposes the most crucial because it both draws in and subsumes the second and the third) is the method of the theory construction.

These concerns enable one to look at the themes through which Marx addresses his two problem complexes:

1   the historical specificity of capitalist society,
2   the evolutionary logics of societal development,

3   the logic of capital,
4   the philosophy of history,
5   the ethico-political dimension: the critique of civil society and
    formulations concerning the constitution of post-capitalist society,
6   the dynamics of class struggles.

Whilst the two problem-complexes or pivots remain constant, these
themes do not. Rather, they are varyingly combined within each of the
problem-complexes to present a particular strategy of critique that
can be identified as lying at the heart of each of Marx's critical
theories. Moreover, the combination of particular themes stabilizes
the problem-complexes into *competing* paradigms from 1845 onwards.
In contemporary sociological literature these two currents are presented
as functional or system theories, and action or power theories.[10] In
Marx, they develop into different conceptualizations and strategies for
the theoretical articulation of a general social theory. On the one hand,
the problem-complex of social production stabilizes into a *paradigm
of production* which gains theoretical articulation from *The German
Ideology* onwards and into which the base–superstructure model
nestles. On the other hand, the problem-complex of class conflict
stabilizes into a *paradigm of class action* which addresses the problematic of class relations or contestation[11] between historically constituted
classes. This paradigm is visible in Marx's historico-political writings of
the late 1840s and early 1850s and draws on a conception of freedom
that has elements of the Kantian notion of practical reason, in
particular the universalist and pedagogical conception of politics
which includes the central category of the public.
   This suggests, importantly, that the paradigm of class action draws
on normative and symbolic features of the human condition for explanatory force – features, it is argued, which are already located
within the Enlightenment's shift towards an anthropology of the self-
defining subject. These features are said to constitute Marx's 'hidden
imaginary' – a reading that suggests that the language of production
does not exhaust an interpretation of Marx's work. What we argue is a
competing, nascent current, not reducible to the categories of labour
and production but paralysed and suppressed by them, which implies
that self-activity presents both the praxistic (telic) and interpretative
dimensions of the human condition. It thus opens onto the problematic
of Hegel's hermeneutically centred historic-interpretative dialectic.
We view Marx's 'hidden imaginary' as an attempt to argue with Marx
against Marx in order to go beyond him possibly to structure another
analysis and critique of capitalism, and develop a philosophical
anthropology flexible enough to conceptualize the heterogeneous

forms and structures through which human beings constitute and typify themselves.

This marxological approach is not a desire to 'save' or 'return' to Marx through idiosyncratic twists and turns of 'The Text'. Rather our interpretation and reconstruction of Marx looks at his work in the light of the nascent and growing self-conscious anthropological turn in the early modern epoch and which points towards an incomplete, yet extensive and heterogeneous cultural modernity. This way of regarding Marx especially enables our interpretation to become an essay in the decomposition and relocation of Marx around the key anthropological problematic of self-definition. It is within this context that his competing paradigms and directions make sense. The critical theories from 1843 can be viewed as attempts by Marx to develop a materio-anthropological conception of freedom. This conception, though, ultimately leads to self-defeating results which immediately problematicize the anthropological basis of his notions of freedom and rationality – the concept of labour and the paradigm of production. These become, both for Marx and the Marxian traditions, the field of tensions and competing interpretations.

Moreover, this anthropologically centred interpretation of not only Marx, but also of Hegel and Kant links them implicitly to contemporary developments in the recasting of philosophical anthropology in social theory. Contemporary social theory shares a common ground that in part draws some insights from both the unfinished and latent aspects of Marx's theorizing in particular, notwithstanding its often intensely critical relation to his work, and the same underlying problematic with which he was concerned – the anthropological determinants of the self-defining subject. Although not all participants would put it in these terms the contemporary developments can be typified by the communication theory of Jürgen Habermas, Cornelius Castoriadis' notion of imaginary significations, Alain Touraine's theory of social movements and the paradigm of objectivation which stems from The Budapest School, in particular Agnes Heller. [12] Each in its own way denotes a turn in contemporary social theory towards viewing culture as a primary constituent in social reality, and the placing of theories of politics and power within this problem-complex. These projects constitute the implicit reference points for this work and the horizon beyond its immediate path.

In the light of the decomposed formal theoretical structures and suppressed insights of Marx in particular and of Kant and Hegel, the respective images and theories of society that emanate from these four contemporary theoretical enterprises can be transposed into three theses (thus also transposing the problematic of self-definition into contemporary socio-theoretic terms). These three theses not only address the dynamics of the socio-historical epoch of modernity that function according to differentiating, systematizing of totalizing logics and the dimensions of conflict through which a society is also constituted, but are also related to general theoretical formulations concerning interpretations of history. These theses are:

1 Society is not only a totality but also a series of power centres, each with its contestatory moments and strategies of societal totalisation.
2 Classes constitute themselves through an identity-forming process typified by a culture, that is, norms, values and a mode of life. These can be either contrasted to, or imposed upon, other classes.
3 Society is also constituted as a series of objectivations that are simultaneously institutional and cultural. The cultural component is cognitively structured and imbedded in linguistic and symbolic forms, and mediated and limited by practical relations with nature and other socially constructed societal reproductive (institutional) mechanisms. This culture carries the socio-historical function of a society's interpretation (or social imaginary) of the world as well as its historical function of communicative self-understanding.

Each of these theses implicitly sustains this work and guides our project of critique and reconstruction, not only of Marx, but also of Kant and Hegel. Through the perspective of these theses the anthropologies through which Kant, Hegel and Marx interpret reason or capital – centreing respectively on language or labour – are seen to be both too specific and not specific enough. Each anthropological determinant is too specific inasmuch as it subsumes the other moments of the human condition under it; and not specific enough inasmuch as it cannot address the complex configurations that constitute the nature and primacy of the social. Each thesis develops the modern paradigms of the human condition in specific ways – through either the socially configured paradigms of system and action, the normatively constituted notion of intersubjectivity, or the notion of culturally located processes of the interpretation of humankind, society and nature – that returns to and problematizes the anthropological constituents of what can be termed the self-defining subject in the works of Kant, Hegel and Marx. As its broadest level, then, this work is a contribution to an understanding of the development and determinants of the anthropology of modern subjectivity, from within attempts to define modern subjectivity in its own terms.

1

Civil Society as the Public: Kant's Conception of Modern Politics

THE ANTHROPOLOGICAL BASIS OF KANT'S CRITICAL PHILOSOPHY
PROGRESS AND KNOWLEDGE

Kant ends Rousseau's ambiguous notion of freedom, which is conceptually embedded in the general will, by making two distinctions. On the one hand, an anthropological distinction which separates culture from nature, thereby establishing culture as the domain of reason. On the other, the notion of reason itself is held distinct from the empirical world, that is, reason is transcendentally constituted and able to legislate to the empirical world. Moreover, Kant bifurcates reason. He does this in an effort to guard against an instrumentalization of all reality, that is to guard against a repetition of the expansion of objectified scientific and mathematical principles to all reality, including humankind, that characterized the Enlightenment. He establishes a categorical and unconditional separation between those principles of reason dealing with the affairs of nature and those dealing with the affairs of humankind. In other words, under the Kantian reformulation of the cognitive basis of freedom all human activity embodies the legislative capacity of reason; either dealing with humankind's technical utilization of nature, pertaining to the principles of theoretical reason, or the moral conduct of a society's citizenry, pertaining to the principles of practical reason.

There are, though, two immediate problems which Kant confronts in his reformulation of the cognitive basis of human action. On the one hand, even in spite of the bifurcation of reason, how is an unacceptable expansion and colonization of either sphere by the other to be avoided? In other words, while the transcendental separation of domains is immanently construed, how do the different regimes of reason know which object domain to investigate? On the other hand, how is humankind itself to be conceptualized if reason, the cognitive form of humankind, is transcendentally construed? These questions implicitly underly Kant's other revolution in thought which accompanies his transcendental investigation of the faculties that construe the world, that is his revolution in philosophical history.[1] This other Copernican Revolution helps to pinpoint a fundamental distinction within his critical philosophy; one which pertains to the principles of cognition as they are abstracted from the human condition, and the second which addresses the problem of theoretical, although in the main *practical*, reason from the viewpoint of their historico-cultural contextualization. It thus also opens onto the second problem that Kant confronts. We will turn to this first.

For Kant, humanity is not a species that exists in a state of permanent homeostasis. Rather, it is one that, because of an orientation towards reason, progresses gradually through many generations where it attains either a sufficient mastery over nature through the use of theoretical reason, or a social, cultural and political stability through the employment of an ethically constituted reason. In this context the questions, which Kant argues should precede the examination of knowledge,[2] are ultimately tied to another one: what is humankind? What are its constituting characteristics?[3] This is the theme that continually pervades Kant's work, and the one to which he will constantly return – sometimes explicitly, often implicitly – through the notions of progress and knowledge. Each is used by Kant to establish a confident narrative concerning humankind's own movement away from self-incurred tutelage and towards the use of the principles of reason. In this context Kant's famous definition of the Enlightenment not only joins his two 'Copernican Revolutions', but does so in a way that establishes a nexus between socio-historical contextualization and political ethics, and thus hints at the primacy of practical reason. For Kant:

> Enlightenment is man's release from the self-incurred tutelage. Tutelage is man's inability to make use of his understanding without direction from another. Self-incurred is this tutelage when its cause lies not in the lack of reason but in the lack of resolution and courage to use it without direction from another. *Sapere aude* 'Have courage to use your own reason!' – that is the motto of enlightenment.[4]

This formulation can be read in two ways: on the one hand, as a species-related notion that refers to humankind's propensity for progress, and on the other, as a notion that refers to the ethics of the political subject. Together they give rise to two interrelated possibilities – education and government. Anthropologically, they are instances of an immanently constituted reason and an active species-being.

The first way of reading this dictum pertains directly to Kant's philosophy of history, which can be interpreted as an evolutionary learning theory. Kant views the civilizing process as a phylogenetic orientation towards progress in a way that situates reason purely within the domain of culture and outside the considerations of a theory of nature (physiology), thereby circumventing arguments from empirical materialism. In this sense, the learning theory continues the Humean break with metaphysics but in a more active and rationalistic way than an empirical scepticism because it implies that the intellectualization of cognition is a prelude to a reflection about the world itself, the logic of which unfolds as a human universal. It is within the capacity of every-body to be reasonable. Kant states:

> Man accordingly was not guided by instinct, not nurtured and instruc-
> ted by ready-made knowledge; rather he should bring forth everything
> out of his own resources. Securing his own shelter, food and defense
> . . . all amusement which can make life pleasant, insight and intelli-
> gence, finally even goodness at heart – all this should be wholly his
> own work.[5]

Nature, then, provides nothing but the backdrop for the ordering of human existence. Humanity is entirely alone – society is the prerogative through which humans establish and maintain the universalizing demands of reason.[6]

The notion of a learning process becomes important precisely in this context of anthropological developments. Because 'reason does not work instinctively but requires trial and instruction in order to gradually progress from one level of insight to another'[7] the developmental process of enlightenment, for Kant, can only be a long-term process in which each generation builds on the knowledge and experience of the previous one. Moreover, the end of history becomes ensured through the way in which each generation prepares the next for a life of moral worth. This preparation is the 'machinery' of progress which the logics of pure and practical reason, as finely honed instruments, keep in order. The moral worth of the species, on the side of practical reason, is transformed by Kant into an end of history; the brave denial and the constraint of authority are all evidence for him of humankind's trans-formation from a creature guided by natural impulses (which still must be fulfilled) to one with a moral value, that is to one imbued with reason. In other words, because reason is imbedded in the ac-culturation process (in which the liberation from instinctual compul-sion through moral rectitude and constraint also entails a conscious expectation of the future), humankind constructs a morally bound culture which develops, through the notion and process of enlighten-ment, an historical reflexivity.[8] In other words, the basis for a pedagogically mediated 'species evolution' is the articulation of the immanent structures of reason itself, even if the essence of the imma-nent structures remains unknown.

In this way, epistemology and anthropology meet. Kant's initial epistemological investigations of the transcendental constitution of the cognitive faculties that construe the world (the *Critique of Pure Reason* and the *Critique of Practical Reason*) can be read, in the context of his later essays, as containing an implicit anthropology. As such his revolution in thought cannot be seen as simply a redefinition of the epistemological parameters of human knowledge. Rather it denotes a 'change in the relationship between the spectator and his object.'[9] In other words, the spectator or subject, which for Kant is ultimately humankind, draws precepts 'out of his own will and not from any external source.'[10] The determining and transforming power of reason also becomes the determining and transforming power of humankind. Kant's anthropological formulation of an active and creative reason immanently present in humankind comes to the fore; it originates a series of events. In positing reason as a transcendental construct, Kant removes humankind from the enslavement of deified and reified systems of causality. Humankind becomes transcendental in the sense that its essence is 'beyond' time and pedagogically uniquely fashioned to reconstruct either the natural empirical world of appearances or the social world dealing with the affairs of humankind. Moreover, the implicit anthropological status which is given to humankind solves, for Kant, the problem of which transcendental principle is to be brought into play with regard to what object-domain reason is faced with – the empirical or the moral–ethical.

In an article 'What is Orientation in Thinking' Kant argues that the transcendental procedure is preceded by reason's own ability to point itself in the proper direction, that is in the direction of its correct use. He takes as his starting point the familiar everyday example of geographical orientation, extending it by analogy to the problem of creating a path into and through the worlds of the sensible and supersensible. While experience is the guide for the sensible, it cannot be so for the supersensible. Here, according to Kant, the objective grounds of knowledge no longer exist for reason to bring a judgement. In the darkened spaces of moral uncertainty the spectator only has a subjective sense, or 'ground of distinction', with which to plot a course. For Kant, this subjective sense 'is nothing else than the feeling of a need belonging to reason.'[11] This 'need belonging to reason' is its compass when faced with the uncertainties of the supersensible world. It is the force that not only sets the mind on its journey but also keeps it from sliding into dogmatism and superstition when faced with uncertainty. The transcendentally constituted cognitive resources that humankind draws on and develops are a result of this orientation. In other words, in analysing the principles by which humankind cognizes its natural and social (moral) worlds, Kant argues that the spectator *orientates* either to 'the starry heavens above . . . [or] the moral law within'; [12] that is, to the specific world that the spectator wishes to investigate. The direction of the orientation dictates which principle of reason is invoked (either the theoretical or the practical).

However, in many respects this remains unsatisfactory. Kant appears to be confronted by the immutability of his transcendental principles once he moves from the terrain of his philosophy of history and confronts both the problem of orientation and the internal composition and dynamic of the conflictual dimension of social life, that is, civil society as a *political universe* and the real domain of practical reason. While there is a gulf separating the empirical world and the domain of reason, the orientation, apprehension and enactment of transcendentally construed laws is, for Kant, still a problem of/for humankind in the world. In other words, Kant's view of human progress as a gradual orientation and thus education of people to rational ends through either pure or practical reason, reveals a permanent tension that permeates the whole of his work. This innermost tension

> may be seen clearly in the contrast between the purely intellectual aspect of philosophy and the moral aspect; between the mechanistic necessity of nature and the moral freedom of human acts and most important in the dual nature of man himself as a participant in both the physical and intelligible worlds. [13]

In order for the likelihood that the requirements for human existence be realized, Kant's formalized and epistemological separation between the noumenal and the phenomenal must be synthesized in a temporary unity. This, in Kant's view, temporary synthesis, occurs in the temporal world of human beings who create an ongoing history of substantiated needs. To be sure while it is history that contains the stock of human knowledge, the movement from a priori concepts to an active understanding and judgement of historical experience, memory and political life is still a problem. In this sense, the application of the transcendental principles becomes the primary task of the philosophy of history.

One could suggest that this process of orientation is Kant's anthropological construction of the notion of teleology that belongs to the faculty of judgement which in itself substantiates a philosophy of history. The need belonging to reason is the faculty of judgement through which humankind ascertains whether or not reason is pointed in the correct direction. The correct outcome of either pure or practical reason (their successful legislation in their spheres) cannot be so correct unless reason is imbued with an orientative-cum-teleological capacity.

In other words, the transcendental principles that ground pure and practical reason are imbued with an orientative-teleological impetus in each of their spheres of knowledge. The faculty of ends imbedded in theoretical reason is evidenced in the outcome of the laws of nature, whilst practical reason presupposes a teleology of, an orientation towards, morality.[14] In effect, Kant subsumes the teleological impulse which belongs to the process of orientation to his own anthropological understanding of humankind. In positing that pure and practical reason are active and causal principles Kant must demonstrate a unity between two apparently incompatible modes – the world of disparate human activity and the transcendental principle that gives it coherence and depth. In the latter, either pure or practical reason become the sole objective principle of causality, while in the former it must posit a necessary being, a subject who takes his or her place in either the empirical domain or the world of social action. In other words; how does reason, as a transcendental category, cross the boundary into empirical realizability?

Kant locates the orientative capacity of reason within the structure of human cognition. As such he opens up to humankind an analysis of its own orientating, both procedurally and substantively, through the faculty of judgement. In *The Critique of Judgement*, Kant is concerned with the logic of a teleological ethical form (that the a priori concept of freedom contains a final end), in an effort to make clear the precise faculty which makes 'the transition from the realm of the concept of nature to that of the concept of freedom.'[15] Judgement now emerges as that faculty which enables the transition to empirical realizability to be made. It simultaneously embodies, through the process of orientation, an anthropological interest as part of the transcendentally constituted 'higher faculty of cognition', that is it also concerns the notion of the subject, humanity and its existence in the world. Whilst Kant argues that:

> the effect in accordance with the concept of freedom is the final end which (or the manifestation of which in the sensible world) is to exist, [then] this presupposes the condition of the possibility of that end in nature (i.e. in the name of the Subject as a being of the sensible world, namely a man). [And,] it is so presupposed *a priori* and without regard to the practical, by judgement.[16]

The connection between the a priori of reason itself, its teleological moment and its concretization, is forged through the mediation of judgement as it transforms people from prerational to rational beings. Kant must invest the character of the species with the property of, and the capacity for, reason to enable it to make this connection. Man, as the self-creator of his character 'insofar as he is capable of perfecting himself according to ends that he himself adopts',[17] and in his transition from nature to culture, substantiates practical reason and produces a distinctly ethical historicity. *Fundamentally, it is this central anthropological image which informs the Kantian project of grounding the immanent logics of the three principles of rationality.*

The three principles or functions of reason to which Kant addresses three specific studies (the *Critique of Pure Reason*, the *Critique of Practical Reason* and the *Critique of Judgement*) can be congregated and arranged according to the *Anthropology from a Practical Point of View* and his philosophy of history. The first critique represents a propaedeutic to the other critiques. This critique establishes transcendentally the knowledge that humankind claims it has of the natural world, following Kant's desire that reason should be presented containing a logical synthesizing structure. The second critique explores and explicates reason's ethical dimension, which, although still transcendentally formulated, demands active realizability, while *The Critique of Judgement* investigates reason's legislative power. In this light, the technical analyses which Kant pursues are only for the purpose of establishing the universal and rational foundation which will ground persons as active subjects. Together, the powers of reason embody the complete capacity of thought, that is, the ability of humankind to capture and order the world, render it meaningful and act. As van de Pitte comments, 'reality is now man's reality, and the Enlightenment is fulfilled. Man is freed from self-imposed minority – he has the courage to use his own intelligence, and to assume his rightful position.'[18] This, it can be argued, remains the programmatic goal of the three *Critiques*.

In this context ethics surfaces as the guiding motif. For Kant, humankind's relation to nature is essentially unproblematic. The 1787 second 'Preface' to the *Critique of Pure Reason* can be read as Kant's brief yet positive exposition concerning the historical maturation of the principles of pure reason. Nevertheless, the intersubjective relationships which constitute the genus humankind are, for him, problematic in the extreme. The technical use of nature through the principles of theoretical reason cannot account for, in Kant's view, the way in which human beings live together and organize their lives in the course of satisfying their basic needs. Hence, while Kant presupposes a technical predisposition within the phylogenetic formation of human evolution, it is subordinated to what he sees as a greater concern: the organizational form of social life and the articulation of the ethical imperatives that should inform it. This problematic of the social is for him a distinctively moral–ethical problematic and is the central focus for a specifically *human* project. In other words, Kant argues that the phylogenetic progress of humanity is developed from within the communality of social life which itself is structured through the formation of regulative ethical norms. It is the recognition of a self-articulating communality that portrays, for Kant, the moral dignity and aspiration of the species. In the *Anthropology* Kant makes this quite clear:

> The character of the species, as it is indicated by all the experience of all ages and of all peoples, is this, that taken, collectively (the human race as a whole), it is a multitude of persons, existing successively and side by side, who cannot *do without* associating peacefully and yet cannot *avoid* constantly offending one another. Hence they feel destined by nature (to form) through mutual compulsion under laws which proceed from themselves, a coalition which, though constantly threatened by dissension, makes progress on the whole.[19]

Kant, then, addresses progress *primarily* from the standpoint of the problematic of the political formation of human life. He does this from the viewpoint or orientation of the transcendental principle of practical reason. This transcendental principle enables him to move from a discourse concerning the 'end of history' to one concerning specifically the socio-ethical formation of the modern world of inter-subjectivity. It is to this discourse that we now turn.

KANT'S CRITICAL ANTHROPOLOGY AND CIVIL SOCIETY
THE PROBLEMATIC OF JUDGEMENT, POLITICS AND THE PUBLIC

Kant recognizes that social progress is more often than not accompanied by social conflicts between people and nations.[20] This entails that his anthropologically construed notion of a 'sphere of needs',[21] is formulated as a *civil union* or civil society that, because it embodies people's intersubjectively mediated needs, takes on an immediate 'political' dimension.[22] Kant addresses the problematic of social conflict by formally separating the realm of civil society into private and public domains (that is, the domain of virtue and the domain of right). In so doing he continues the post-Reformation distinction between the inner world of religious, moral and personal legitimation, and the outer world of institutionalized order legitimized through constitution and the formal laws of the state. Kant, in 'The Metaphysics of Morals' makes a division within the framework of a theory of ethics: the doctrine of virtue is rendered distinct from the doctrine of right in that the concept of freedom divides itself into (through the notion of duty), 'inner freedom' or 'outer freedom', depending on the type of subjective action under scrutiny. In Kant's view, only duties of inner freedom are to be considered as the constituent field for ethical enquiry This, then, becomes the domain of the Doctrine of Virtue. All areas *not* resting upon inner legislation pertain to actions made in accordance with moral right, that is, duties acted upon in accordance with the law. These include property, the relation between people as objects of the will, contract, the household, civil conduct and its relation to the state (as embodied in laws for the nation), and the laws between states. For Kant, this 'outer life' is the prerogative of the Doctrine of Right. Within this, freedom as far as Kant is concerned, is constituted through two simultaneous movements; on the one hand, through the recognition of individual autonomy and particularity, and on the other, through the universally constituted notion of practical reason which mediates the formation of intersubjectivity and the formation of political will.

Leaving aside the question of the nature of Kant's Doctrine of Virtue and its relation to the Doctrine of Right, we will look specifically at his political theory.

The domain of right pertains to the specifically political nature of social life, and is further addressed by Kant in three ways; first, according to the notion of individual action, secondly, according to the notion of the commonwealth or civil constitution, and thirdly according to the notion of the public. This, then, introduces our second reading of enlightenment; a more conventional one which addresses the relation between political activity and critical judgement.

For Kant, politics is interpreted as part of an ongoing ethical project in which the articulation of moral law indicates the progressive development of humankind. But while he denotes the species rather than individuals as bearers of the pedagogical impetus, it is (as Kant indicates) acting subjects themselves who compete for all needs in the realm of necessity. This socially constituted world of necessity is, according to Kant, a world of 'unsociableness and mutual opposition from which so many evils arise.'[23] It presents itself to humankind as its great challenge, that is the challenge to create laws to ameliorate the conflict. In recognizing the conflictual nature of social life, Kant goes on to argue that humankind needs an immanent authority – a master – to tame its drives and passions. In the spirit of the Enlightenment he further argues that the master is humankind itself.[24] The spectator becomes the player.

If though, Kant enquires, humankind is its own immanent authority, how then is it going to insulate itself against the vagaries of human nature? In answering, he invokes the notion of practical reason, of a transcendental a priori that resides within, and construes the nature of immant authority.[25] According to Kant practical reason engenders

> practical principles which are propositions which contain a general determination of the will, having under it several practical rules. They are subjectives or maxims, when the condition is regarded by the subject as valid for his own will. They are objective, or practical, laws when they are recognized as objective; i.e. as valid for the will of every rational being.[26]

Moreover, the maxim which most concretely typifies the Enlightenment's *political* claim is expressed as the fundamental right of persons to the recognition of autonomy, which in turn leads to security and the pursuit of their needs. This takes place through the articulation of freedom which is structured as a two-sided reciprocating norm. Right, for Kant, becomes on the one hand 'the restriction of each individual's freedom so that it harmonises with the freedom of everyone else (in so far as this is possible within the terms of a general law)'.[27] On the other hand, right also means that persons in the general movement from nature to culture implicitly enter into a relation of freedom and equality with all other people on the basis of a single anthropological claim: that each is an end to himself, 'respected as such by everyone, a being which no one might treat as mere means to ulterior ends'.[28] Through this maxim reason is given an objective existence which rational persons come to know because they too are autonomous – neither reliant upon, nor reduced to, empirically or historically determined grounds for moral certainty. Thus this maxim which rational persons assert is established as an ethical norm which is in accord with the objectively constituted moral law, but subjectively enacted by them by virtue of their autonomy and self-deliberation. The articulation of the moral law, then, denotes that the consciousness of the freedom of the will is identical to the subject's autonomy. Reason now involves the will thinking in universal terms, thinking consistently and thinking freely. The maxims are constructed by the will, complied with (through the notion of duty)[29] and judged critically. The latter pertains explictly to Kant's anthropological insight. Practical reason generates norms for social action in a way that both unites and mediates its objectivity with the subjectivity of the social actor. The mediation occurs through the faculty of reflective judgement. In other words, in having shown that a 'free and pure will' is not only objectively determined, but also subjectively responsible, Kant demands neither passivity nor subserviance, but active judgement.

Likewise the activity of reflective judgement mediates subjectivity and objectivity: humankind with the transcendental quality of reason. This transcendental principle enables actors to judge practical problematics in terms of an 'ought'. In this way, it does not matter if the action is enacted empirically; what does matter is that the 'ought' signals a potential judgement of the event in a way that articulates the determinate nature of reason itself. And, for Kant, the determining principle of freedom can be expressed concretely. The will can, through the faculty of reflective judgement, accept or reject a moral law just as long as it recognizes the universal status of other wills and does not turn them into a pure means – an instrument without rights. According to Kant:

> He is the subject of the moral law which is holy because of the autonomy of his freedom. Because of the latter, every will, even the private will of each person directed to himself, is restricted to the condition of agreement with the autonomy of the rational being, namely, that it be subjected to no purpose which is not possible by a law which could arise from the will of the passive subject itself. This condition thus requires that the person never be used as a means except when it is at the same time an end.[30]

This practical expression of reason gives substance, universality and meaning to all human conduct. This ethical maxim is double sided. On the one hand, it holds to a distinction between a transcendental determination and a subjective will, and thus overcomes, in Kant's view, the subjectivist motivations of desire and caprice. On the other, the categorial imperative of the ethical maxim entails that persons recognize, through the use of reflective judgement, the autonomous existence of others and hence that they live in a society. The moral teleology concerns the role of human beings in the world, and therefore persons interacting with other persons. As Meld Shell points out in her commentary on Kant's Doctrine of Right:

> To treat another as an end-in-himself, is to treat him as a being for whom our action, when it affects him, could also be an end. It is, in other words, to recognize him as a person with intentions like ourselves. Those activities through which we make use of other persons ought to serve their purposes as well. *Our use of others ought to await their (rational) consent.* The notion of reason as an end-in-itself translates practically into a duty to treat others in a way to which they can (prudently) agree. The ideal consensus of a rational community translates externally into a duty to secure the consent of others in all one's social dealings. We cannot establish the 'kingdom of ends' without first securing a juridical community of means. The moral idea of an end-in-itself entails the juridical notion of a means in general.

Fully perfected, the concept of right implies a system of reciprocally related equal selves.[31] [my emphasis]

In other words, for Kant, this double-sided ethical maxim functions as a regulative principle. Moreover it does so in three ways that for him ensure that humankind ameliorates, or at least minimizes, its predisposition for conflict: through the notion of personal will; through the construction of civic law through a constitution that gives legitimacy to the state and through the public sphere, the sphere of criticism. Together through the regulative principle they function as a complete and open-ended civil state that entails and ensures both negative and positive freedoms.

As analysed elsewhere, each of these formulations compete with one another to guide the developmental impulses of the modern conception of politics in three directions: individualism; the reliance on the formal status of the law; or a notion of enlightenment through a strengthened and radicalised idea of the public.[32] It is this latter point which interests us, and which guides our own subsequent reconstruction of a possible version of Kant's conception of politics.

In positing a unity of transcendence, action and knowledge and turning his back on metaphysics, Kant invests practical reason in critical subjects who can only realize autonomy and freedom through active participation in a civil state. The conflicts that arise between social actors and their resolution (as more than a mere moment within the Kantian philosophy of history), should, according to Kant, take place there. As he puts it, 'the greatest problem of the human race, to the situation of which Nature drives man, is the achievement of a universal civic society which administers law among men.'[33] Kant's notion of reflective judgement which mediates the distinctions between the noumenal and the phenomenal, passivity and activity, morality and opportunistic expediency, denotes his own move from the immanent logic of practical reason to the problematics of realizability and critical enlightenment, that is to the problem of politics and its organizational forms. In this sense politics, embodied in a civil state, is an a priori principle because it belongs not only to the teleological nature of practical reason but also to its immanent logic.[34]

Organizationally, Kant argues that any civil state that develops to solve the problem of conflict in terms of autonomy should be a republic. In it 'the legislative power can belong only to the united will of the people.'[35] Through this united will, and by it being grounded in the transcendental a priori of practical reason, legislation which is passed gains an objective and universal legitimacy. This universal legitimacy guarantees the three rightful attributes which are inseparable from the nature of a citizen . . . [these are] firstly, lawful *freedom* to obey no law other than that to which he has given his consent; secondly, civil *equality* in recognising no-one among the people as superior to himself, unless it be someone whom he is just as morally entitled to bind by law as the other is to bind him; and thirdly, the attribute of civil *independence* which allows him to owe his existence and sustenance not to the arbitrary will of anyone else among the people, but purely to his own rights and powers as a member of the commonwealth (so that he may not, as a civil personality, be represented by anyone else in matters of right).[36]

In other words, acting subjects participate in the civil, that is, institutional aspect of political life.

However, this institutional aspect of political life is informed by a crucial twofold notion of the public which Kant builds into his notion of enlightenment. The two aspects are the publicity of political life, and the existence of a public sphere outside the domain of both the state and domestic life. It is this twofold notion of the public we suggest, that is the cornerstone of Kant's political philosophy. To be sure, the notion of the public that emerges from Kant's essay 'What is Enlightenment' pertains specifically to the problem of the 'scholar before the reading public'.[37] However, Kant's *problematic* of public reasoning pertains to a wider problem (and has wider application), that is, to the constitutive nature of thinking as such. In this context, the notion of the public belongs to the problem area of freedom in general and to political life in particular. Hannah Arendt, in her *Lectures on Kant's Political Philosophy*, argues that, for Kant, the public is the central animating feature of his work; 'publicness is the "transcendental principle" that should rule all action.'[38] For her 'the reading public' is not a limiting concept or practice; rather it focuses our attention on public opinion and politics as 'observation', for which the faculty of judgement is central. Her interpretation suggests (implicitly) that Kant's construction of the public and his notion of judgement can be extended to embrace the more general problem of the subordination of empirical political life to the communicative ability of all people who reside in the political state. In other words, we suggest that Kant gives to the public an extended meaning that lies beyond the instance of 'the reading public'. It is, in the language of contemporary theory, a sphere of critical discourse free from domination.[39]

There are some important indications of this in Kant's own work. Both philosophically and as a social process, enlightenment embodies and expresses, for Kant, 'the freedom to make public use of one's own reason at every point'.[40] The subject becomes an active critic when she or he learns to use understanding and judgement without the guidance of others. Without this, criticism is inconceivable. The person who is uncritical is one who does not think for him/herself but relies on the 'alien' guidance of other persons. For Kant, this indicates the immaturity of civilization, the 'end of history' has not been reached; that is, in terms of his own philosophy of history, the capacity for politico-ethical judgement has not been universalized. A (political) culture of tutelage remains and people cannot distance themselves from the expectations and evaluations of others, nor can they judge whether such expectations are valid or warranted. They are always in a position of ethical dependence, never politically independent from the guardians of the good, the protectors of the public.

As a learning process, enlightenment starts from the general form-ulation of reason as a species-project in which the actual justification and logic for the development of the 'public' as a category is generated from the transcendental constitution of freedom itself. As we have seen, enlightenment entails the freedom to make public use of one's own reason, to make judgements. By 'public use' Kant formally means the unhindered use of reason in the cause of argument and criticism – the injunction 'do not argue' does not apply.[41] Freedom to think is opposed to both civil constraint and the 'prescribed formulas of belief'.[42] In the case of the former:

> the external power which wrests from man the freedom publicly to communicate his thoughts also takes away the freedom to think – the sole jewel that remains to us under all civil repression and through which alone counsel against all the evils of that state can be taken.

In the case of the latter:

> some citizens set themselves up as guardians in matters of religion. Instead of arguing, they know how, by prescribed formulas of belief ac-companied by scrupulous fear of the danger of private inquisition, to banish all rational examination by making an early impression on the mind.[43]

Freedom in thought avoids these restrictions, because, in Kant's view, it lies under the jurisdiction of reason which prescribes the principles of the use of freedom.

What we have portrayed as Kant's expanded notion of enlighten-ment with its relation to practical reason, carries within it an implied political message: remove the restrictions to enlightenment and a culture of reason will flourish.[44] For Kant, then, the notion of the public signifies a major development in the political life of the modern age. It denotes the functional separation of spheres of social activity which were previously the prerogative of the absolutist state: specifically, the division of politics between separate spheres of power – legitimate authority and public discourse and critique. As such, while Kant recognized that authority (and the seat of power) ultimately remained with the state, the emergence of an independent 'space' outside its direct influence and power in which subjects participated in a political society distinct from the prerogatives of the state, indicated for him the emergence of a 'public sphere' in which rational discourse between subjects could take place.

Moreover, this public space entails *publicity*, that is, that the form that politics takes is public, rather than private, in nature. Kant, in fact proposes the notion of publicity as a transcendental principle of public law for the reason that it concerns actions pertaining to the rights of others. He states: 'All maxims which *stand in need* of publicity in order not to fail their end, agree with politics and right combined.'[45] In this way a political commonwealth of free, acting subjects emerges. Through the transcendental principle embodied in the public, the constitution signifies the embodiment of an expressed general will.

The validity of the constitution for Kant, depends on whether the laws which issue from it and embrace civil conduct have been issued in accordance with the model of legislation encompassed in the *idea* of an original 'political will-formation' between reasoning individuals. For Kant, the law represents:

> an *idea* of reason, which nonetheless has undoubted practical value; for it can oblige every legislator to frame his laws in such a way that they could have been produced by the united will of the whole nation, and to regard each subject, in so far as he can claim citizenship, as if he had been represented within the general will. This is the test of rightfulness of every public law.[46]

In this way, the idea of the constitution signifies that civil laws are the combined will of all members of the state, in which the 'united will of all' functions as a hypothetical standard of legislative legitimacy. The demand is put, then, that the laws promulgated by legislators be seen *as if* they had been decided by each and each had been decided for all, because 'in deciding whether or not the law harmonises with the principle of right . . .[they] have already to hand as an infallible a priori standard the idea of the original contract.'[47] Any restriction on civil conduct (which Kant accepts as a form of positive coercion) becomes legitimate because it takes place through a civil constitution, which becomes the legislative and institutional domain of practical reason,

thus situating it beyond the empirical intentions of capricious individuals. As Kant points out, 'public right in a commonwealth is
simply a state of affairs regulated by a real legislation which conforms
to this principle and is backed up by power, and under which a whole
people live as subjects in a lawful state.' [48] In this way, Kant joins right,
freedom and the restriction of freedom to the formal ethical condition
of practical reason. Objectively, practical reason is embodied in the institutional form of the post-absolutist modern state which he calls 'a
civil state, and it is characterised by equality in the effects and
countereffects of freely willed actions which limit one another in
accordance with the general law of freedom.' [49] Subjectively, its status
is situated in accord with the maxims which are generated and acted
upon dutifully. In this way the law can be considered to be just and
social actors can be expected to respect it dutifully.

Moreover, Kant's insistence that the constitution is a norm generated
from the ethical imperative of practical reason, means that it becomes
the standard by which civil society is judged in its historical manifestation. Civil society is the *result* of the will of all unified in the
idea – a conception that signals Kant's departure from Rousseau.[50]

Civil society and the actions of political subjects in it (if we read it
as an anthropological construct) unites Kant's two different conceptual level – his philosophy of history and his concept of reason – both
of which embody the move from nature to culture as a species-project
and the articulation of immanently generated substantive claims to
reason by social actors themselves. What emerges is a concept of
reason based on the notion of an absolute and realizable freedom,
bound neither to the necessities of nature nor to the oppression of
tyrannical governments. On the contrary, reason is bound to the
ethical and moral struggle of a humankind possessed with a 'will to
be free'. Through this, the sense of a social actor emerges as the
bearer of personal ends:

> Man is a being who has the power of practical reason and is conscious
> that his choice is free (a person); and in his consciousness of freedom
> and in his feeling (which is called moral feeling) that justice and in-
> justice is done to him, or by him, to others, he sees himself as subject
> to the law of duty no matter how obscure his ideas may be.[51]

Our reading of the concept of enlightenment, which builds into it
both (self-) learning and (self-) government, strongly captures the
notion of reason in its practical relation to political action. Whilst as
members of the species social actors bear the responsibility for their
own actions, they also have a responsibility to act as enlightened
critics, and by so doing learn to orientate themselves to reason (and

hence freedom) through the faculty of judgement and thus become *real* and *rational* sovereigns. The twofold notion of the public that pertains to Kant's politics, with its emphasis on critical judgement in which the actor is *both* spectator and player, in fact becomes the central requisite of the civil state. Kant defends the right of subjects in a commonwealth to make use of their reason, against the ambitions of the rulers who seek to suppress all opportunity to express public criticism. The public grounded in the principle of practical reason also ensures the subjects' entry into the domain of power, their universal participation in the exercise of legislative right. As a social process, enlightenment begins from the phylogenetic capacity for intersubjectively structured discourse in which critically motivated social actors can discuss, argue and resolve questions of general political concern. The notion of the public, in this sense, facilitates discourse outside the domain of the household as well as the state, and between and among persons who learn to become political actors.

Despite his suspicions towards democracy, Kant generates a model of a democratic social form that is guided by the notions of universal participation and critical judgement. Our reading of the Kantian construction of the public realm suggests that it is constituted not only by actors who proclaim and make the law, but also by critics and spectators who reside both *in* the public and *inside* every actor. As Arendt argues in her tenth lecture on Kant's political philosophy: 'without this critical judging faculty the doer or the maker would be so isolated from the spectator that he would not even be perceived . . . the faculty they have in common is the faculty of judgement.' [52]

However, in spite of constructing a twofold notion of the public on transcendental grounds Kant undermines this very transcendentalism by introducing an unacknowledged empirical formulation into his formal criterion of right. It is to this that we now turn.

THE ANTHROPOLOGICAL 'LOSS' OF POLITICS
KANT'S RESTRICTED NOTION OF THE PUBLIC

It is here that the full force of the conceptual tension in Kant's anthropology surfaces. His conceptualization of enlightenment – which we suggested simultaneously moves in the two directions of education and (self-) government – comes into conflict with its own formalistic transcendental nature once it takes its place in the social world. This occurs in two ways; first through the limitations that Kant places on criticism and protest against a government. [53] And secondly, through the criteria which are used to establish the social actor's legitimate right to participate in political life. This right, for Kant, *ought* to be generated from the transcendental category of reason as the universal ground against which the historical development of humankind is judged. However, it is filtered through an 'empirical slippage' that introduces an unacknowledged historicism into the a priori conception of the law of freedom. We shall concentrate on the latter because it has an important bearing on the way in which the Kantian notion of civil society moves away from a notion of the public based on unrestricted universalism, to a version in which it appears to be the venue for privilege based in economic and not *political* right.

At first sight it seems that Kant's transformation of the notion of the original contract as the basis for legitimate authority (the realm of appearance) merges with his transcendental principles of pure practical reason. The sovereign ground of right establishes freedom as the basis for human existence, which is expressed through the equal and open membership of all in a civil society. The legal validity of the constitution originates solely in the externalization of the concept of freedom. For Kant, the civil state regarded as a lawful state, is based on the following principles:

1   the *freedom* of every member of society as a human being,
2   the *equality* of each with all the others as a subject,
3   the *independence* of each member of a commonwealth as a citizen.[54]

The first and second principles oppose the traditional legalism of the absolutist state, which was philosophically justified in terms of nature and natural law, as well as being hierarchically structured.[55] The right of freedom, which for Kant, every member of a *civil* state possesses, denies the traditional rights and freedoms of the corporations, the cities and communities, landowners and merchant classes. It is the right of the emancipated and free person, who is concerned with him- or herself, and having eliminated the privileges that functioned under absolutism, pursues personal happiness and acts and judges according to his or her own will. This, as Kant points out, becomes an objectivation of practical reason:

> No-one can compel me to be happy in accordance with his conception of the welfare of others, for each may seek happiness in whatever way he sees fit, so long as he does not infringe upon the freedom of others to pursue a similar end which can be reconciled with the freedom of everyone else within a general workable law – i.e. he must accord to others the same right as he enjoys himself . . . This right of freedom belongs to each member of the commonwealth as a human being, in so far as each is a being capable of possessing rights.[56]

The second principle, too, indicates that right is tied to freedom as a transcendental principle. It includes legal equality and the equality of persons as uniform subjects before the universal laws which have been codified by the modern constitutional state.

However, it is in the third principle that the claims to universality are undermined by the introduction of criteria for practical political life other than those based on the transcendental grounding of freedom and legal justice in the principles of pure practical reason. The notion of independence, which Kant introduces as a predicate in the third principle and which functions as an a priori construct, moves the criteria for the right to co-legislation away from practical reason itself. 'Independence' becomes the sole adjudicator concerning membership to the civil state. Kant denotes it thus:

> the *independence* of a member of a commonwealth as *a citizen* i.e. as a co-legislator, may be defined as follows. In the question of actual legislation, all who are free and equal under existing public laws may be considered equal, *but not as regards the right to make the laws.*[57]

The right to legislate emerges as the most important right, but Kant ties this not to the a priori lawful constitution of civil society, but to the ability to participate as a citizen, that is, to the historical and empirical criterion of independent citizenship. For Kant, this criterion (whilst related to the earlier maxim of not using others as means to ulterior ends) is based on the empirical reality of the economically and legally independent citizen who is in a position to serve no other except the commonwealth. This means that

> he must be his own master and must have some property (which can include any skill, trade, fine art or science) to support himself. In the case where he must earn his living from others, he must earn it only by selling that which is his, and not by allowing others to make use of him.[58]

In an attempt to be consistent with the maxim of practical reason Kant brings into his transcendental formulation the historically generated class and gender basis for closed political and economic relations. In other words, 'the domestic servant, the shop assistant, the labourer or even the barber, are merely labourers, not artists or members of the state, and are thus unqualified to be citizens.'[59] This is argued precisely on transcendental grounds: the artisan 'in pursuing his trade, exchanges his property with someone else, while (the labourer) allows someone else to make use of him'.[60] As Reidel points out, this shift 'conceals the exercise of domination behind the universality of compulsion without succeeding in making it universal.'[61] The economic dependency of non-property owners means that their political right is appropriated by a citizenry from which they are excluded. They become passive members of the commonwealth, excluded from civil society with no legitimate participatory role to play in the legislative process. While all citizens are equal before the law, they are unequal in their right to make the law. Moreover, they cannot participate in the learning process embodied within the *movement* of practical reason: their lives as political beings remain unfulfilled. Refused entry to public life and relegated to the private domain of the household and workshop, they can only obey.[62]

This immanent shift in transcendentally construed presuppositions informs Kant's characterization of the public of critics. It is, it can be argued,[63] indicative of a general political weakness of the Enlightenment: a general pessimism and despair of the condition of the lower orders (the heterogeneity of which they tended to collapse into *the people*) which the *philosophes* often developed philosophically into a denial of a place of *the people* in any project of enlightenment. Whilst some of the *philosophes* retained a commitment to the education of all humankind, their sense of despair (which Gay presents in his book *The Enlightenment An Interpretation*), was related to a misconceived and overly pessimistic realization (given the existence of heterogeneous publics in England, Holland and Switzerland) of the daunting nature of the task of enlightenment outside the small educated circles of the early modern age. Kant's cautious optimism, which he builds into his theory of progress as a *Bildungsprozess*,[64] is matched by a circumscribed notion of the public that also replicates the general pessimism of the *philosophes* who preceded him. Describing the '*Volk*' as idiots,[65] and invoking the transcendental requisites of the public (against the public) means that the spectator as critic is represented by a minority.

In terms of his own philosophical anthropology Kant circumvents his demand for a realizable practical reason: 'The *a priori* legal construction of the original contract *prescribing* communicative action free from domination describes at the same time a society which no longer coincides with its own name.'[66] It is no longer (in strictly Kantian terms) a publicly constituted civil state.

The concept of enlightenment as both a *publicly constituted* procedural ethics and social process, which Kant retains and normatively justifies as an a priori principle founded on the constitutive elements of pure practical reason, is undermined a posteriori at its foundation, through the category of independence which is rendered and legitimized through property ownership. Independence as a privilege of citizenship is surreptitiously transformed into a right which persons must acquire:

> For Kant, this sphere is only a secondary consequence of the a priori legal construction of civil society; and this is why he does not realize that this society suddenly assumes a new form – that the concept of right which merely seems to imply mutual freedom and equality has as its consequence one-sided dependency and renewed inequality.[67]

In presupposing a social sphere of unobstructed political will formations which would anthropologically mediate its own formalism, Kant constructs a transcendental concept of pure reason that lacks the capacity to represent itself because the political conception of the public is undermined and denied real criticality. Anthropologically, reason becomes an empty shell into which politics retreats.

This is the legacy Kant left to Hegel, a legacy which also affects the critical thrust of Marx's own theoretical enterprises. Hegel's problematic of civil society is already informed by Kant's own limiting conception of it, in which politics 'retreats' to the safety of an internal history of the mind where the end of history is played out neatly through the logic of pure reason.

2
The Dialectical
Anthropology of Freedom

THE VIEW FROM THE BRIDGE
HEGEL'S PROBLEMATICIZING OF THE KANTIAN LEGACY

Hegel addresses two major antinomies which he sees emerging from Kantian philosophy. The first, and certainly the continuing reference point for Hegel is Kant's formulation of reason; the second is the - dissolution of the notion of the subject into two spheres of subjectivity. Over, against and within these antinomies is Hegel's own positive reading of Kant. According to Hegel, Kant's strength is that he posits the idea of freedom as a regulative principle that articulates the possibility of a normatively based society. Within this, freedom is constituted through two simultaneous movements: on the one hand, through the recognition of individual autonomy and particularity, and on the other, through the universally constituted notion of practical reason which mediates the formation of intersubjectivity and the formation of political will.[1] Hegel, in this sense, suggests that the strength of the modern state lies in this very principle: self-subsistent personal particularity and substantive unity through the objective forms of civil sovereignty. But for Hegel, this very unity within the Kantian context is itself problematic. The unity is only temporary. Reason is never completely substantiated, articulated or known. Moreover, the differentiation of the notion of the subject into spheres of subjectivity also makes the temporary unity even more fragile. Right, in this sense, relies only upon the recognition of practical reason to legitimize publicly orientated duty, whilst morality as virtue has no real substantiation through the formal structure of reason itself. For Kant, the private world of inner life has no public or institutional framework to which it can refer – it only has a regulative idea.

Hegel addresses this problem-complex in two ways. On the one hand, he abolishes the separation between right and morality and situates them within the context of an ethically constituted social order

(*Sittlichkeit*). On the other hand, this dissolution of separate spheres is immanently related to the very constitution of the idea of freedom itself. Freedom, for Hegel, is not only located within the domain of an ethical community in which its institutional framework also embodies both right *and* ethics, but it is also generated from the notion of reason itself. Hegel's notion of reason, while like Kant's in being actively engaged in the world, is different from Kant's in that it manifests itself completely in the world. Reason is self-actualizing and self-revealing through that very ethical community. Hegel directs two interconnected arguments against the Kantian notion of reason. On the one hand, Hegel sees it as being too absolute in that the noumenal becomes an empty formalism in the face of phenomenal reality. The formalistic criteria for ethical judgement, that is its transcendental purity, denies reason itself real and sustained worldly intervention and the development of a sustainable, ethically constituted social order (*Sittlichkeit*). It is in Hegel's mind a dialectic which does not get its hands dirty in the toil of humanity's striving for consciousness, that is, it lacks concreteness by being too absolute. For Hegel, reason must generate a content out of itself to engage the phenomenal level. Following Taylor this involves a 'historical dialectic' through which the ethical life unfolds.[2] This further entails that the separation between right and virtue is abolished. On the other hand, Kant's formulation of reason is seen to be not absolute enough. By lacking concreteness, Kant's free and pure will can never understand itself completely. But for Hegel, the possibility of complete self-understanding is grounded in the logic of being-in-itself. It is an 'ontological dialectic' which articulates the hidden, yet real, process of becoming self-conscious. The tiny, momentary glimpses of a spirit in progress which become memorized, immanently informing an ongoing historicity, entails that reason's own logic becomes gradually visible and understood. Its own internal formations, from naive consciousness to absolute consciousness, are but instances of reason's self-learning and self-articulation. In this way, too, the antinomy between inner and outer freedom is dissolved though reason's own systematization and totalization of the disparate world of social life, thus demonstrating reason's own inner logic. Reason is self-revealing and self-articulating through the ethical community.

Moreover, Hegel assumes that the historico-phenomenological and ontological dialectics manifest themselves in a simultaneous unity. Ontology meets unproblematically with history, each presupposing the other, and together dissolve the Kantian antinomies in a circle of necessity.[3] The historical dialectic articulates the way in which the purpose of reason realizes itself. To be able to do this effectively, the historical dialectic needs the ontological dialectic to immanently question the standards which history judges itself by. In this case, the movement in ontology forces a change in either the conception of the standard or in the conception of the reality in which it is filled to enable a coherent account of this fulfilment to be given. In this way, Hegel can show (for example in the 'Introduction' to the *Philosophy of History*) that the logic of reason requires a series of realities through which it can work, and that these require reason itself to be explicated. This inner articulation distinguishes between what is being aimed at or meant, and what exists phenomenologically, that is, between the standard and the reality. In the process of this articulated difference, the two moments move into contradiction and are subsequently transformed.

We preliminarily suggest, however, that Hegel's dual argumentation concerning the resolution of the Kantian antinomies (too absolute/not absolute enough) evolves into competing strategies for the articulation and construction of his social theory as it takes place under the auspices of dialectical reason (and for Marx's response to it). Following Taylor, we also suggest that these strategies can be seen as two readings of the genesis and development of dialectical reason, each presupposing a shift of emphasis in the assumed unity of the historico-ontological dialectics. This unity, it will be argued, devolves into the competing strategies which rely either on the primacy of an ontological vision of history and society or a historical and developmental view of humankind that historically reflects upon its past, present and future.

In the 'not absolute enough' reading/strategy a shift occurs in favour of the ontological dialectic. Here, a philosophical anthropology takes a less central place than in the historical dialectic. Reason functions as a series of self-creating and unifying instances which bring together the *practice* of knowledge and its conceptualization (the dialectic of historical forms of consciousness and the dialectic of the theories of knowledge), but in a way in which the anthropological image is a mere backdrop for the outplay of the dialectical interaction. The dialectical interaction itself takes place within the realm of categories that partially denude the significance of humankind as a plurality of actors who form the world through their own reasoned actions. Humankind becomes only a subordinate moment of *Geist* which mediates the teleological impetus of the ever-present and unfolding *Geist* with *Geist's* own understanding and knowledge of itself. This means that the notion of humankind is relativized. The teleological *logos* of reason is actually metasocial – society and the human life which encapsulates it are but intermediary stages or stations on the way to reason's self-knowledge. In this context, spirit/reason is both evolutionary and systemic. The truth of reason can only be grasped as a whole in which all elements, because they too issue from reason, are interdependent moments of the whole. This becomes particularly clear when Hegel discusses the aporias of modernity and the formation of the modern state. For him particularity and autonomy are achieved only within the context of the universalizing nature of reason. The state, then, is an 'organism',[4] it is both unity and difference, unfolding yet constant. System and evolution become complementary manifestations of *Geist*, because it knows itself as its own subject – it becomes self-identified. The exposition of the system of reason can only be expressed as the truth realizing that it is not only the substance, but also its own selfsame (teleological) movement.[5] The totalizing, ontological dialectic, because of its immensity and depth and all-embracing character, can never posit the possibility of a positive decomposition or detotalization.

But there is also the alternative 'too absolute' strategy. Once humankind is established as the central, although relativized, subject, it is imbued with self-activity. This is the essential element of the historical dialectic. This moreover, presents quite a different problematic from the preceding strategy because it desires a direct purpose that is imputed to real historical actors. For Hegel, like Kant, this imputed purpose is reason, that is it becomes humankind's journey with *Geist* in its historical self-development. But as Taylor points out, 'the imputation of purpose can never be self-authenticating as a starting point,'[6] and it is this problem which sits at the core of the historical dialectic.

Unlike the ontological dialectic which begins with a realized goal or standard, the historical one begins with no realized purpose, it only finishes with one. This makes the reading of history problematic – we cannot read with certainty a particular purpose. This means that an exposition essentially different from that of the ontological one is involved. The historical dialectic functions hermeneutically – it is an interpretative dialectic which must convince its audience, by the overall plausibility of its historical interpretation, that reason has proceeded in the most rational and necessary course through the study of world history. Although history is looked at with the eye of reason, it is substantiated reason made visible, because it is being made conscious through an interpretation of it.

This project is ultimately more reliant upon a philosophical anthropology than the former. Humankind now engages much more forcefully with history, it becomes a substantial actor that generates a reflective historicity out of itself. Hegel's philosophy of reason, within this context, becomes an action theory. Freedom is translated into action categories which subjectivities themselves use to establish their right as political actors. Human activity, although grounded in an objectivating reason, creates the possibilities for freedoms that are brought forward as *real* historical moments (for example the Athenian world of antiquity and the development of the modern state). In this latter perspective, the action theory becomes a strategy which mediates the conflictual configurations that are historically generated by reason's self-defining and self-positing activity. Humankind becomes action, the activity of negating the given, the activity of fighting and work where history mediates past, present and future and where humankind transforms the given to make it conform with a consciousness of what ought to be. This entails a shift, then, to a phenomenological interpretation of reason that subsumes the ontological dialectic to the historical one. It also brings the latent anthropological content of Hegel's philosophy to the fore.

In analysing what we argue are the dual and competing strategies developed by Hegel to resolve the Kantian antinomies, we shall invert the procedure with which we have opened our discussion. We shall begin with the interpretative dialectic rather than the ontological one. Hegel's philosophy, at first glance, appears comprehensible only as a fundamentally all-embracing and ontological system. Through this, Hegel constructs and develops the notion of self-positing spirit. However, in the broader context of the anthropological problematic of modernity, with which we (following Taylor) introduced this work – the nature of the modern self-defining subject – an analysis of the interpretative dialectic seems more fruitful. It is through this that the subject speaks; brings him or herself to life in relation to others, acts and forms society. In this context, the self-defining subject has a relative primacy which, as we shall see, is transformed (or transposed) under the auspices of the ontology that Hegel invokes to address the problems that the interpretative approach brings forward.

REASON THROUGH AN ACTIVE HISTORY
THE MASTER AND THE SLAVE AS TRANSFORMATIVE MYTH

Hegel proposes the dialectical overcoming of transcendental philosophy in a way which, like Kant but distinct from him, speaks about and to a humanity that struggles for itself. For Hegel, Kant's journey with reason opens the *possibility* of a realizable freedom for humanity in which the spirit of this freedom (as a value-idea and its evolution as part of human experience and historicity),[7] posits the logical conditions for its self-consciousness, i.e. autonomy, particularity, universality and interdependence. Hegel transposes the central Kantian insight, that humanity has an inherent capacity for reason, by asserting that not only does the 'free and pure will' judge the criteria of inner actions or construct a constitution bound to negative freedoms, but that it also exists in the historico-social world as part of a positive forming process. Freedom is both concept and realization as Hegel states in the Introduction to the *Philosophy of Right*: 'the subject matter of the philosophical science of right is the Idea of right, i.e. the concept of right together with the actualization of the concept.'[8] In the *Philosophy of History* Hegel understands freedom to be '*self-contained existence* . . . [which is] none other than self-consciousness of one's own being. Two things must be distinguished in consciousness; first, the fact *that I know*; secondly *what I know*. In *self*-consciousness these are merged in one; for Spirit *knows itself.*'[9] The historical-interpretative dialectic manifests itself in an attempt to bring the work of this conception of freedom to the fore. Anthropologically, freedom becomes the condition through which humankind can realize itself fully.

In this light it is useful to postpone momentarily the analysis of Hegel's internal dialogue with Kant as he generates his own philosophy of right, and firstly establish the primacy of Hegel's visible anthropology which sits between history and action. Instead of analysing the *Philosophy of History* (which on first glance might be the best place to begin) we shall turn to the dialectic of the master and slave.

We can interpret the dialectic of the master and the slave as Hegel's use of myth or symbolic narrative in a similar way to that in which Kant interprets *Genesis* as humankind's acquisition of the transcendental principles of reason and the transition from nature to culture in 'Conjectural Beginning of Human History'. The categories of the master and the slave hermeneutically reconstruct reason's passage through world history as it intersects and combines with a specific human capacity for making and transforming its own historicity, in which the problematics of freedom and foundation and constituency of political right come to the fore. Hegel's exposition of the relation between the master and the slave, then, sits on these two interconnected levels – history and action.

On the level of action it follows the process of consciousness as it moves from the privileged position of a generic subject to a form which posits two subjects – a one with the other. For Hegel, an autonomously constituted intersubjectivity becomes the necessary feature of the generic form of humankind:

Although as consciousness, it does indeed come out of *itself*, yet, though out of itself it is at the same time kept back within *itself*, and the self outside it is for it . . . They *recognize* themselves as *mutually recognizing* one another.[10]

To properly posit itself independently, autonomous self-consciousness must exist for another, not in a subservient manner, but in a way in which the *right* of autonomy is recognized for each and in each.[11] This signifies, for Hegel, the double dialectic of recognition. In the first instance, each action, each moment is recognized and reciprocated as necessary for the other. Behind the double dialectic of recognition Hegel outlines the central idea which functions as the normative ground for recognition – freedom. The notion of recognition posits a reason which, although self-derived, self-transforming and self-judging, takes place within the context of continuous conflict (that is of the conflictual nature of social relations). Freedom's recognition always entails a struggle.

Kojève's interpretation of the master–slave dialectic is of interest here.[12] In his view, Hegel's anthropology becomes clearly visible in this dialectic. Moreover, it becomes visible as *action*. In the negation of the domination of the master, the very act of negation signifies the human capacity for self-creation, for freedom that forms an active juxtaposition with the evolutionary move from nature to culture. In this way, the *difference* between master and the slave cannot be located at the level of nature, rather it has a history in which enslavement is overcome by no longer being recognized as a legitimate *social* category. It is struggled against. Freedom is actively fought for.

This leads to the second level – history – reason's own becoming self-consciousness. The master – slave dialectic is, for Hegel, an abbreviated historical reconstruction of reason's own desire for recognition and freedom. It also contains in Hegel's view, historical authenticity (the world of Greek antiquity) which can be symbolically generalized to the level of a politically significant dialectical anthropology. In other words, in defining freedom as human consciousness, Hegel interprets world history (via the master – slave dialectic) as the development of the consciousness of freedom in which humankind is established as an object for itself.[13] In this context, it not only plots reason's historical development, but also the possibility of its normative institutionalization against a background of domination and subjugation.

The active and historical struggle for recognition and freedom becomes the ground for Hegel's basic imputed anthropological claim. Moreover, he proceeds to give it substance – to make it live historically –

by imbuing it with three types of activity: language, fighting and work.[14] Fighting precedes work, not because it implies a more primitive state of consciousness that belongs to first nature, but rather because it articulates a principle of recognition based on a context free of substantive domination. In the arena of the fight the adversaries are equal. The second instance of the double-sided dialectic, then, acknowledges that the *value* of the equality of recognition can only be realized if it is maintained at all costs. For Hegel, the dialectic is also a fight for recognition in which the adversaries, because they are able to lay down their lives, restate their recognition of, and autonomy from one another.[15] This 'abstract negation', as Hegel terms it, leaves its mark, however, in the denial of reality. Kojève disagrees – it is not the fight to the death which is important, but the 'risk of life' which preserves autonomy by articulating, that is externalizing, the value-content of freedom. In other words, the value-ladenness of the risk marks the action as human and immanently related to the objectivation of reason.[16]

The master – slave relation also counterpoints the counterfactual dialectic of recognition in the context of the phenomenological boundedness of humankind's relation with nature. For Hegel, this relation is not rooted in the techniques that humankind may use to separate itself from nature; rather *work* like the fight is constituted socially. It is this social dimension that denotes work's humanness. Hegel establishes it as a historically contextualized social form that bears upon the manifestation and experience of reason.

The *denial* of recognition, like the fight, exposes the normative grounding of intersubjectivity, first as negation, as hostile, separated indifference engendered through a relation of domination. Through the negation of recognition, consciousness is reduced to a mere object, a thing that has no humanity, a thing whose only use is to toil, to work.[17] The master consciously exists for himself. His is the world of consumption, and although his existence is bound to another (the slave) this other is rendered, through the master's domination, as an independent thing, an object whose only purpose is to satisfy the master's needs. This *objectification* does not deny consciousness as such, but it does deny recognized self-consciousness. However, the process of objectification means that the 'other' no longer corresponds to reason's own criteria. Rather,

> the object in which the lord has achieved his lordship has in reality turned out to be something quite different from an independent consciousness. What now really confronts him is not an independent consciousness but a dependent one. He is, therefore, not certain of

being-for-self as the truth of himself. On the contrary, his truth is in reality the unessential consciousness and its unessential action. The truth of the independent consciousness is accordingly the servile consciousness of the bondsman.[18]

According to Hegel, though, the servile dependence of the slave has its own strength. Negativity, in the first instance, is almost a flight from reason; the anxiety of dependence joins hands with the threat of death. However, the slave must still exist, if for nothing else, for the lord. In this meagre existence among the goods and chattels of the lord's worldy baggage, consciousness still exists, prompted by the lord's own need. The freedom of a once recognized self-identity, as a hidden, yet permanently active memory, is achieved through fulfilling the master's needs, by work. Through this, the *memory* of recognition is restated in a new way. The seemingly negative activity of work becomes the self-formative activity of the slave through which 'the pure being-for-itself of the servile consciousness'[19] acquires an element of permanence. The slave is no longer unessential, 'work forms and shapes the thing.'[20] In externalizing him- or herself through work, in creating objects, the slave exists in his- or her hands. It is both negating and creating. In this way, the slave establishes his or her humanity (despite the domination of the lord). She or he becomes self-conscious of what she or he has done and is doing.[21]

Moreover, in the process of continued externalization, consciousness remembers its once-cherished independence. It begins to *think* it is free. This other process, thought, utilizes or belongs to Hegel's other anthropological impulse, language. The enunciation of words represents, for Hegel, the co-constituting movement from the zoological and one-dimensional attachment to and containment by nature to a world of an intersubjectively constituted humanity. It is more than the mere stepping out from nature though naming, through the passive indifference of an immediacy that has been given a *figurative representation*; it is also, and more importantly, the process of becoming-other which is both mediating and reflecting. Hegel puts it thus: 'Whatever is more than such a word, even the transition to a mere proposition, contains a *becoming-other* that has to be taken back, or is a mediation.'[22] This activity of linguistic symbolizing is also 'directed against the representation thus formed, against this (mere) familiarity; knowing is the activity of the *universal self*, the concern of thinking.'[23] Hegel thus gives language a double function – naming and knowing (or representation and reflective mediation). Representation presents something or a state of affairs for us, for humankind, 'that is not immediately given through

something else that is immediately given, but which stands for
something other than itself.' [24] In so doing, the meaning that it has
for humankind (or at least amongst its specific groupings) is also
declared. This entails that humankind itself produces the symbols,
and by so doing, its consciousness and knowledge of itself becomes an
object for itself. This enables consciousness to distance itself from its
immediate objects and reflects upon itself in its own right.[25] This
process of reflection on and through notional formulations, which for
Hegel constitute the patterns of consciousness, signifies the development of cultural objectivations.

The master – slave dialectic has value as a heuristic construction in
which history is simultaneously suspended, abbreviated and construed
mythologically (but not abolished). It represents, for Hegel, the conjunction of action and dialectics. The heterogeneous actions of
fighting, work and linguistic symbolizing signify that, at the deepest
anthropological level, an acculturated humankind proceeds, not only
through negation, but also through a positive transformation.
Moreover, this is achieved within the domain of conflictual social
relations, that is a society whose members have competing needs. The
conflict can be articulated in three ways. While fighting means that
the conflict engendered from the struggle for recognition tests the
value of life to the fullest, its real importance is that the articulation and
possible resolution of the conflict takes place according to a value
criterion. This becomes, for Hegel, the basis for persons as *political*
actors. It signals the transformation of fighting into politics. In a
similar way *work*, although initially performed in servitude to another
or to nature, creates and maintains a newly formed interdependent
series or relations. Hegel's sphere of material needs ultimately
demolishes the 'slavish' utilitarian and individualistic imagery, well
exemplified in Defoe's *Robinson Crusoe*. In its place is established an
interdependent relation between ethically motivated and articulate
subjectivities. For Hegel, this becomes the basis of social actors as
producers. Moreover, the dialectic of recognition renders the social
actor as a being who also dispels the fear of using language consciously.
Language, already implicitly imbued with the universe of reason, is
given over to reason entirely. Once she or he begins to *think* , the slave
is a self-conscious being and forces the lord into a new relationship of
freedom, autonomy and equality.[26] This is the basis of social actors as
reasoners. Language joins hands with politics and work. Together they
realize and maintain freedom.

Through each of these moments history proper also begins. For
Hegel, the story-teller, the memory of freedom becomes part of the
conscious process of reflection in which an identity is preserved in the

flight towards reason. This separates humankind from the animal and natural worlds and signifies the shift to second nature through the use of reason in labour, politics and language. Labour and politics entail the diversification and multiplication of needs and an ongoing socio-organizational complexity (private property and division of labour) that facilitates their satisfaction. The expression of humanness, for Hegel, is irreducibly tied to society's progressive rational domination of nature and the rational articulation of political life through the development of statehood. This entails, though, that consciousness itself mediates and unifies the heterogeneous self-formative processes of the species. Language as the unthematicized anthropological domain of consciousness emerges as the central medium of self-expression, especially as it takes objective form as a culture that articulates freedom as the core value. The notion of freedom, then, informs the real 'imagination' of human life in general.

A culturally impregnated and expressive history, then, becomes the place where the contradiction between the master and the slave is overcome. The allegorical tale, whilst abbreviating history's course as strict narrative, posits a historiography (particularly if one reads the *Philosophy of History* in conjunction with the master – slave dialectic) where the slave and the master supersede their particular universes and become free human beings – real human beings who encompass the universality of a free state. The memory and culture of freedom denotes a human consciousness that has moved to a higher level of mediated unity between a subjective action in history as a deed and an objective narration of it.[27] The two come together when Mnemosyne moves from formless impulses to those which produce history out of itself and become institutionalized in the state and articulated through a constitution. The master – slave myth represents the watershed between the prehistory of humankind and its own historicity. For Hegel, prehistoric periods (and here he cites India as one example) signify epochs in which reason is not heard. For him, they are not acts of will becoming self-conscious of freedom, mirroring itself in a phenomenal form and creating for itself a proper reality. Not partaking in this element of substantial, veritable existence, those nations – notwithstanding the development of language (culture) among them – never advanced to the possession of a history.[28] Rather, history or more properly, modern history, begins when the rationality of freedom starts to be manifested as a universal norm by social actors in the conduct of national affairs. And for Hegel, this means specifically when the modern state takes and produces from itself the rationality principles of freedom, institutionalizing them in universalistic formal commands, laws and constituted rights in which the subjects too constitute themselves as a universal citizenry. The state, then, is the culmination of political society. It is not only the pre-eminent objective embodiment of freedom, but also the means through which freedom is obtained by individual men and women. Together these confer permanency upon statehood itself.[29] Together they represent the recognition of the state's own identity as objectively self-conscious. In this way, the modern state represents for Hegel, the concrete expression of rationality, and as such becomes the form through which the universal and the particular, the subject and the object are integrated.[30]

However we still have to ask: how, in Hegel's view, is the self-conscious and self-determining identity of the modern state manifested in the political and working lives of acting subjects and in the organizational life of society?

THE LIFE OF THE SUBJECT
FREEDOM MADE OBJECTIVE

The *Philosophy of Right* 'transposes' the dialectic of the master and the slave (as an action-orientated philosophical anthropology) into the history of the modern age. The *Philosophy of Right* is a modern book. Freedom moves beyond the particular discourse of the absolute monarch to become actualized in the discourses of many. This multiple articulation of social and political life, however, becomes problematic for Hegel. Is political life now the articulation of many single individuals, is it formed into an aggregate of classes, is it the voice of the crowd? In other words, the multiplicity of discourses raises the problem, for Hegel, of a cohesive political identity and reality. For him, a cohesive and rational political identity should manifest itself in both the free will of the acting subject and the will of the state. In their conscious recognition of each other they both gain legitimacy and an objective existence which can be readily identified. The objective existence resides in the manifestation of the norms of freedom which become part of the cultural and institutional life of society as a whole. They become the framework for the self-identity of both the subject, as the autonomous individual, and the state.

In Hegel's view, freedom begins with subjectivity. Conscious freedom is the exercise of free will. However, for Hegel, a self-conscious life cannot be divided into the Kantian spheres of subjectivity. To be sure, in Hegel's eyes, modern philosophy has a debt to Kant. He can be thanked for firmly establishing 'the pure unconditioned self-determination of the will' as the starting point for any analysis of moral autonomy,[31] and it is on this ground that Hegel establishes an internal dialogue with him. Kant's notion of morality places individual action firmly within the domain of reason. The freedom of the individual is grounded in the notion of a person as the bearer of self-legitimation through which he or she recognizes him- or herself as a free willing subjectivity.

While this certainly establishes the individual subject as the possessor of moral autonomy, Hegel argues that the guarantee of autonomy remains incomplete and thus illusory – it remains subjective and particular, removed from the possibility of *real* objectivation, and because of this lacks genuine identification with the universal Idea of freedom. Kantian philosophy, in Hegel's view, cannot establish, yet alone maintain, an institutional objective form that is required for the subjective will to achieve fully realized self-reflective consciousness and identity. The real goal of the free mind, for Hegel, should be to make freedom *objective*, 'in annulling the contradiction between subjectivity and objectivity and in giving its aims an objective instead of subjective character, while at the same time remaining by itself even in objectivity'.[32] In this way, the Idea of freedom *could* be substantiated despite a real difference in form between subjectivity and objectivity. For Hegel, though, this is exactly what Kant's concept of freedom cannot achieve. It delimits freedom rather than posits it. Hegel's 'crucial point' against Kant is that in separating the spheres of inner and outer freedom both are denied real objectivated substance.[33] The determination and prerogative of the particular will's duty and the determination and prerogative of the subject's self-certain conscience are immanently problematic if they remain formally separate. In other words, Kant's temporary unity between the noumenal idea of freedom and its phenomenal forms separates freedom's universality as an ideal from the particular instances of its realization. Ethics is reduced to an 'empty formalism'.[34] This formalism, in Hegel's view, generates two fundamental problems that establish an antinomic cul-de-sac in which the politics of universality and reason cannot be fully articulated, only partially so. On the one hand, moral autonomy is entrapped within the internalized structure of the ego unable to be objectified through the veracity of laws and principles. On the other hand, the structure of external relations on the basis of the formal logic of practical reason lack permanent institutional substantiation.[35]

Furthermore, for Hegel, even in a partial and negatively prescribed form, freedom is open to vicious and tragic curtailment. The non-actualization of the transcendental Idea of freedom, creates, in Hegel's view, a vacuum into which rushes Jacobinism. Hegel's critique of Kant, then, is woven into his own continual and ambivalent sighting of the French Revolution.[36]

While Hegel welcomed it enthusiastically as denoting the political realization of freedom related to the notion of reason and a concomitant universalization of citizenship, he recognized well the extent of the unresolved antinomies of these gains, particularly in the face of the Terror of 1793. Positively, the Revolution raised freedom 'to an "intellectual principle of the state" and set it in the "*droits de l'homme et du citoyen*" as a "natural right"'[37] The 'old framework of injustice', unable to offer any resistance, evaporates, melting into air. Hegel establishes this very principle of freedom as both his philosophical *point d'appui* and the standpoint from which the outcome of the Revolution is judged.

Hegel's negative assessment of the Revolution rests fundamentally upon the vicissitudes of freedom itself. This, moreover, indicates the way in which he sees that a political price was paid by Kant's grounding of ethics in the distinction between the noumenal and the phenomenal. The Jacobin negation of freedom manifests itself in two ways, through the universalization of a self-certain conscience (outwardly parading as virtue) or through rendering universal freedom absolute.[38] Each can lead, either one by itself, or both together, to the formation of a perverse political culture.[39] The important point for Hegel is that both these forms of 'evil' take place during the French Revolution and give the Jacobin phase its distinct political and philosophical character. The foundation of freedom on virtue *and* a concomitant absolutization of the universality of freedom denotes the second route of the revolutionary period which circumvents freedom as a *real* universal. Each presupposes and buttresses the other.

The Jacobinization of virtue dissolves the whole determinate character of right, duty and existence into itself, thereby establishing itself as the sole power and prerogative of judgement of what is good, what ought-to-be and what is actual.[40] Moreover, Hegel recognizes it as a particular path of modernity within the context of the separation between morality and political institutionalization.[41] Morality, as the basis for Jacobinism's philosophical conception and articulation of the world, relies not on the institutional mechanisms of conflict mediation, but rather on the certainty of immediate and strategic action which divorces itself from the principles of practical reason.[42] It is here, too, that Hegel perceives the rise of the 'new personality'; the rise of passionate spleen – so central to an egoistic self-certainty – springs from the politicization of virtue. The Rousseauesque rendition of politics is activated by the intensity of self-righteousness, by the condensation of subjectivity into itself.

Moreover, this 'taking shape in the world', this worldly ascetization of politics is also established through the absolutization of the universality of freedom. Absolute freedom becomes the auspice under which the revolutionary transformation of society takes place. The Jacobin consciousness, in 'good faith', defines the ought-to-be of this universalization, its form and its content. Rousseau's 'general will', in Hegel's view, brings together the universality of absolute freedom and the politicization of personal virtue – the one collapses into the other.[43] In an attempt to articulate the will of all, each 'free' will genuflects before the will of the state, the embodiment of generalizable will-formation and rationality.[44] This further entails that the differentiation and individuation that Hegel sees as so important for the continual and progressive development of the modern era, is also annihilated. The inner life of personal needs is sublimated and subsumed to an identification with the general will to the point where

there [is] no reciprocal action between a consciousness that is immersed in the complexities of existence, or that sets itself specific aims and thoughts, and a valid *external* world, whether of reality or thought; instead, the world [is] absolutely in the form of consciousness as a universal will, and equally self-consiousness [is] drawn together out of the whole expanse of existence or manifested aims and judgements, and concentrated into the simple self.[45]

It 'effaces all distinction and all continuance of distinction within it'.[46] In this way, the objectivity of freedom undergoes an elliptical postponement. The objective determinants of absolute freedom can, for Hegel, only be negative. It releases a 'fury of destruction' in its *desire* to pursue a *total* social transformation which proceeds in two directions.[47] On the one hand, all *difference* is recognized in its non-identity with a generalizable, yet abstract freedom, and annihilated. The reign of Terror can begin. On the other, the formation of lasting institutional forms that articulate and mediate freedom as an actual social relation cannot be established because of an inner tension between the logic of the general will, which homogenizes and totalizes social life, and the recognition that absolute freedom *itself* is established through a particularity that utilizes power against any order (even its own),[48] in the name of an unsubstantiated rationality of freedom.

To be sure, while Hegel directs his analysis concerning this second version of negative freedom towards the Rousseauesque impulse in the French Revolution, he also has in mind the Kantian version which, he argues, is incapable of guarding against the universalization of the individual will.[49] The transcendental form of freedom which Kant posits, in Hegel's view, cannot, through a legislative act, protect itself against the vagaries of individual consciousness and generalized absolute freedom, because it lacks actuality.

Hegel's alternative solution to both these forms of freedom (the negative and the absolute) is to posit a notion of freedom which defines itself through actualization, i.e. an enduring institutionalization.[50] In other words, and as he states in the later *Philosophy of Right*, the universality of freedom is both conjoined and constituted through particularity and in being so constituted particularity itself is 'brought back to universality'.[51] This then becomes Hegel's solution to the Jacobinization of modernity in the face of the (purported) irresolution of the Kantian antinomies. The formation of *Sittlichkeit* is precisely this, to universalize freedom whilst maintaining the differentiation and heterogeneity of social life which the modern epoch has brought forward, but reintegrating this back into the institutional or objective forms of freedom itself.

REASON IN ACTION
THE FORMATION OF SITTLICHKEIT

In Hegel's view an ethical community should both mediate right and morality and articulate reason. The authenticity of moral life then becomes its ability to express itself not only as particularity, but also as universality.

In this way, Hegel reinterprets and restructures four of the fundamental political problematics of modernity. For him, the value of moral autonomy of individuals is simultaneously encapsulated within the domain of society, the public life of which should be an expression of its civil membership. The four problems that he addresses, then, are moral autonomy, society, the public (as against the private) sphere within that society and lastly the (democratic) articulation and recognition of demands (that is, that society's members engage in politics and as such are political beings and practice politics in a particular way). The core social forms that Hegel sees as mediating these modern types of social and democratic differentiations are the state and civil society, each presupposing the other. The state represents both the functional and ethical totality of its civil membership, which in turn is comprehensive and self-defining in its expression of the public life of society which is articulated through the state. The state thereby embodies the normative expression of society's objective life. Society, then, is the focus for its own self-articulation and self-activation. Its members (through and in civil society and the state) act to articulate demands and resolve conflicts, the procedures of which become the objective reality in the lives and actions of individuals. Ethical authenticity and strength is demonstrated through a capacity of each of the spheres to mediate, situate and universalize social conduct. So, while Hegel begins his analysis of the structure of *Sittlichkeit* with the family, that private and immediate sphere of desire, love and trust (the rudimentary elements of ethical life), he quickly moves to analyse civil society, which, for him, constitutes the basic expression of realizable and objective freedom in modernity.

However, for Hegel, civil society represents only a limited and indefinite stage of the actualization of freedom itself. The freedoms which the members of civil society express, and which are meaningful to them, require further supplementation to confirm their lasting objectivity. This supplementation and final definition of freedom will for Hegel take place within the sphere of the state. Hegel's analysis of civil society presents us with two tasks, then, which are related to our primary question: first, why does Hegel conceive civil society as a realization of human freedom, and secondly, why is this realization seen to be incomplete?[52]

For Hegel, the freedoms that civil society articulate are special. They are special in the sense that they indicate a sphere that exists independently of the state as a self-sustaining and self-defining sphere, as a sphere-in-itself. This is what establishes it as a positive modern phenomenon. For the first time, according to Hegel, all determinations of the Idea are given their due,[53] formed according to two principles that are inherent within civil society. On the one hand, civil society gives *all* subjects their due right and recognition in their idiosyncratic lives and, on the other, it can only do this if civil society is constituted intersubjectively and not through an individualistic ethos.[54] Hegel is concerned with much more than the development of identity, of egoistic subjectivity, *per se*. He is concerned with the reproduction of a stable normative order that facilitates the universalization of social individuation. This can only occur if the identity-formation is tied to those intersubjectively constituted and located processes of objectivation – work and effort and 'things' (property, products of needs and the will of others)[55] – which are seen as *social* projects. Through these and within the social space called civil society the two forms of the modern epoch – the authentic recognition of particularity (the universalization of the autonomy of the subject) and the institutionalization of the universal idea of freedom – find their first real and clear expression.

Given that Hegel has already posited work as an anthropological category (humans as producers), he now transforms this anthropology into a sociology, guided by the Idea of freedom. The existence of civil society gives Hegel a framework in which to transpose action categories of labour (informed as it is by mutually reciprocating inter-subjectivity) into the historical epoch of the modern world. Society, for him, has to be evidence of a realization of human freedoms that are situated within the ethical veracity of social life as a whole. For him, the answer to the problem of individual productions as a *social* activity lies in productivity being concerned as the objective production of *social wealth* – wealth is seen as a common social possession. It is 'beyond' family capital because through work and possession this social wealth is transformed into an ethical moment which becomes permanent.[56] In producing wealth, individuals, in their self-interest, produce a social product. In this sense, for Hegel, political economy provides the hermeneutical key with which to understand the already emerging social relations of bourgeois society (although the key is both integrated into and subsumed under the normative systematizing logic of *Geist*).[57] Its presence and importance is interpreted according to the two principles of civil society. Property in the first instance signifies the process of individual autonomy and personal freedom. The ownership of property signifies individuals as possessors of juridical rights because, for Hegel, in linking property ownership to the manifest forms of reason, it shows that owners have become self-conscious through imposing their will on material objects, and in so doing confront their own humanized world which they can use for their own purpose.[58] Political economy, in the second instance and through the system of needs, theoretically establishes both principles that determine modernity's inner logic. This, for Hegel, signifies the strength of political economy's analysis of the sphere of needs. It coherently interprets the endless detail of modern economic life, showing that behind the mass of accidents a rational law functions into which is drawn the 'mutual interlocking of particulars'.[59] Political economy is *the* modern science of society because it shows the rationality principle that lies behind the every-day production and consumption of needs. Hegel builds upon and transforms the Smithian image of the 'invisible hand' to argue that it is *wealth* as a *social product* that forms the basis for the actualization of freedom in civil society.[60] Wealth is an ethico-social category precisely because it is 'rooted in the complex interdependence of each on all'[61] that is, it is dependent upon individuals working together to produce it. In other words, it is grounded in labour *as a social activity*. This means that the universalizing Idea of freedom is carried beyond the particularity of need satisfaction as such, to establish the structures of normative inter-pretation in which the particular is reintegrated into the life of univer-sality. The increasing complexity of production, expanding needs and the social *capacity* for wealth, means that the division of labour (which arises, in Hegel's view, in the shift to second nature) now becomes a vehicle for identity-formation. Production, in that it is performed perforce socially, entails that the different types and spheres of productive activity become the basis for the collective and systematiz-ing symbiosis of civil society.

In this way, wealth and the articulation of needs simultaneously hold another moment – the dialectic of recognition. Freedom is expressed through the mutual and *recognition* of reciprocating objec-tivity.[62] The modern type of freedom, for Hegel, ostensibly begins not only with the independence of particularities, but also with their mutual recognition and interpenetration in all the moments which coalesce in civil society. However, the maxim that also holds the invisible Smithian hand – 'that each member can be his own end' – can annihilate the social existence of a society's membership. Hegel realizes that bourgeois self-seeking and capitalist enterprise, if they are universalized as *the* social norms, create social crises and not only social wealth. The net result, and as we interpret Hegel's argument, is a *crisis of social integration* that takes the form of pauperization and general alienation from civil society.[63] The poor (a social category which for Hegel includes the itinerant worker and the day-labourer) and the pauperized cannot, or can no longer, participate in society's productive life or its products. In so analysing the poor's misery and plight Hegel responds to it in two ways that could be seen to restate the ethical and normative imperatives of civil society in an action perspective. On the one hand, society must alleviate poverty in the long-term expansion of the wealth of society through trade, markets and colonization.[64] On the other hand, society must minimize suffering through welfare measures which demonstrate its ethics *publicly*.[65] For Hegel, reason rendered as a form of practical and public wisdom through welfare *is* social action.[66] The social actor now has freedom rendered as a conscious activity – as a realization and a recognition of a social crisis.

However, this is only half the story. Despite his analysis of the social effects of poverty, Hegel ultimately sees no way that civil society can satisfy the claims brought against it by the poor, even though their claims are legitimate. Certainly he is adamantly clear that poverty is a social condition which society as a whole must account for. Furthermore, the claims not only signal the imbeddedness of reason in the move to second nature, but that also in this move there emerge new relations of subjugation and domination. 'Against nature man can claim no right, but once society is established, poverty immediately takes the form of a wrong done to one class by another.'[67] Hegel, in explicitly recognizing the aporetic nature of a burgeoning modern (capitalist) society, also implicitly acknowledges a new class-relation 'in the making'. The poor's lack of property and dismemberment in the face of the vagaries of economic life means that, for Hegel, they form a class, rather than constitute an estate. Hegel's differentiation between class and estate is a significant recognition of the weakness of civil society, in that it stratifies its productive life, and relegates part of its real productive membership to the periphery. 'This results in', as he points out, 'the dependence and distress of the *class* tied to work of that sort, and these again entail inability to feel and enjoy the broader freedoms and especially the intellectual benefits of civil society'.[68] However, this implicit recognition lies dormant – it is not until Marx that this becomes the ground upon which a *theoretical* analysis of society is based.

Why? Hegel's fundamental thesis is that society is the ground for the actualization and articulation of reason.[69] This can only take place if, in Hegel's view, the members of society are totally integrated into and identify with, the project of reason. Civil society, then, must subsume its own demands to the more ultimate demands of society as a whole (the apex of which is found in the state).

Within this context the poor have no place; poverty threatens the existence of a unified and self-identifiable definition of society as reason/freedom. It threatens social integration, conflict becomes visible. Moreover, the experience of pauperization annihilates the potentiality of reason. Torn from their customary environment of family, village and parish, the poor are always in danger of becoming a rabble, a crowd, which with vengeful anger turns against society, against government itself.[79] It is this concern (at its most abstract – the destruction of reason) which propels Hegel, with the *memory* of the Terror fully in mind, to see the poor as the real threat to social stability. Having criticized the *lack of property* as the central problem of civil society, Hegel though, reabsorbs this 'weakness', restating it through a circumscription rather than 'radicalization' of the category of recognition. The property-centred interpretation of this central category indicates whether one is contributing legitimately to the production of social wealth. This means though that the poor are not recognized as having a place in society. Furthermore, unlike Kant's (purportedly universalistic) criteria for the participation in the commonwealth, Hegel's category of recognition dictates that all those who are not recognized become one single ontologized and generic negative subject – the rabble of paupers. The implicit heterogeneity of the Kantian disclosure, which recognized an empirical plurality of social groups, is forfeited. These series of antinomies and elisions, though, point to a deeper theoretical movement in Hegel's dialectical reasoning – his preoccupation with an ontological response to Kant, which to be sure is structured immanently in the *Phenomenology of Spirit*, but is fully explicated in the work on logic.

3

The Science of Society

FROM HISTORICITY TO DIALECTICAL HOLISM

Hegel thinks he solves the problem of poverty by absorbing the *nature* of civil society under the auspices of reason itself. This means that the substantive problem of social integration is approached in three ways that culminate in an ontological holism that subsumes a genuine social theory. First, he posits civil society as the preliminary stage in the overall integration of people into society as a whole and, secondly, he sees the state as the place where the process is completed. Thirdly, these two aspects are subsumed under Hegel's ultimate claim that reason be fully visible, self-explicating and self-knowing. Through this the antinomy between subject and object is ultimately and finally resolved.

This claim absorbs the action perspective which surrounds the dialectic of recognition and its existent consciousness and gives to it two interrelated frameworks through which to proceed. Both these frameworks come together under the co-ordinating agency of reason and present Hegel as a *systems theorist* in whose work all elements of the whole are submerged under the capacity of the system to function as a whole. This system-theoretic approach rests on the Hegelian view that '*What is rational is actual and what is actual is rational.*' [1] In fact this pithy statement from the preface of the *Philosophy of Right* summarizes Hegel's programmatic response to Kant, as well as indicating the underlying current of the work itself.

On the one hand, under the auspices of 'reason as system' an institutional infrastructure is generated that mediates the activities of the free-willing subject. This is termed the ethical order and is the representative feature of the first framework. For Hegel, this 'is the system of those specific determinations of the idea which constitutes its rationality'. [2] It replaces the Kantian abstract notion of the good to become an 'objective circle of necessity whose moments are the ethical powers which regulate the life of the individuals',[3] in which 'the absolutely valid laws and constitutions' provide its stable and independent context.[4] The *labour* of civil society and the *politics* of the *'fight'* (with their concomitant norm of recognition) are subsumed variously under the system of the economy (the sphere of 'unimpeded activity . . . expanding internally in population and industry'),[5] and under the 'organism of the state . . . and its constitution'.[6] The state is seen as the concretization of rational freedom because it unifies subjective freedom and objective freedom. In other words, Hegel 'invents' a series of institutional reference points for collective and individual identity and will-formation that ensure the stable integration of action and system. These are the corporations and the institutions of the state (the legislature, the executive and the crown). They come together in a mediated unity that presents society as a corporatistic entity.

The second framework refers to reason's stake as an ontology. Hegel is more than only interested in constructing a parable concerning the transformation of slaves into free persons. He is also interested in the *reason* for their transformation – that is their place within the internal ontological structure of reason itself, and the way in which the free individualities and their institutions embody or encompass the different moments of *Geist*. This constitutes Hegel's second interrelated, yet constitutionally distinctive conceptual strategy which also embodies his other argument against Kant, that is that Kant's transcendental philosophy is *not absolute enough*. We are not arguing that this is a new version which surfaces in the later Hegel's work, but that it has an immanent place even in his early (but not first) systematic work the *Phenomenology of Spirit* and sits 'beside' the historical dialectic. It does, however, have the effect of *decentring* the philosophical anthropology of the historical dialectic. The anthropology of an active humankind, which utilizes reason in its conflictual path to freedom and autonomous self-consciousness, is displaced by the demands of 'method', that is by the immanent ontological structure of reason itself. Hegel has a basic ontological claim, an *ontological dialectic* that establishes both the procedures and the categorizations that order the world. In other words, Hegel transposes the dialectic of recognition into the categories of logic. In this way, he maintains the melodious harmony of the earlier *Phenomenology* yet adds a categorial counterpoint which exposes the inner movement of world history. In this context, Hegel's *Science of Logic* becomes *Geist's* own self-exposition which both informs and explores the composition of historico-social analysis.

This ontological structure of the *Geist*-philosophy is thus the starting-point for the analysis of Hegel's holistic response to the multi-dimensional antinomies of modern life, which Kant's theoretical and practical philosophies represent. It is their bifurcation as well as their transcendental grounding that Hegel objects to – the splintering of areas of life and thought into separately constituted and autonomous object domains. Hence, the unity of pure and practical thought under the auspices of a self-explicating and self-authenticating reason, which Hegel posits and the *Logic* attempts to detail, is the unity of life in general and the transposition of the differentiated moments of social life into an integrated and harmonious ethical community in particular. For Hegel, to be sure, this substantiated unity occurs through opposition. The dialectical play of opposites (of subject and object, of the universal and the particular, of form and content) and their sublation and reconciliation denotes, for him, two things. On the one hand, reason's self-authenticating self-knowledge, and on the other hand, and because of the latter, the cognitive and logical articulation of a whole life which is expressed either culturally (in the *Phenomenology*) or politically (in the *Philosophy of Right*). The *Logic* then, can be read as the culmination of Hegel's vision of modernity. In this work the tensions and contradictions in both the epistemological and politico-ethical formulations of the Enlightenment's (real or imagined) post-absolutist world are resolved, for Hegel at least. The *Logic*, as ultimately a discourse on freedom, quickly absorbs the domain of nature in its quest for an ontology of society. It is in this context, then, that we wish to establish that the *Logic* is a sociological text and not only a philosophical one; that it establishes both the metatheoretical rationality and the implicit forms of structural and intersubjective interaction within which Hegel's argument concerning society unfolds.

REASON'S CIRCLE OF NECESSITY

For Hegel, Kant's construction of freedom is a spectral illusion produced by the Kantian insistence on the separation between form and content, subject and object, the phenomenal and the noumenal.[7] To be sure, the transcendental construct becomes the ground from which Hegel proceeds. This means that he accepts Kant's idea concerning the original unity of apperception.[8] However, he vehemently refuses the dualism which this entails, that there is no necessary relation between phenomena and things-in-themselves. Kant's formalization of the function of logic denies a content to the categorical thing-in-itself, thus also denying reason's access to it despite the fact that the thing-in-itself is part of the synthetic process of cognitive formation. This is the essential element in the dispute between Kant and Hegel. Kant's disjunction between the rational reconstruction of knowledge through the transcendental categories of reason and the thing-in-itself (reason) is, for Hegel, untenable. It is derived from the problematic formulation of transcendental philosophy, which is unable to answer satisfactorily the questions 'What is truth?' and 'What is an ethical life?' because they have been posed incorrectly.[9]

Hegel's response to Kant's transcendental philosophy can be seen to proceed in two stages, one of which is reminiscent of the historical dialectic, the other of which is anchored firmly in ontology. He introduces and at the same time tries to defuse what later writers would call the hermeneutical circle. Hegel renders the problematic of the constitution of reason as a problem for the construction of all types of knowledge – the traditional, the everyday, the empirico-rationalistic (scientific), the practico-normative. Habermas notes that there are three primary presuppositions that Hegel uncovers in his critique of Kant's dogmatic exercise of faith in mathematics and physics in his *Critique of Pure Reason*.[10] These are the normative concept of science's own scientificity, the criteria of judgement, and the formal and categorical distinction between the theoretical and the practical.

In the first level of analysis, and leaving aside his arguments concerning the problem of judgement in Kant, Hegel's critique exposes the historico-hermeneutical dimension that is irreducibly part of the formation of knowledge and is always prior to its various theoretical formulations. Epistemology unknowingly has a normative concept of the type of knowledge that is specifically identified as scientifically cogent and accepted a priori. As such it may hide from view the particular domain that is claimed to represent scientific thinking. In so doing it also closes other knowledges from consideration as scientific and sets the parameters for judging the scientific status of other cognitive domains. Hegel argues that a philosophy of knowledge (science) confronts in the first instance, only competing claims to knowledge and scientific truth.[11] Hence, the investigation of knowledge *itself* must abstain from prejudgements concerning what accounts for knowledge, from any quarter whatsoever.[12]

Moreover, this demarcation effectively and explicitly decentres pure reason from a reflection concerning its own genealogy. For this reason Hegel argues 'that an exposition of how knowledge makes its appearance [must] be undertaken'.[13] In this sense, the problem, for Hegel is not the generation of the *type* of knowledge. In an obvious reply to the Kantian construction of mathematical or ethico-historical truths in the preface to the second edition of the *Critique of Pure Reason*, Hegel argues that the truths that transcendentally grounded knowledge give are only bare results, lifeless and defective; defective because there is no reflective necessity in their construction. Their beginning and end-points are arbitrary and their efficacy vacuous.[14] Rather, these truths should be understood in terms of their own historicity.

> Philosophy . . . has to do . . . [with] the *actual*, that which posits itself and is alive within itself - existence within its own Notion. It is the process which begets and traverses its own moments, and this whole movement constitutes what is positive [in it] and its truth . . . In the *whole* of the movement, seen as a state of repose, what distinguishes itself therein, and gives itself particular existence, is preserved as something that recollects itself, whose existence is self-knowledge, and whose self-knowledge is just as immediately existence.[15]

As Habermas comments in obvious approbation of the reflective aspect that Hegel brings to the process of cognitive self-formation:

> unlike empirical existence, phenomenological experience does not keep within the bounds of transcendentally grounded schemata. Rather, the construction of consciousness in its manifestations incorporates the fundamental experiences in which transformations of such schemata of apprehending the world and of action themselves have been deposited. The experience of reflection preserves those outstanding moments in which the subject looks back over its own shoulder, so to speak, and perceives how the transcendental relation between subject and object alters behind its back. It recollects the emancipation thresholds of the history of mankind.[16]

The development of new knowledge contains the memory of past knowledge and the seeds of a future one, for both domains of cognition. This to be sure, is precisely the motif of the historical dialectic. The realm of freedom is reflected upon, a *memory* is activated, the world is changed.[17] Moreover, it is also the element that finds its way into what will be termed Marx's 'hidden imaginary'. The epochal clashes that occur in the history of humankind, as well as the stabilization of the epochs themselves, take place in the sphere of consciousness, in the cultural objectivations that are historically generated. Through this, the distinction, which Kant formalizes, between theoretical and practical reason, disappears. They belong not to specific object domains, but to the overall self-development of cognition itself.

However, hegel brings something more to the process of a reflective spirit - the immanency of its own absolute knowledge. This ultimately becomes the pivot around which Hegel's critique proceeds. The problem of the self-formation of consciousness is subsumed under the logical self-explication of Absolute Spirit itself; *Geist knows* the direction that consciousness should take because *Geist* is not only 'watching' but also positing. The criterion for truth is structured immanently into reason itself. Hegel clarifies this when he argues in *The Logic* that 'in order to be true [the science of cognition] must possess in its own self a *content* adequate to its form.'[18] But as Habermas has pointed out, this programmatic statement that surrounds the Hegelian objection to Kant, is only valid 'presupposing *that there can be* something like knowledge in itself or absolute knowledge'.[19] It is through this that the ultimate form that knowledge finally takes becomes both determinant and actual, confident in its self-possessing veracity.

This means, though, that the reflectiveness of the 'patterns of consciousness' with which the historical dialectic is ultimately concerned (and which establishes the framework for the analysis of the evolutionary self-formation of the species) is unproblematically absorbed by the requirement demanded by Hegel that this process must also denote the immanent explication of reason itself.[20] With this in mind, Hegel now transposes the world of phenomenological reflection into the world of logic. The problem becomes, for him, not the reconstruction of the long process of the coming-to-consciousness to Absolute Spirit but the investigation and clarification of its immanent structure. This presupposes 'a liberation from the opposition of consciousness'[21] which frees reason from 'all sensuous concreteness'[22] (that is the *experience* of overcoming and reflecting upon the distinctions that consciousness must face) to enable it to 'dwell and labour in [its own] shadowy realm' of pure thought.[23] In other words, 'the true method of philosophical science', for Hegel, can only 'fall within the treatment of logic itself; for the method is the consciousness of the form of the inner self-movement of the content of logic'.[24] In Hegel's view, the a priori synthetic constitution of knowledge denotes that thought itself has a logical content that can be reconstructed. Hence, questions concerning the nature of truth and freedom can only be raised within the ontological construction of reason itself.

To achieve the veracity and depth of the ontological dialectic Hegel must posit two things. First that all thought, as it is objectified through language which is made up of notions or concepts, embodies the universality of reason, and that each particular notion contains universality inscribed within it. In other words, there is an 'essence' or 'nature' of things that is constituted under general notions or concepts.[25] Secondly this can only be established through the process of worldly actualization. Hegel argues, then, that reason, through notions, fills out phenomenal reality because the world is the contingent and multiple mode or externality of reason. The actual world denotes the perpetuity, yet real existence of reason, that is, it is infinite, alive and in action: 'What is actual can *act*; something manifests its actuality through that which it produces.' [26] For Hegel the analysis of reason 'becomes a comparison of consciousness with itself', [27] as it manifests itself in the world propelled and judged by the principle of the universality of the notion of freedom. The history of the world, for Hegel, is this precisely – the actualization of freedoms in the world is evidence of reason's presence. These are judged by the standard of the universal notion of freedom.

This ontological formulation of reason, however, entails a change of emphasis within Hegel's formulations of history and (implicit) anthropology. The function of history is transformed from the interpretative, hermeneutically centred, historical dialectic to the reconstructivist version of an ontological dialectic. Historical development can be spelled out through the categories of reason because it, like nature, is one part of the structure of reason. Moreover, the philosophical anthropology of heterogeneous actions which informs the category of reason becomes a subservient and secondary feature once Hegel utilizes reason in its strong sense as an ontology. Philosophical anthropology is less important as an activity-forming constituent in the world than either Kant's later anthropology or the Hegelian anthropology imbedded in the historical dialectic.

The main change, though, is evidenced by the way Hegel presents the anthropological principle of language. In the historical dialectic, language functions as the mediating link between the moments of the heterogeneously constituted anthropological triad. Within this, one could argue that while language is ultimately posited as the predominantly important form that human action takes, the other forms are given due recognition regarding their constitutive importance. Together they form the totality of mediations through which humankind firstly demarcates itself from the zoology of nature, thus leaving instinct behind and, secondly, expresses and transforms its life through reflections on the notional contents as they are formalized both institutionally and culturally.

However, in the context of the ontological dialectic, language is posited, by Hegel, as *the* central principle of all human objectivations against labour and politics. It moves from a position of relative centrality to one of real centrality where it is both the keystone and apex within the system of reason. Categories, because they *are* the self-expression of language, not only 'permeate every relationship of man

to nature, his sensation, intuition, desire, need, instinct and simply by
so doing transforms it into something human, even though only
formally human, into ideas and purposes',[28] but also 'serve for the
more exact determination and discovery of *objective* relations'.[29]
Language objectifies thought, thus allowing thought to play upon
itself with categories that are not only both abstract and real, but also
can become both conscious and actual. In this way, reason does not
stand alone and self-subsistent beyond the world to order it. All
forms of thought, for Hegel, are an inherent manifestation of reason,
'the immanent universal'. This is, in his view, the indispensable
foundation that animates, moves and works in the mind of every
person and unites them into a community. The word is not only *the*
deed, it is also, for Hegel, the avenue along which reason travels
towards actuality and self-knowing, stopping only briefly at the
byways of the profane and the mundane, soon to return to 'the loftier
business of logic . . . to clarify [the] categories and in them raise mind
to freedom and truth'.[30] In other words the categories become the
keys that unlock the immanent structure of 'the circle of necessity'
and make it visible. For Hegel, the 'blindness' of an opaque reason is
lifted when reality becomes visible (understandable) through the
forms of notions that preserve the content of reason's universality.
Through these the Hegelian circle of necessity can assume that reason
is both simultaneously the subject, the ultimately real in its coming-
to-self-consciousness, and the object, because it is acting on itself as
the foundation of self-consciousness.[31] Subject and object exhibit the
same processes and come together to provide a clear enunciation of
each, an enunciation that dissolves the Kantian distinction between a
universality preserved exclusively for the domain of reason (the Idea)
and the particularities (Notions) that make up the totality of the
world. The rationality of the world, then, can only be ascertained
through an investigation of 'the immanent development of the
Notion'.[32]

Moreover, the ontological status of reason, for Hegel, resolves the
problematic of the subjectivistic status of judgement in its Kantian
formulation. In Hegel's construction judgement becomes a problem
of, and for, reason itself.[33]

The notions are given a self-reflecting objective or externalizing
existence that absorbs the subject into itself. The correct judgement
of the efficacy of knowledge (objectified in notions) by the subject has
to coincide, if one reads back (so to speak) from the works on logic to
the *Phenomenology*, with the self-consciousness of consciousness
itself. Reason establishes *the logic* of its own efficacy by reflecting on
itself and its own development. The criteria, then, for judgement, as

well as the act of judging, belong, in Hegel's view, to the notions themselves: 'Consciousness provides its own criterion from within itself, so that the investigation becomes a comparison of consciousness with itself.' [34] The categories or notions that language brings forth themselves bring to the surface the principles that are the universal expression of reason's logic. The categories designate the method through which the absolute knowledge of the world is attained – the method of the dialectic, the mainspring of reason's advance. [35]

For Hegel, the methodical aspect of reason is found in its inner movement – the dialectical outplay of the categories. Reason's desire for absolute knowledge is propelled by a series of 'ontological conflicts' or necessary contradictions. [36] These constitute the inner self-movement of reason. In this context, *method* is a misnomer. Hegel, in his discussion on dialectical method, asserts that it does not sit outside the 'substantive' task of forming knowledge – it is not something which is brought and applied to knowledge from a tool-box fully equipped with a ready-made and indifferent organon. [37] Rather as already indicated the method belongs to the very process of knowledge-formation. Hegel makes this quite clear:

> The method is the knowing itself, for which the Notion is not merely
> the subject matter, but knowing's own subjective act, the *instrument*
> and means of the cognising activity, distinguished from that activity,
> but only as the activity's own essentiality. [38]

It is not a predeveloped procedure (like Kant's transcendental deduction) nor does it derive from arbitary decisions of the empirical subject; it stems from the very developmental processes that take place in the formation of reason. It is the modality of cognition through which reason attains a conscious grasp of itself, or to put it more correctly, reason attains its own coming-to-consciousness about its cognitive formation.

The dialectical outplay of the categories or the 'ontological conflicts' are themselves formed and organized through three essential and interrelated conditions or principles of movement. The first two are organized according to different conceptual strategies. Reason is first and secondly the universal infinite out of which finite reality evolves, and the universal process through which identity is formed out of contradiction. Thirdly, it constitutes a totality or all-encompassing whole in which each diffentiated part is both an autonomous moment and a necessary link in a conceptual chain leading to self-consciousness. These come together in complementary movements to form the inner circle of absolute truth that not only closes the hermeneutical circle but also makes it an irrelevant problematic. The dialectic is both *negative* and *positive*, infinite and total. Each simultaneously and necessarily presuppose the other to enable the universality of reason to exist *for itself*, that is to posit and articulate its own determinate existence. This entails that dialectics should be recognized as the unrestrictedly universal, internal and external method for everything that

> exhibits itself as a *circle* returning upon itself, the end being wound back into the beginning, the simple ground, by the mediation; this circle is moreover a *circle or circles*, for each individual member as ensouled by the method is reflected into itself, so that in returning into the beginning it is at the same time the beginning of a new member. Links in this chain are the individual sciences (of logic, nature and spirit), each of which has an *antecedent* and a *successor* – or expressed more accurately, has only the antecedent and indicates its successor in its conclusion.[39]

Geist is, *firstly*, the universal, absolute subject that exists as an infinite cosmic entity. It is an infinity or rationality out of which a finite reality, as its own self-embodiment, is established. *Geist* establishes the rational and necessary relations for everything that exists because it is posited as rationality *per se*. Hegel's task is to make explicit the implicit rationality and intelligibility of phenomena, which because they exist are already imbued with a rational core. This strategy of a *descending dialectical* exposition (as Taylor puts it)[40] demonstrates that *Geist* must posit the structure of the things that are known. In other words, *Geist* as the cosmic spirit lays down the conditions of its own existence and posits the structure of finite reality.

Hegel's ontology, then, posits both the necessary conditions for, and the necessity of, a finite reality. Rationality, to be seen as immanent to the world must be embodied in it. Hegel's *Geist* philosophy is, in this sense, 'a this-sided ontology'.[41] The world is both subject and object – a subject which breathes life and acts upon itself 'is something enunciated, has an empirical existence in general and stands therefore in the field of limitation and the negative';[42] it suffers and it dies. Reality becomes its own object.

In this way, the finite and temporal world is the domain of *Geist's* self-realization and self-identification. Through this, reality too establishes its identity. There is though an opposition between the reality that is established and becomes identifiable as 'this' or 'that', and the inherent authenticity of *Geist's* self-consciousness. In other words, a contradiction exists between a dispersed, incoherent and unconscious reality and the reality that *Geist* wishes to posit categorically. The contradiction is between *Geist's* claim to adequacy and reality's *de facto in*-adequacy in the light of this.[43]

This establishes the *second condition* which exhibits its own principle of movement – the dialectic of identity. Moreover, this also denotes the transposition of the phenomenologically centred dialectic of recognition into the categories of logic. When confronted with finite, temporal reality Hegel's ontological *Geist* moves according to a different strategy – it moves according to the principle of *ascendence* from the abstract to the concrete. Beginning with the most elusive, singular and incoherent concept – being – *Geist* both establishes identity and the list of categories which describe, *identify* and come into opposition with reality and hence itself. The movement from the abstract to the concrete is then simultaneously negative and positive, positive because the categories are both concepts and forms of existence that establish *Geist's* reality, negative because *Geist* itself judges its own adequacy and authenticity.[44]

The negative dialectic essentially problematizes the identity of self-asserted, abstract universality. In Hegel's view, this form of indeterminate universality denies a realizable truth-content to itself and its judgement of reality. It lacks authenticity precisely because it is indeterminate. The *recognition*, though, of this indeterminacy provides the impetus for reason's movement towards self-authentication. For Hegel, this can only come about if reason in its first act, recognizes that it 'attains an existence (only) by means of *other* corporeal individuals',[45] that is, it is 'differentiated within itself'.[46] The act of negation which reason manifests is not, for Hegel, an annihilation, but rather a positing.

The immediate relation of being and nothing uncovers the necessary relation of interdependence, differentiation, yet unity. For Hegel, the world in general cannot be conceived of as rational if its parts are presumed to be completely separate. It is the 'unseparateness of being and nothing',[47] which, in having recognized the necessity of each in the other, lose their initial confident and imagined self-subsistence to become moments in each other's existence. In this way, the formation of identity signifies a double relation and purpose in which inherent negativity posits self-identity.[48] Both particularities form their identities only in relation to the other and in so doing dissolve their own particular perceptions. Each particularity transcends the boundaries of its own self-subsistent existence and puts itself into a relation with others. It is through this that the universality which is initially inscribed only implicitly is made explicit. In other words, each particularity finds 'its proper identity only in those relations that are in effect the negation of his isolated particularity'.[49] For Hegel this movement is the necessary and contingent feature of reality that establishes the foundation of reason's authentic identity.[50] The construction and actualization of universality assumes and sublates the dialectic of recognition. This is the central pivot of the entire negative aspect of the dialectic. Reason now exists for itself, in a unification of form and content and theory and method.[51] In other words, each particularity manifests its immanent universality not by a separate existence, but by identifying *itself* through another that on first meeting is perceived to be in opposition to it. For Hegel, this initial perception of conflictual opposition constitutes the beginning of reason's identity, and the process through which this is formed. It constitutes the primary identity-forming process of the universal *tout court*.

Moreover, this comprehension of concrete intersubjectivity also denotes the transition from negativity into positivity. Reason's positive dialectic exists in fulfilling its own promise of being-for-itself.[52] This is certainly realized at the beginning but it is *in reality* the result of a long process in which the universal is shaped in the construction of the notion. Reason is not fully actualized until the ground is cognitively prepared for its explication. In this sense, dialectical thinking is positive precisely 'because it generates the universal and comprehends the particular therein'.[53] The process of intersubjectively constituted identity-formation takes place through a series of determinations that 'work up' to the realization of reason. In the language of *The Logic* (which explicates the order of the categories that envelop a reflective cultural objectivation – not by themselves, but as a totality), reason is not realized until it makes itself its own subject and object through its own discourse. This discourse belongs properly, for Hegel, to the language of the notional form itself in which 'the *presupposed* or *implicit* originativeness becomes *explicit* or *for itself*.'[54] Discourse originates in and around an immanent reconstruction of the categories rather than the phenomenological relations of the social actors. Reason constructs its own self-sufficient principles of explanation through which it constitutes and addresses the world.

The concepts and categories become objectivated forms of life, each with its own history, each setting the stage for the succeeding period through which reason articulates and judges its own worldly formations and efficacy. In other words, reason cultivates itself[55] through an explication of its internal categories that manifest themselves as objectivations in either the natural or human worlds. As a result, the focus of the historical dialectic shifts from an interpretation of cultural symbols and constellations where the narrative told of a 'timeless historicity', to the ontological discourse in which the possibility for reason's actualization is both teleologically posited and internally constructed.

History, which signifies the expression of the human world, can be reconstructed because it follows the same rational pattern as reason – it is the outward and visible sign, a mark of reason's logic. Hegel reconstructs the self-formative and developmental process of reason as it moves from naive indeterminancy to the stage where it posits itself through notions that articulate freedom as the principle of life. The Notion is the category through which the 'language' of freedom is centralized. In its true form of existence the Notion belongs to 'the free, self-subsistent and self-determining subject'.[56] Freedom, then belongs to the Notion. It is the world of realizable and self-authenticating practical reason.[57] The ideologically posited processes of reason set about establishing historically the conceptual structures that contain the germinating seeds which can become the principle of freedom. These become the genus (or more properly, ground), from which freedom evolves from a period of indeterminant or accidental flowering (the Greek *polis*) to the more permanent and actual expression of the Notion. The first seminal forms of freedom in antiquity are 'recaptured' or recast in more modern forms – the world of the Notion made explicit. Here reason has achieved real externality and determinateness in a form in which the totality of its parts is both subsumed and identifiable within the whole structure of reason.

In the world of logic, the Notion is divided into three parts in ascending succession – the Subjective Notion, the Objective Notion and the Idea. These categories are used by Hegel to simultaneously posit both the resolution of the Kantian antinomy between subject and object and the authentic coming-to-truth of reason's self-knowing and self-actualization. It has already been established that, for Hegel, the world of subjectivity is an inadequate expression of reason's capacity in the world and is open to vicissitudes that work against reason itself.[58] The problem, for him, becomes to demonstrate the development of reason in terms of further externalized and objectified forms that give credence and permanency to reason's existence, by taking on institutional forms. Hence, the Hegelian Notion, which has within itself the world of the free-willing subject, must also include two other essential 'parts' that maintain and sustain the subjective life.[59] These are, the world of objectivity (the Objective Notion) which provides an objective determinacy for the subject (this is the world of civil society, the formation of *Sittlichkeit*),[60] and the realm where they (subjectivity and objectivity) come together – the Idea:

> The Idea is truth in itself and for itself – the absolute unity of the notion and objectivity. Its 'ideal' content is nothing but the Notion in

its detailed terms: its real content is only the exhibition which the Notion gives itself in the form of external existence, whilst yet, by enclosing this shape in its ideality, it keeps in its power, and so keeps itself in it.[61]

Concretely, this is represented, for Hegel, by the modern (Prussian) state. Reason now authenticates itself subjectively and objectively, actually.

Furthermore, because 'the Notion *is* the power of substance self-realised',[62] it is also the place where the harmonization and integration of disparate realities or particularities takes place. To be sure, Hegel, in the *Philosophy of Right*, views differentiation as a strength of the modern age.[63] In the *Logic* (and the *Philosophy of Right*), this strength can only be steeled through a higher unity. Nothing should have a separate, differentiated existence. There is an 'essential relation' between the whole of the constitution of reason and its parts. 'The whole and the parts *condition* each other.'[64] The whole cannot exist on its own as an independent thing; rather it can exist only in relation to its parts, as a self-subsistent totality in which the parts have an autonomous interdependence with the whole.[65] This is the *third principle and condition* for *Geist's* self-realizing ontology. In an effort to maintain the notion of diverse autonomy, yet divest it of the alienating characteristic of separateness, Hegel invests the whole with the power of integration and systematization. And the whole can, for him, only denote the world of the Notion in which the parts come together to form an objectifying unity and totality,[66] which unifies subject and object in a series of objectivations that bring the real and ideal into harmony.[67]

The totalizing dialectical movements between the real and the ideal, form and content, subject and object constitute, for Hegel, the basic structure of human cognition and the social world as a whole. 'The whole is a totality built up out of the dynamic interconnections' of autonomous, relative and partial realities.[68] Reason can only exist by negating these as negations, thereby sweeping them into the 'circle' of its explication. Finite reality, then, is the fulfilment of a plan, the articulation of which is determined by rational necessity. The plan – the map of the world – is externalizing, self-knowing, all-encompassing, total.[69]

THE SCIENCE OF SOCIETY
HEGEL'S FORMATION OF THE CORPORATIST STATE

It is in his interpretation of the modern state that Hegel's substantive and formal resolutions to the crisis of modernity combine and coalesce.

The notion of totality indicates that the dialectics of recognition and the whole and the parts have been transposed into an ontologically constituted *science of society* in which the structures of society are interpreted and reconstructed as categories of reason. The expressed ontological substructure of the *Philosophy of Right* is now clearly visible. *Sittlichkeit* becomes a system.

The totalistic self-explication of reason is not achieved by abandoning the philosophico-anthropological categories of fighting and work. Rather, Hegel transposes them into systemic categories of politics and economy. The objectivation of freedom takes place (in order to over-come or sublate its alienation from the subject) in the institutions of politics (the state) and the economy (the corporations of civil society). These become the legitimate and sanctioned forms that mediate the conflictually configured, yet intersubjectively constituted, social relations. To be sure, the modern state, for Hegel, represents the definitive although not final resolution of this movement towards reason's actualization. It is 'the actuality of the ethical idea',[70] the real concretization of freedom in its most rational form because 'the particular self-consciousness . . . has been raised to consciousness of its universality.'[71] This is reiterated in Hegel's interpretation of the con-stitution of the modern state. It is, in essence, a higher form which sublates the dialectics of recognition and the whole and the parts. As Hegel states:

> The constitution is rational in so far as the state inwardly differentiates and determines its activity in accordance with the nature of the concept. The result of this is that each of these powers is in itself the totality of the constitution, because each contains the other.moments and has them effective in itself, and because the moments, being expressions of the differentiation of the concept, simply abide in their ideality and constitute nothing but a single individual whole.[72]

In Hegel's view, the idea of the Idea is now both preserved and given an explicit *concrete* expression.

The dialectic of reason's self-explication immanently informs the formation of the state. The actualization of reason can only be achieved if its method 'expands into a system'.[73] This ensures that the move from indeterminacy to determinacy

> *maintains* itself in its otherness, the universal in its particularization, in judgement and reality; at each stage of its further determination it raises the entire mass of its preceding content and by its dialectical advance it not only does not lose anything or leave anything behind, but carries along with it all it has gained, and inwardly enriches and consolidates itself.[74]

Hegel adds proudly, 'this it accomplishes as *a system of totality*.' [75] This is what establishes the state's *rationality* criteria. In this context, a passage of the *Philosophy of Right* (which has already been referred to, but in the framework of the action-centred historical dialectic)[76] takes on a different meaning. While rationality consists, for Hegel, 'in the unity of objective freedom . . . and subjective freedom . . . and consequently . . . in self-determining action on laws and principles which are thoughts and so universal',[77] this can only occur if Hegel conceptualizes society as a functional and systemic totality itself – as an organism. The metaphor is important for Hegel on two levels; on the level of logic it signifies the mediated resolution of the whole and the parts, the recognition of the one with the other, as well as the manifestation of finitude out of infinity.[78] As a substantive or contextualizing metaphor (to use the language of contemporary systems theory)[79] it enables Hegel to solve the problematic relation between the desire for free autonomous individuals who *should* be political actors, the institutional forms in which their activities become manifest and the need for the systematic and integrated management of differentiated institutions. This is achieved, though, in a manner that surreptitiously introduces an instrumentalist criterion which undermines the norm of freedom. The metaphor of the organism is, in these terms, translated into the world of the corporations. They, in Hegel's view, sit in the belly of the organism, assert their independence, yet set aside this independence to be absorbed into the whole.[80]

The corporation becomes the basis and model for Hegel's organizing principle for the modern state as a whole. It fulfils the requirement that reason be fully realized and known, integrated yet differentiated. Reason's different moments – immediate unity, separation and mediated unity that constitute its triplicity – are realized in separate groups, achieve relative autonomy and come together, as a differentiated, sublated unity, in the legislature of the state. Hence, Hegel structures civil society into three moments that reflect the manner in which individuals participate in the production and sharing of social wealth. These are, the (already mentioned) system of needs, the administration of justice (which is tied to the normative and contractual recognition of property), and the police (that is public authority and corporations).[81] This scheme is further divided into estates constituted and defined by the type of work performed (agriculture, business functions of the state – public service).[82]

For Hegel, the functional separation of civil society into estates 'makes' identities and facilitates social cohesion. Class analysis (if it can be called this) is important, for Hegel, only inasmuch as it is indicative of the level of social integration. Classes, or more properly, estates, mediate the particular personality with the universality of the social, and by so doing become the second normative precondition for the formation of a cohesive and viable state.[83] For Hegel, because a person is actualized only in becoming something definite,[84] the proper place for this actualization is the system of the estates.[85]

Social integration is stabilized systemically because each estate is given a concrete institutional framework which defines and actualizes its participants. Actors are only social actors inasmuch as they act through their designated institutions. The agricultural class is substantiated in 'natural family life',[86] whereas the class of Civil Servants dwells in the public authorities of the state which look after the 'universal interests of the community',[87] and is thus completely absorbed into the life of the state. The business class establishes its own identity and institutional framework within corporations, which become, for Hegel, the proper and legitimate institutions of civil society not only because of their integrating capacity, but because it is they, *as organizations*, which overcome the dysfunctional effects of the crises of civil society. Corporations have a *character* that cannot be developed let alone sustained by labourers or the poor. The corporation is 'the second family of civil society [which envelops] the whole range, the universality, of the [subject's] livelihood.'[88] By being integrated and constituted through objectivity, the subject learns and practices a normative content, not by reverently genuflecting before it in a manner reminiscent of prior subservience, but rather through positively accepting the constraint of duty, which then becomes the subjects' liberation. In this sense, Hegel's notion of duty is for him more substantial than the Kantian version; in this liberation the ethical order gains its own legitimacy and right. The subject recognizes that his or her own rights are embedded in the universalizing constituencies of *Sittlichkeit*. They not only give a determinant framework for individual action but also become the real agencies for social assistance in times of crisis. The corporate structure of civil society, then, becomes Hegel's solution to the problem of poverty.[89]

Moreover, the corporation not only signifies Hegel's substantive solution to a partial and practical, but not yet theoretical, recognition that a new class is being formed and that this formation leads to conflict that is systemically dysfunctional; it also signifies his *political* solution. It denotes the model for the substantive organization of political relations within the state. Politics as the fight now takes place within the state which constitutes the fight's (only) arena. The resolution of more general social crises becomes the prerogative of the state; it is the place of political activity, it is the place of reason. Formally, the corporatist model sits inside reason's syllogisms and denotes the state's organization of all spheres of public politics under the auspices of either legislation or administration.

The state, as the domain of fully objectivated reason, is constituted through an immanent organizational logic that shows the capacity of reason to articulate itself fully. Composed of the sovereign, the executive and the estates general, each political moment is intersected by another institutional component to ensure the true articulation of the whole. By representation in the lower house of the estates general or on an advisory committee, civil society is incorporated in a series of syllogisms.[90] This incorporation unites those who live in the private sphere of civil society with the public life of society as a whole, so that as Taylor points out, 'they identify with this life and its acts.'[91] Corporate identity constitutes the substantive process of publicly manifest 'political will-formation', and hence the recognition of the social actor as citizen. Access to the dominions of power and legitimate authority is dictated and enfranchised by membership of either the universal estate or a corporation. Hence, it is not civil society as such that is represented or enfranchised. Rather, the legislative represent-atives are elected to office by the corporations, communities and associations. This is where their constituent responsibilities reside and where public life and public scrutiny begin and end.[92] The actor as a political being demonstrates not so much a public use of reason (Kant) but rather expresses it through his or her practices as they become objectified in the state institutions (be they the legislature or the executive committees) in which the actor participates. This constitutes the form of society's public life.[93] To put it another way, the corporate organization of society (as against the corporations of civil society) takes over the public articulation and mediation of political life and its administration. The corporations then, are not only

the components of the constitution (i.e. of rationality developed and actualized) in the sphere of particularity, [but also] the firm foundation of the state [and] of citizen's trust in it and the sentiment towards it. They are the pillars of public freedom since in them particular freedom is realized and rational, and therefore there is *implicitly* present even in them the union of freedom and necessity.[94]

As far as Hegel is concerned the isolation of the individual is overcome. Rights and duties are balanced and are visible. The particularity of the individual is mediated by a recognition that she or he is part of an ethical community that finds its fulfilment in the state. Or as Hegel puts it:

the isolated individual, so far as his duties are concerned is in subjec-tion; but as a member of *civil society* he finds in fulfilling his duties to it protection of his person and property, regard for his private welfare, the satisfaction of the depths of his being, the consciousness and feeling of himself as a member of the whole; and in so far as he completely fulfils his duties by performing tasks and services for the *state*, he is upheld and preserved.[95]

The claims laid out in constitutional law – that the state is the most rational of political forms because through it human freedom is actualized by the mediation of the particular with the objective institutions of civil society and the state – are grounded in the logic of reason and actualized as a teleological movement through history.

The 'freedom made actual', which in terms of the Kantian project demanded both the liberation of civil society from the absolutist state and civil society's sovereignty over it, becomes, for Hegel, the immanent movement of the 'Idea of freedom'. It is here that Hegel glides past the historical dialectic with its anthropology of action to embrace the ontological dialectic. Within this context, Hegel dramatically reinterprets the Kantian formulation of civil society and the concomitant notions of 'the public' and the 'enlightened use of reason'. The Kantian version of politics views civil society (or more specifically the concept of the public that resides within it) as the representative symbol and notion for universal citizenry, the membership of which is recognized as free wills. As such, civil society (through the concept of the public) constitutes, for Kant, both the institutional and critical domain for and of the political activity of the citizen. In the politico-social domain, which is the one we are primarily interested in, Kant establishes the transcendental status of practical reason as the criterion for the judgement of ethical claims which actors put forward in their own political and everyday lives. Moreover, in the realm of politics, judgement is a matter of *public* life. It should, as far as Kant is concerned, be part of an increasing movement towards enlightenment through the use of reason, which takes place in public spaces as well as being institutionalized in state constitutions. The tribunal and final arbiter of public political disputes is the transcendental status of the norm of practical reason.

This is the politico-philosophical background to Hegel's own interpretation of the modern world and modern subjectivity. Civil society, according to Hegel though, is simply the sphere of economic and corporate life where 'the public' is formulated as a functional homology of concern which becomes part of the state's administrative apparatus. The Kantian 'public' as the free voice of reason in civil society no longer appears in Hegel. The public, as a sphere of *political* activity, which resides more properly in the life of civil society where people come together to form a political will through the public use and show of reason separate from the dominions of state *power*, is closed. Public opinion, as a power imbued with the force of reason which challenges the state, no longer exists. While to be sure, Hegel retains the belief that the free expression of public opinion is the gift of the modern rational political order, he also sees it as the potential agency for ignorance, error and irrational mass politics.[96]

More importantly though, according to Hegel, public opinion only approximates the use of reason because of the former's capricious and unpredictable nature. Its (reason's) true ground and appropriate articulation is the state, 'the actuality of the ethical idea'.[97] Hegel ties the use of reason to the ontological status of reason as a category which judges the world. Judgement is presented as the unity of subject and object prescribed within the system of reason. As such, it either falls under the spell of, and is thus subsumed under, the logic of contradiction and objectified through the structures of society, or it is given over to the world-historical individual.[98] The latter, a strange, unique yet august being, who at times unknowingly does the work of reason, now represents the context of human action within Hegel's ontologized system. For those who are not heroic but merely mortal, and thus come under Hegel's categorization of the former actualization of judgement, the public use of reason can only take place within the state because the state is absolutely rational.[99] Because Hegel conceptualizes the free will as being imbedded in the law of the development of society, freedom and judgement are beyond civil society, they are outside Kant's own notion of the public. Hegel's Notion of freedom becomes a purely objectivistic entity unto itself and thus swallows whole the problematic of the acting, judging subject. For him, society is not only reason made actual, it is part of reason's own immanent ontological and teleological self-explication.

Hegel's unity of the world of reason which humankind inhabits is now complete (at least as far as we have analysed it in its political form). However, it is not achieved, as he supposes, through the absolute interrelatedness of the historical and ontological dialectics. Rather, Hegel's ontological dialectic comes into its own and sublates the world of phenomenological experience and interpretation. Ontology forms a totally integrated system of reason that configures the social world in a way qualitatively different from that of the historico-interpretative dialectic. As such, it effectively decentres the claims that the self-defining subject had to relative primacy.

As a *science of society* the ontological dialectic constructs the social world of intersubjectivity, that is, the actualizing world of the self-defining subject in its three images, according to three interrelated principles of movement. These are, as we have mentioned: the primacy of the infinite over the finite with its descending dialectic, out of which finite reality develops and achieves an authentic existence; the universal nature of contradiction or ontological conflict through which identity is formed by the ascending dialectic of triplicity that moves from the most abstract universal to the most concrete *universalized* form; the principle of totality or the dialectic of the whole and the parts which gives primacy to the whole over the parts. Each buttresses the other.

However, for the purpose of locating Hegel within the anthropological problematic of the modern shift towards self-defining subjectivity (and of viewing Marx's relation both to this problematic and to Hegel), the principles of contradiction and totality are the most important. Once transposed into the language of society these two principles together construct society as a systemic whole in which everybody gives voice to the universality of freedom because everybody has 'a home' and is clearly visible. The important point, though, is that society and the lives of the subjects are conceptualized, by Hegel, as vehicles for reason's *own* self-actualization and movement towards self-consciousness. This hands priority and primacy over to the principals through which reason moves, and, hence, to the categories through which the principles construct the social world according to reason.

The teleological movement that Hegel imputes to the principle of contradiction emerges as one driving force behind the construction of his science of society. The notion of self-actualization is conceptualized in terms of a prefigured end that only gives legitimacy, authenticity and recognition to the human world by mythologically absorbing its components – history and society – into *Geist*. Reason stands above, and thus becomes independent from, individual acts (except in the case of the world-historical individual) and the reality of society. Its ultimate interest is only in its own movement towards the Absolute.

This entails that history becomes unified, and in so doing its constituting actor (the dialectic of intersubjectivity and the domain of society) is unified also. History and society are constructed according to the principles of absolute identity, which simultaneously draw in the principles of totality. The ontological dialectic constructs the world according to the principles and categories of reason's circle of necessity. In this way, the *Notion* of freedom becomes both self-defining and all-encompassing. It subsumes all parts under the whole and restates itself as a self-constituting totality. As such, the development of the category of the Notion, as it structures Objective Spirit and comes to rest in the Idea, exhausts the composition of social reality (but not itself). Social reality, according to Hegel, is coextensive with the categories of Reason; as we have seen with the problem of poverty, Reason 'systematically forbids the admission of anything that eludes [its] closed circle'.[100] Conversely, it systematically forbids the expression of social conflict. Society is in harmony with itself and the structure of reason; the system is integrated.

Hegel's reconceptualization of the self-determining subject, notwithstanding its formulation under the historico-interpretative dialectic, leaves the subject not so much disembodied (because it is now completely embodied in *Geist*) but *disinherited*. The subject, humankind, or more specifically, the composite of hetereogeneous social actors (classes, groups, individuals) cannot claim for themselves the anthropological determinants with which Hegel forged the world of Objective Spirit. Labour, politics and language, as anthropological categories, are constituted and mediated according to ontological principles. This leaves them bereft of both real subjectivity and a conceptual structure through which they can be analysed. It is not until Marx one-sidedly constructs an anthropologically centred paradigm that humankind 'speaks' on its own terms. It is to this that we now turn.

4

From the Politics of Strangers to the World of Estranged Needs

THE TENSIONS AND DIRECTIONS OF THE WORKS OF 1843

It is appropriate to introduce the 1843 works through the general problematic that Marx is confronted with. Generally, it is the separation of state and civil society. However, more specifically, this is informed by an ethical imperative that not only guides Marx's early investigations, but also becomes the central maxim that helps to structure all of Marx's critical theories. This is found, not in the 1843 'Critique of Hegel's Doctrine of the State', but in the slightly later 'On the Jewish Question':

> Man leads a double life . . . He lives in the *political community*, where he regards himself as a *communal being*, and in *civil society*, where he is active as a *private individual*, regards other men as means, debases himself to a means and becomes a plaything of alien powers.[1]

This maxim is first formulated by both Kant, as the maxim for practical reason, and Hegel, through the dialectic of recognition, to become the ground of freedom. Marx consciously separates himself from these two thinkers. He accepts neither the Kantian image of the actor as a citizen of two worlds, nor the Hegelian image of humankind as a vehicle of Absolute Spirit. This separation is formulated at this stage in terms of a not yet crystallized anthropology through which he addresses the central maxim in two ways. His anthropology implies, first, that an ethical maxim denotes a practical relation to the world by social actors, and secondly, that the world is constituted by human beings. These already *implicitly* inform the way in which Marx establishes his analysis of Hegel's *Philosophy of Right*, although Marx simultaneously draws on Kantian and Hegelian formulations in an effort to give the maxim both theoretical veracity and practical, that is political, significance. But in so doing (and with an anthropological reading of philosophy in mind), he radically departs from, as well as deeply adheres to them.

Marx is singularly unconvinced by Hegel's corporatist solution to the problem of the modern state. While he acknowledges Hegel's positive pronouncement that the separation of the state from civil society is part of the realization of freedom in modernity,[2] Marx views as illusory Hegel's attempts to posit corporatist intermediary institutions which aim to facilitate political practice by a free citizenry. Hegel's harmonization of individual and society is, for Marx nothing but 'the *romanticism* of the political state, it contains its dreams of its essential unity, its harmony with itself.'[3] Moreover, this 'harmonization' also means that society is viewed as being total and transparent.

Marx seizes upon and presents Hegel's corporatism as an *allegory* that signifies an unresolved antinomy between civil society and the state. In so doing he develops his double-sided criticism of Hegel – that society is both transparent and harmonious – by seemingly separating the two sides of the argument into (apparently) distinct problem-domains. First, there is the formation of political will in the modern civil or constitutional state, and second the constituted basis of the sphere of needs, or more specifically how civil society reproduces itself. In an effort to come to terms with the *former problem* Marx generates two types of universalistic arguments. One is grounded on the notion of freedom derived from Kant (the notion of freedom as a transcendental norm), the other from Hegel's idea of holism.

The Kantian argument provides one basis from which Marx seeks to radicalize and concretize the already universalistic principles for political life, i.e. the normatively grounded practical philosophy which Hegel also absorbed. From this, and if one reads 'On the Jewish Question' and the September 1843 'Letter to Arnold Ruge' in the light of the slightly earlier 'Critique of Hegel's Doctrine of the State' one can argue that Marx is developing a quasi-transcendental strategy of radicalized enlightenment. Echoing a version of Kant's 'What is Enlightenment?' thesis, but one which explicitly revokes the restrictions on criticism as public activity, Marx instructs his audience that the present task is '*the ruthless criticism of the existing order*, ruthless in that it will shrink neither from its own discoveries nor from conflict with the powers that be'.[4] This radicalization of enlightenment which is by its very nature a radicalization of democracy, is, for Marx, a process in which his addressee, at this time an active humanity, becomes conscious of the disjuncture between its real condition and a historically generated possible alternative. If critique thematizes the normative and universalistic principles that are already historically present and which *should give content* to modern political institutions, it should also address the systemic or institutional constraints and blockages that prevent their actualization. As Marx states:

> Reason has always existed, but not always in a rational form. Hence the critic can take his cue from every existing form of theoretical and practical consciousness and from this ideal and final goal implicit in the *actual* forms of existing reality he can deduce a true reality. Now as far as real life is concerned, it is *precisely* the *political* state which contains the postulates of reason in all *modern* forms, even where it has not been the conscious repository of socialist requirements. But it does not stop there. It consistently assumes that reason has been realized and just as consistently it becomes embroiled at every point in a conflict between its ideal vocation and its actually existing premises.[5]

The norm of the freely expressed autonomous person already formulated by Hegel (via Kant) in the 'dialectic of recognition' (as well as the democratic Constitutions of France and the United States) provides the starting-point for Marx's critical appropriation of the universalistic principles of freedom, equality, justice, autonomous individuality and personhood which are used for the self-legitimation of the modern state. Marx's invocation of these formal criteria for freedom that both inspired and were voiced in the democratic revolutions, sits beside a second – that of substantiated unity. This argument relies implicitly on Hegel's notion of the Universal which is both the prefigurative and necessary form that closes the gap between the objective conditions of people's existence and their own subjectivity. Marx's charge of formalism against Hegel rests upon a basic acceptance of this Hegelian notion of the Universal, the creation of a whole being. Marx however, does not agree that this holism is *actually*, or *in essence*, created either in Hegel's corporatist formulation, or out of the esoteric air of *The Logic*.

Both universalitic arguments inform and *contest* the basis, the realm proper, of the first problem-complex – the way in which Marx addresses and problematizes the Hegelian formulation of the sphere of needs. This too, as we shall see, transforms the way in which the maxim itself is interpreted.

THE FIRST PROBLEM-COMPLEX
MARX'S POLITICAL ANALYSIS OF MODERNITY

Marx recognizes that the problems which emerge from the *Philosophy of Right* are in themselves immanently related to Hegel's *Geist-*

philosophy. They denote the illusory, phantasmagorical nature of Hegel's resolution of the conflictual separation of state and civil society – they are categorizations of the inner logic of *Geist* on its way to absolute self-knowledge. Hegel's corporatism, because its fundament is *Geist*, assigns the real subjects of freedom to purely formal significance and in so doing abolishes the opposition between state and civil society as a *real* political conflict.[6] In other words, Marx essentially argues, by way of a left-Hegelianism, that the estates are not categories of logic but instances of the social life of humankind. The Feuerbachian atheistic God as humankind, in all its consciousness, entails that it is left alone in all its inglorious reality to struggle with and realize the promise of the modern epoch. Moreover, it has been left alone within the domain of civil society after its real or imagined separation from the state. The positive aspect of this historical separation lies, for Marx, in the way in which civil society frees itself from the prerogatives of the state, absolutist or otherwise, by becoming the sovereign power of a society as a whole, formalized through a constituted democracy.[7] Furthermore, civil society also represents the true sphere of needs, the sphere of non-politicized subjectivity, into which the state cannot penetrate. It is the sphere of negative freedoms.

But for Marx, this double-sided nature of civil society that finds its way into Hegel's corporation typifies and prolongs the contradiction between the autonomous political personality who should participate formally and freely in political life, and the private citizen who has no claim to universality, but lives a separate and atomistic life in civil society itself. This division is the source of the critical weight that Marx brings to bear upon civil society itself. For Marx, a civil existence entails that the modern individual '*must . . . divide up his own essence*' and become subject and part of a bureaucratic order that belongs to the state and a social order that belongs to privatized civil society.[8] Both of these moments, in Marx's view, ensure that the political fragmentation and the indeterminate sovereignty of civil society posited by Hegel's formulation is *guaranteed*, not overcome. Corporate identity continues the separate existence of *both* civil society from the state – an existence that occludes or obstructs civil society's potential sovereign dominion over the state – and the fractured existence of *man*, who is perceived to be simultaneously a *Burgerstand* with particular interests and a *citoyen* with a political life of *public* concerns. Corporate representation robs the individual of his (not yet her, and by no means universal) recently won autonomy, by institutionalizing his functionally derived civil privatism as well as fulfilling his political essentialness, *only* by subsuming his political life to the will of the integrated state.[9] Moreover, in Marx's view, Hegel also collapses the corporation into bureaucratic rationality and corporatist organization into the constitutional state. Both sets of determinations have a devastating and immediate effect on the political life and composite structuring of society as a whole. The transformation of the civil corporation into a state bureaucracy amounts to the depoliticization of public affairs. The separation between state and civil society disappears in the legislature's muted deference to the empirical universality of administration. The bureaucracy, as the representative form of the universal interest, asserts its predominance by transforming any universalistic claims into purposive and administrative offices and thus monopolizes political life.[10] This rationalization preserves rather than abolishes (in a historical sleight of hand) the official castes which typify pre-modern stratified societies. This ensures that the bureaucracy becomes 'a magic circle from which no one can escape'[11] – a magic circle of self-enclosed (secret) knowledge which the individual bureaucrat utilizes in hunting for a career. Moreover, the monopolization of political life by a bureaucracy that imposes its own image on society, is for Marx the sign of the totalized yet depoliticized society, not the politico-ethical community, as Hegel would have it. The permanence and the power of the bureaucracy indicates to Marx that the state functions without politics; what are taken as universal interests are merely the functions of the state in the hands of Civil Servants, who either render superfluous the corporate representatives of civil society as they take their place in the legislature or transform them into administrators.

Marx's rejection of corporatism is due to his disdain for particularistic politics as well as corporatism's inability to overcome the contradictory separation of state and civil society. Marx, in fact, interprets Hegel sociologically – the *Geist*-philosophy is a theory which is supposed to reveal the complete truth about society's functioning, and that this truth is gained or attained in a completed form, that is that society is completely transparent. In this way, there are no hidden corners, no hidden histories. Marx treats this totalization *ideologically*, that is he views this as Hegel's ideological legitimation of the German state. The actual state of affairs (and Marx does not essentially disagree with the Hegelian holistic notion of truth, only its truth-content – something which underpins his method of ideology critique, especially as it takes another shape years later in *Capital*) is that the revealed truth is *concealed*. Corporatism is the hidden tension, the unrevealed conflict between the composition of civil society, the reality of its sovereignty and the domain of effective power, the state.[12]

Marx is at a theoretical watershed – the interesting aspect of the 1843 'Critique of Hegel's Doctrine of the State' is that it contains three directions. The three directions though cannot be developed very far from within the framework of the 1843 writings. The immaturity of the project corresponds to the lack of development of all three themes, the tension of which fractures Marx's attempt to generate a distinctive *political* philosophy.

In the first instance there are the largely unformulated and unspecified ways in which Marx wishes to solve the dilemma of a normative yet institutionalized democratic politics, which is related secondly to Marx's own analysis of the Hegelian version of civil society; which remains unproblematicized as the representational form of a specific historico-institutional reality, despite an immanent critique that exposes the constraints generated by civil society itself. These two aspects are in turn informed by a third, an albeit tentative anthropology that emerges to articulate the constituent elements of societally located human action.

What would Marx have in place of the corporatistically organized and bureaucratically structured state?

In Marx's view, the organizing principle of modern society *should* be democracy. For him 'the democratic element should . . . be the real element which confers a *rational* form on the organism of the state as a *whole.*' [13] It is the form that should transform civil society's partial and hidden sovereignty over the state into an actual one, and thus expresses the idea of freedom.

Although Marx's commentary and arguments for democracy have an elusive quality, it is here that his Kantianism comes into its own. In response to Hegel's abstraction of the estates from their political roots in civil society Marx basically asks: 'who participates in the political process?' [14] His argument hinges on an interpretation of a paragraph of the *Philosophy of Right* in which Hegel argues against popular participation in electoral and state affairs and for corporate deputization of legislators. Hegel's argument is thus:

> To hold that every single person should share in deliberating and deciding on potential matters of general concern on the ground that all individuals are members of the state, that its concerns are their concerns, and that it is their right that what is done should be done with their knowledge and vocation, is tantamount to a proposal to put the democratic element without any rational form into the organism of the state. [15]

Marx counters Hegel's dismissal of democracy by universalizing the right on which even Hegel's estates are based – the universalistic criterion for participation: '"All" should "as individuals share in

deliberating and deciding on political matters of general concern";
i.e. *all* people should play their part, not as all but as "individuals".'[16]
In other words, or in Kantian terms, all members of the state already
participate in its affairs by virtue of their existence in it, and participate
in it as free and autonomous persons. The task is to remove the restrictions placed on *real* participation and to do so in conformity with
universalistic principles. In addressing this problem in a similar way to
Kant in his essay 'On the Common Saying: "This May be True in
Theory, but it does not Apply in Practice"', and removing Kant's
unacknowledged historicism lying within it,[17] Marx concretizes and
thereby radicalizes the already universalistic criteria. For him, 'What is
crucial is the extension and greatest possible *universalization* of the
vote, i.e. of both *active* and passive suffrage.'[18] The question in this
context is not, as Hegel presumes, the substantive problem of either
direct or representative democracy, but the *right* of participation in the
affairs of state, as a universal value. It matters not if this *right* is
actualized as a 'mere' member of an electorate, as an elected participant
in the state's institutional complex, or as a public voice; in all instances
it is carried out as a free and conscious *political* activity. It is the realization of *homo politicus*. In this light, Marx's critique of property is
essentially political. In other words, the critique of property is based on
its *use* as a criterion of exclusion from political life, that is it becomes
part of Marx's 'transcendental' critique of access to participation in
politics and the possible democratic control over the power of the state.

   This extension of democracy, as Marx argues correctly, would
significantly and radically transform the relation between state and
civil society – it would invert Hegel's 'managerial' relation and assert
civil society's primacy over the state.[19] In becoming the primary and
anthropological source of political life, civil society is itself transformed.
The values that would inform this transformed sphere (the core ethical
value is the maxim prohibiting the transformation of people into mere
means) are constituted through a radically democratic *Sittlichkeit*.

   The elusive nature of the 1843 'Critique' also suggests that Marx
offers a fleeting and momentary alternative to Hegel's corporatism
that tentatively addresses the question of how the complex institutional
arrangements of modern society might be organized around the norm
of democracy. Already mindful, through Hegel's own analysis, of the
problems of direct democracy, the Rousseauesque formulation of the
'general will' and the liberal constitution, Marx favours a participatory
democracy which at the very least articulates all conflicts that originate
in civil society. This is, for him, against the Rousseauesque formulation,
the strength of the representative constitution – it is an open, logical
and undistorted expression of the contradictory nature of modern

life,[20] that raises the possibility of transforming civil society into a political society through as general a participation as possible.[21] One might interpret Marx as suggesting that this could take place through a pluralization of legislatures within both civil society and the state. It could entail that the corporate entities become universalized and self-managing through their own legislatures. This subsequently results in a concomitant decentralization and democratization of both state and corporate power. It is worth quoting the relevant passage at some length because it is incongruent in the context of the work as a whole. Moreover it also draws our attention to the main underlying problem in Marx's work at this time.

> Hegel refers to the 'Estates' as the 'extreme position of empirical universality', which actually properly applies to civil society itself. (Hence it was pointless for Hegel to cause the political Estates to arise out of the Corporations and the different classes. This would only have been meaningful if the different classes as such were the Estates and if the determination of civil life were in reality identical with that of political life. In that case we would not have a *legislature* of the state as a whole, but a legislature of the different Estates, corporations and classes over the state as a whole. In that event the classes of civil society would not receive their political determination from elsewhere, but instead they would determine the political state. They would turn their *particularity* into the power determining the whole. They would represent the power of the particular over the universal. We would not have a single legislature but a plurality of legislative powers which would come to an understanding among themselves and with the executive . . .)[22]

Marx, though, basically bypasses this rudimentary yet potentially fruitful idea of a self-managing society, remaining instead with the Rousseauesque image of direct democracy or an alternative later version of planned socialism inherited from Saint-Simon. This model does two crucial things. First it maintains and extends the institutional basis of formal democracy, thus drawing more people into political life. Secondly, it abolishes the administrative monopoly of the bureaucracy and executive government by ensuring that the politics of decision-making are publicly accountable and based on principles of election. However, it is driven by an underlying logic – a logic that Marx himself recognizes as problematic, especially in his analysis of the period of the Terror in 'On the Jewish Question' and *The Holy Family*,[23] but simultaneously mythologizes – the logic of the re-unification of everyday life and political life, of civil society and the state.

THE SECOND PROBLEM-COMPLEX
THE CONSTITUTED BASIS OF THE SPHERE OF NEEDS

What surfaces immediately in the 1843 'Critique' is an internal tension between the precise meaning of the two models of universalistic philosophy and the way in which they coalesce in Marx's own analysis of civil society. So while the tentative anthropology that emerges from the *'Critique'* is fundamentally a *political* one which is not yet informed as its innermost core by the categories of political economy, there is an internal strain that reflects these two interpretations of universalism (the Kantian and the Hegelian).

Marx, in an almost Kantian guise, concentrates on the normative principles that the Enlightenment had already constitutionalized.[24] In this light, he sees the problem of sovereignty, as well as civil society itself, as being *tied categorically* to the capacities of people to organize their lives freely. The problematic of civil society that Marx opposed to Hegel's modern corporatist formulation of the estates, then, belongs to an underlying Kantian anthropology of generic self-enlightenment or emancipation. The constitution in *this* sense is read as a document concerning the positive anthropological status and evolution of humankind. It denotes humankind's capacity to move from zoological dependence to free and determining political consciousness. This is also why, for Marx, Hegel is so fundamentally incorrect to utilize the corporate institutions as the organizing principle of society. It denies both individual autonomy as well as universal participation and restates instead the medieval 'zoology' of human life in which the estate transforms the human being 'into an animal that is identical with its own immediate determinate nature'.[25] For Marx, the modern age has yet to capture the message of the Enlightenment anthropologically. *'Civilization . . .* does not treat the content of man as his true reality'[26] and, for Marx, the true reality at this stage of his intellectual life consists of the free and conscious (and thus really human) articulation of political wills, guided by the ethical maxim of the due recognition of the other.[27]

Moreover, this Kantian element continues to constitute Marx's critical perspective, at least in his substantive analysis of one world-historical event – the French Revolution. The importance of civil society's *claim* of sovereignty over the state is not lost. Civil sovereignty is the critical basis for two of Marx's rare non-mythologized references to the French Revolutionary period. Beginning with the question of Jewish civil rights as the starting-point Marx, in 'On the Jewish Question' and *The Holy Family*, analyses the anti-capitalist and despotic tendencies within the Revolution. This is interpreted against the background of civil society's emancipatory disposition which has decentred the state's power.[28]

If Marx is ambivalent towards the *nature* of civil society and its negative freedoms, which may indicate civil privatism, the Terror for him results in a double negation that destroys their albeit partial yet *real* emancipatory quality. On the one hand, the recognition of the egoism of civil society is abstracted to a *negative* anthropological principle. Marx realizes that Jacobinism grounds its own myth of the republic of virtue on the egoism that is found in the bourgeois life of civil society.[29] Jacobinism merely reproduces this egoism through the invocation of a supreme ego, the 'general will', that declares these things to be non-virtuous. On the other hand, this results in the total absorption of civil society by the state.[30] The power of the state becomes its own prerogative; it emerges unfettered, *omnipotent*, *theological*, annihilating negative freedoms altogether with the ease of signing a death warrant.[31] Furthermore, Marx argues that Napoleon's defeat of the Jacobin dictatorship on 18th Brumaire resulted, not in civil society's renewed sovereignty, but in the continuation of the *logic of statism* already established under the dictatorship. Both the logics of democracy and bourgeois life-interests are circumscribed under Napoleon's regard of the state as 'an *end in itself* and civil life only as a treasurer and his *subordinate* which must have no will of its own'.[32]

However, the other (Hegelian) strain also echoes throughout these works of this early period, to give a countervailing tendency that forces this distinctly *political* analysis in another direction. Hegel's formulation of the self-made historicity of human life is absorbed into Marx's own critical theory. This pertains to both Hegel's emphasis on the integrated nature of the social totality and the underlying necessity of ontological holism which conceptually structures the world of Objective Spirit. Marx's initial response to the *Philosophy of Right*, not yet an independent theoretical strategy, is then, also informed by Hegel's dual anthropological undercurrents of *homo politicus* and *homo economicus* that propel Hegel's formation of *Sittlichkeit*. Whilst both of these anthropologies are grounded on Hegel's dialectic of recognition they also represent his systemic or functional separation of society into separate spheres; civil society as the systemic domain of *homo economicus*, and the state as the systemic domain of *homo politicus*.

It is here that the Hegelian current runs strongest and has a lasting effect on the internal logic of Marx's theory. Contrary to those who wish to emphasize the Feuerbachian influence on Marx,[33] it is contended that it is this specific feature – the interpretation of civil society

– that denotes Marx's *real* departure from Feuerbach's short cut from theology to anthropology. Moreover it places Marx's own relation to Hegel in a more central and crucial light.

In ultimately addressing the same problem as Hegel, that is the nature of modern civil life, Marx creates, or more properly restates, a double illusion concerning civil society; that of the alienated separateness of human existence and that civil society is only the sphere of needs. In this context, Marx's references to 'species-will' lose their specifically Kantian tone, and respond instead to the sway of Hegel's dialectical holism. The basic thrust of this alternative anthropology is made more explicit in 'On the Jewish Question'. For Marx, political and religious emancipation are inadequate when viewed in the context of a strained and contradictory existence that signifies continued human subjugation and bondage, slavish and 'Jewish' obedience to the power of money.[34] Marx uses the Jew for the same allegorical purpose as Hegel uses corporatism. Whilst corporatism pinpointed the undemocratic and ultimately *anti-modern* nature of the *Philosophy of Right* (and the German state in general), the Jew pinpoints, for Marx, the same logic of bondage within civil society itself. The Jew, the allegorical caricature of a bourgeoisie that Marx had not yet posited *theoretically*, moves in a world of ethical vacuity, vocationally enslaved to, but actively engaged in, the power of money. Money is the opposing system of value to the Enlightenment's own ethical anthropology. It debases 'all the gods of mankind and turns them into commodities. Money is the universal and self-constituted *value* of all things. It has therefore deprived the entire world – both the world of man and the world of nature – of its specific value. Money is the estranged essence of man's work and existence; this alien existence dominates him and he worships it'.[35]

The 'discovery' that the ethical vacuity of modern everyday life originates *in* civil society propels Marx to posit freedom as a category that is no longer tied to the domain of a democratized state. For him this can only be a limited form of emancipation, 'apparent from the fact that the state can liberate itself from a restriction without man himself being *truly* free of it, that a state can be a *free state* without man himself being a *free man*'.[36] Democracy, to be sure, whilst it denotes a *human* existence, can only posit it partially. Human existence is only fully emancipated once the separation between a political and 'material' existence is transcended, and the distinction between civil society and the state disappears.[37] This means that, for Marx, there is an immanent tension in the way in which Hegel differentiates the anthropological categories of labour and politics and objectifies them institutionally. The problem, for Marx, is not that a reunification should *not* take place, but rather that it should be materially grounded, that is, grounded in the dynamics of material life and by the societal members themselves.

However, Marx is in need of an acting subject that is able to unite and add substantiality to his own universalistic philosophy. The proletariat is constructed philosophically and anthropologically by him as such an actor.

Marx's investigation of a historically derived and antagonistic society propels him by the end of 1843 to theoretically conceptualise social actors who are the embodiment of both universality and particularized exclusion. Marx's earlier question of 'who participates in the determination of civil society's sovereignty over the state?', is transformed into 'who participates in society in general?' Through such a question Marx discovers that a process of exclusion, of disrecognition is mounted within the system of needs itself and is duplicated politically and philosophically by Hegel. There *are* those who labour (the social actors who empirically enact the anthropological category of labour) and are excluded from recognition in civil and political societies. This discovery enables Marx to give final, or more specifically a finalist, content to the Kantian-inspired ethical imperative. The identification of the proletariat enables Marx to posit a solution to the Enlightenment's problematic of an ethics that is situated in, and belongs to, a practically orientated humankind. Ethics, or the problematic of the normative transformation of society (which, within the Kantian discourse, is also a self-learning process by the social actors themselves), is located within the context of an anthropological concept (labour) that denotes or captures the essence of humankind's historicity. The proletariat represents this ethico-anthropological complex because it fashions the world through its labour (on behalf of 'another' humankind), and yet is *denied recognition*. It is the representative feature of the zoology of civilization, a zoology that can only be transcended by transforming society as a whole. In answer to the question 'where is the *positive* possibility of German emancipation?', Marx can only reply:

> In the formation of a class with *radical chains*, a class of civil society which is not a class of civil society, a class (*Stand*) which is the dissolution of all classes, a sphere which has a universal character because of its universal suffering and which lays claim to no *particular right* because the wrong it suffers is not a *particular wrong* but *wrong in general*; a sphere of society which can no longer lay claim to a *historical* title, but merely to a *human* one, which does not stand in one-sided opposition to the consequences but in all-sided opposition to the premises of the

German political system; and finally a sphere which cannot emancipate itself from – and thereby emancipating – all other spheres of society, which is, in a word, the *total loss* of humanity and which can therefore redeem itself only through a *total redemption of humanity*. The dissolution of society as a particular class is the proletariat.[38]

Marx now locates the problematic of the free and autonomous subject to an imputed universal class. The proletariat becomes not just a collective actor with (just) claims, but the universal and world-historical actor who carries emancipatory action within.

All of this rests on Marx's deep acceptance of the structure of Hegel's formulation and analysis of civil society. The categories of Objective Spirit, together with their context-specific categories of politics and labour, are absorbed unproblematically by Marx. He inherits the Hegelian formulation of civil society upon which is constructed a model, a mirror, of the functionality of the sphere of needs. This is the second illusion that Marx creates, and which the Marxist tradition as a whole basically accepts. Civil society *already*, for Marx, represents the groundwork of both society in general and the state in particular. Society, through the system of needs, establishes and mediates a metabolism with nature and with itself through its labouring capacity. A universalistic discourse concerning a redemptive reconciliation of differentiated parts is established and absorbed unproblematically by a discourse that reproduces a specific image of society, which generates from it the structural locations of its functional units, one of which resides outside society. For Marx, civil society is the circle of necessity, the totality of objective existence. It is simply their component parts that require examination – not the reordering of the discourse as such. In so arguing, and discovering the proletariat *against* and *within* the sphere of Objective Spirit Marx presents them as the vehicles for a universal philosophy of reconciliation that has both political relevance and substantial material reality.

This, though, signals the collapse of the Kantian version of categorial universalism into the universalism of reason's ontology, interpreted by a Hegelianized Marx as a holistic image of humankind. This circumvents the Kantian formulations of modernity as bounded by the principles of publicly orientated radicalized enlightenment that is neither conflatable to a priviledged empirical addressee nor dependent upon strictly determined and anthropologically located onto-logical principles for their enactment.

There are three immediate practical and theoretical consequences of this. First, that the functional reproduction of society by the work-ing class denotes the *total* frame of reference for politics itself. This entails that other emancipatory struggles that do not belong to the locale of the working class are either neglected or viewed as marginal or derivative conflict zones by Marx. Secondly, Marx refuses the 'primacy' of politics as the philosophical apex of freedom because he basically incorporates into his own anthropology some of the functional delimitations that are found in the Hegelian formulation of civil society because of Hegel's construction of *Geist*. In the early Marx we witness the competition for functional or systemic *analytic* primacy between two of the possible three 'logics of modernity'.[39] The logic of economy with its capitalist organization competes with the logic of politics organized around either democratic or statist institutions. (The logic of the productive forces – industrialization – has no theorized significance at this time.) In other words, the rationality of Marx's position pushes him to focus primarily on the *functional* reproduction of the economic sphere.[40] Thirdly, a radicalized Kantian response that could have concentrated on politicizing civil society, is blocked, thus simultaneously addressing the working class as an excluded social actor. This could have thus politicized the realm of production, or the sphere of needs, around the problem of *organization* and self-management, in a way similar to that in which the problematic of sovereignty was momentarily addressed.

The 1843 critiques of Hegel's *Philosophy of Right* initially concerned with concrete issues, finish with an (albeit incomplete) anthropological critique of modernity in which Marx's vision of a possible reconciliation of the particular and the universal buries the Kantian distinction, and by so doing collapses together the universalistic claims which the Enlightenment generated, with the practices and conflicts that ensue in their realization and obstruction. Marx's unique contribution in openly and theoretically acknowledging the contestatory and class-divided nature of modern society is circumvented by a Hegelianized imputation of a universal class as well as a holistic systemics. Moreover, in his analysis of the historically substantiated tension between two competing logics of modernity, Marx conflates the differentiated constituting elements of social action to a unified anthropological substrate. This substrate is now provisionally interpreted through the notion of the creation of *material* life, albeit under the positive idea of human self-creation. Marx, in effect gives Hegel's owl of Minerva a practical side. It spreads its wings, not at the falling of dusk (not with the sigh of resignation as it reflects on the dialectic of cultural and normative transformation), but with the dawning of a new era, the 'materialist' critique of the industrialization and capitalization of society. The philosophical and 'heavenly' owl of Minerva is transformed into the earthly and proletarian *Gallic cock*.[41]

1844: CONFRONTING CAPITAL WITH LABOUR

Marx, in his identification of the proletariat as the bearer of world-historical action that fulfils the promise of universal values, realizes that his philosophical critique could remain a limited form of ideology critique which may not identify 'the irreconcilable and potentially system-breaking antagonism in the foundation of civil society itself'. [42] It was not enough, for Marx, to have identified the proletariat as the class with radical chains and radical needs. Rather as Wellmer points out,

> the existence of this class, 'which owns nothing but its ability to work' had to be shown to be at one and the same time 'a necessary prerequisite of capital' as well as the factor determining the abolition of capital. [43]

Like Hegel, Marx now views political economy as the hermeneutical key for the analysis of modern society. [44] Marx analyses political economy with the assumption that it gives a 'correct description of the empirical reality of capitalist economy because, first, it depicts the economic life of capitalist society as a closed system with its own logic and finality'. [45] Political economy portrays the separation of economic motives, which in turn, as Marx will show, are rooted in the separation of economic structures from their traditional context and their universalization over society as a whole. This separation reduces all persons to the role of mere instruments of production, subordinated to its aim, alienated from control over the economy. Secondly, these theories are seen to be equally false because they presume an absolute validity as to their rationality status (and hence their truth-content). For them, labour is nothing but an abstraction, a thing to be measured and quantified within the overall production of the national economy. [46] This criterion of rationality is, for Marx, an uncritical expression of the logic of capital – it reifies economic activity into a law whilst simultaneously disregarding (or actively arguing against) the needs of real subjects.

The radical critique of this ideology takes place though in a way methodologically different from Marx's 'Critique of Hegel's *Doctrine of the State*'. Whereas in the first 1843 'Critique' there was a tendency to argue and judge in terms of universalistic political claims that were being put forward, and although Marx still sees philosophy as *the* indispensable form that critique should take, it (critical philosophy) now traces back the reification of bourgeois economy to the living activity of the subjects directly involved, through historical necessity, in the production process. It is no longer Hegel's political philosophy that is the point of departure for Marx, but is now the *Phenomenology of Spirit* read as the *final idealist* version of Vernunft's anthropological heritage of the Enlightenment. Hegel's interpretation of civil society remains unproblematic because what Marx takes or radicalizes from Hegel is *not* the substantive analysis of a historical form, that is civil society, but a theoretical critique through an anthropological unmasking. This *'unmasking critique'* as Cohen puts it,[47] presupposes that the system of needs, the institutional problematic of political life and the free-willing individual are all representations of a deeper reality, the world of labour and property. The method of the unmasking critique is different from the immanent critique of the 1843 works in its basic attributes. It not only purports to articulate the unexamined presuppositions of political economy through a correct description of it, but is also supposed to point towards the self-transcendence of capitalism in terms of radical needs based on rationality and freedom. This self-transcendence of capitalism is supposed to be derived from and articulated and activated by the working class, which is able to understand its own radical needs. Moreover, this can now be linked to a *quasi-transcendental critique*,[48] in which all categories of political economy are transcendentally deduced from the species-activity of labour.

This entails that the ethical injunction of universal freedom which informed the 1843 works is now approached from a changed theorized terrain, that of the economy. At the heart of this change is Marx's perception that the imperative itself remains problematic in two ways. First, despite its universality, the imperative depends on the moral experience of single individuals and cannot, according to Marx, guard against the individualistic calculations of an emergent capitalist society. Secondly, it cannot properly address the constituting moments of humankind because as an a priori construct it is 'beyond' the domain of a humankind that makes its own history. Marx responds to these two problems by deepening his anthropological form and constructing a 'materialist phenomenology'.[49] The Feuerbachian notion of the generic self-affirmation of needs becomes his point of departure. Through him, Marx inteprets Hegel's historical dialectic as a progressivist allegory that reveals humankind's coming-to-consciousness of its *needs*.[50] This notion not only links each of the manuscripts and their apparently specific object-domains, but is also expanded to enhance the analytical and anthropological power of the allegory. Although the three 1844 *Manuscripts* constitute specific problem-areas,[51] Marx utilizes the concept of need in three ways that overlap in all the *Manuscripts* and which structure them as a whole.

These are, as a normative concept which underpins the ethical injunction, as a 'material'-analytic concept for the investigation of 'living
standards' and a critical concept that propels his analysis of political
economy, Jacobinism and his notion of communism.

The initial meaning of the concept of need goes beyond the
naturalistic meaning of the production of wants. It provides an anthropologically derived and coherent category through which to
analyse the process of objectification. Humankind is directly an objective being in that it is equipped with object-making capacities, that is
it creates an objective world,[52] firstly and naively within the context of
its own drives and, secondly, though the recognition that it makes its
own history. In so arguing, Marx effectively dismantles Hegel's identification between objectification and alienation. The immediately
cognitively structured object–subject relation (as an externaliza-
tion/alienation/reconciliation of consciousness) is replaced by a
practical–material (praxistic) relation of the empirical subject to the
products of labour which have objective status as human creations
whether or not they are alienated. The category of labour functions,
for Marx, as the core anthropological notion that creates a structural
homology between all human life-activities. However the homology
is sustained through the way Marx utilizes the concept of need, instill-
ing into it a multi-dimensional complexity. Objectification always
implies a cognitive, normative and practical relation to the world. It is
this process of producing for the *conscious* satisfaction of needs that
typifies or marks humankind as a species and denotes its life-
activity.[53] Through the free and conscious production and appropriation of objects, Marx argues, humankind identifies itself as both
part of nature and separate from it, that is, identifies itself as a
positing species.[54] The concepts of need and labour together denote
the way in which humankind freely and consciously fashions an
organic world out of organic nature. Moreover, for Marx, these also
embody the normative condition for the practical emancipation from
nature through the recognition of the other as an autonomous yet
mutually dependent being. Labour activity embodies the articulation
of societal and individual needs, which are grounded in the active
recognition of the other. Marx reiterates Hegel's insight of the
master–slave dialectic – which itself is structured into the *Philosophy
of Right* – that no matter how strained civil society is, it is always
grounded intersubjectively. The notions of consciousness and
freedom, as categories from which Marx attacks the 'zoology' of
human life, are now absorbed into a *generalizable* anthropological
notion of the production of needs. This notion is now posited
transcendentally as a species-essence.[55]

Marx's reformulation of the dialectic of recognition that centres and privileges the notion of labour that underlies it, enables him to connect two levels of argumentation from which he interprets the Kantian injunction and develops his first critique of capitalism. In other words, the concept of labour, with its phenomenological debt to Hegel, which establishes the primacy of intersubjectivity, is linked to the analysis of objective material conditions. This anthropological underpinning of Marx's critical programme provides him with the perspective through which to analyse both the nature of political economy and the Jacobinization of emerging socialist and anti-capitalist movements.

The modern world which political economy represents – capitalism – denies precisely the realization of the anthropology of intersubjectively through the social organization of the social division of labour and social expression of symbolic forms. The purported individualistic self-seeking that political economy assumes fuels the engine of civil society, is unmasked by Marx to reveal precisely what it is – a myth which falsely posits the anthropology of individualism, an anthropology which Jacobinism also posits.[56] In this context, the structuring of human needs is analysed by Marx through the derivative notions of poverty and wealth. Through them need can function both as the value-normative category which denotes the processes of structural and symbolic '*dis-recognition*' that occur under the regime of capital, and the analytical framework through which Marx describes the way in which the working class is denied the requirements of daily life whilst social wealth increases. This typology of social inequality is not analysed by Marx as a problem of equality as such. Rather, this social inequality as a process of *denial* is, for Marx, necessarily a modern type of unfreedom. Modern society and its division of labour increases social wealth through the accumulation of capital because it simultaneously places the labourer in a position of dependence and tutelage. This tutelage and pauperization stems from the power of capital 'to command labour and its products'.[57] This is grounded, according to Marx, on the *privatization* of human labour; in the ability of capital and political economy to regard 'labour abstractly as a thing; labour as a commodity'.[58] This ethical vacuity, which is structured as a social relation, is also replicated and represented symbolically. Marx's early analysis of money is indicative of this. It is 'the chemical power of society' that both binds and separates people from each other.[59] It represents, because it is the medium of exchange, the universally modern crisis of individual need, in that it transforms and inverts an ontologically posited species-essence.[60]

Together, the division of labour and exchange denote the totality and expression of social relations under political economy. Furthermore, for Marx, they also indicate the totality of alienated human activity. Marx, because he has established human labour as an ontological species-essence through the notion of the objectification of needs, argues that capitalism alienates this species-essence through its rule over labour-power. Capital buys and sells labour as its *private* property. For Marx, this entails that both the objectivity and subjectivity of human life, and their *unity* are in permanent crisis. Alienation, in this respect, details the crisis-complex that political economy creates for both the subjective and objective determinants of the human condition. Subjectively,

> we have the production of human activity as *labour,* i.e. as an activity wholly alien to itself, to man and to nature, and hence to consciousness and vital expression, the *abstract* existence of many as a mere *workman* who therefore tumbles day after day from his fulfilled nothingness into absolute nothingness, into his social and hence real non-existence; [objectively], the production of the object of human labour as *capital*, in which all the natural and social individuality of the object is *extinguished* and private property has lost its natural and social quality (i.e. has lost all political and social appearances and is not even *apparently* tainted with any human relationships), in which the *same* capital says the *same* in the most varied natural and social circumstances, totally indifferent to its real content.[61]

The important point, though, is that Marx analyses and presents the processes of privatization, commodification and alienation phenomenologically. The categories of the master and the slave are transposed into the categories of capital and wage-labour. According to Marx, this phenomenological reading unmasks political economy's own mythology to reveal an antagonistic relation that connects anthropology and critique.

> The relation of *private property* is labour, capital and the connections between these two. The movement through which these parts have to pass is:
> *First - Immediate or mediated unity of the two*. Capital and labour at first still united; later separated and estranged, but reciprocally developing and furthering each other as *positive* conditions.
> *Second - Opposition of the two*. They mutually exclude each other; the worker sees in the capitalist his own non-existence, and vice-versa; each attempts to wrench from the other his existence.
> *Third - Opposition* of each *to* itself. Capital = stored-up labour = labour. As such it divides into *itself* (capital) and its *interest*; this latter

divides into *interest* and *profit*. Complete sacrifice of the capitalist. He sinks into the working class, just as the worker – but only by way of exception – becomes a capitalist. Labour as a moment of capital, its *costs*. I.e. wages a sacrifice of capital.
Labour divides into *labour itself* and *wages of labour*. The worker himself a capital, a commodity.
Hostile reciprocal opposition.[62]

Marx, then, is faced with the self-contradictory nature of civil society. On the one hand, it is capable of expanding and fulfilling the horizon of human needs through self-production and its metabolism with nature (thus increasing social wealth, even though this is appropriated by the capitalist and not the worker). On the other hand, this increase in needs is bought at the cost of destroying modernity's own ethical injunction, which for Marx is grounded in the inalienability of human species-activity.

What is Marx's solution? The notion of species-essence, also grounds Marx's response to this 'dialectic of enlightenment'. The question of the structural and symbolic 'crudity' of political economy is transformed into the question of the relation of the satisfaction of the wealth of human needs in the course of human development. In this way, too, the notion of need is harnessed to the self-objectification of human life. This grounds both Marx's vision of the Communist Utopia and deepens his continuing critique of Jacobinism. It is, so to speak, the 'other side' of his 'political' critique of the Terror.

The generalized envy of the crude and despotic Babeuvist Communists does nothing, as far as Marx is concerned, but extend the form of private property to everyone by force in the name of the equalization of 'communal property'. For Marx, this postscript to Jacobinism turns out to be a blind alley that draws upon the self-destructive potential of the Enlightenment. It consciously turns its back on the positive emancipatory forces of the modern world, the things which mark it as *being* civilized, as well as singling out the unrefined poor who have no needs as both the revolutionary addressee and the symbol of the post-revolutionary world. It is in this context that we can place Marx's (at first sight) strange championship of the achievements of the bourgeoisie that appear in *The Communist Manifesto*, written four years later with Engels. This strangeness is evidence, though, of only an apparent paradox, and indicates Marx's recognition of the aporetic nature of the development of modernity. Marx, in fact, recognizes the contradictory nature of 'civilization' in the 1847 article 'wages' in which civilization is seen as both the historical 'here and now' of large-scale industrial production which commodifies time and pauperizes labour, as well as the place of real public wealth and the starting-point of possible emancipation.[63] In 1848 he is more forthcoming in his praise for large-scale industry and its owners and 'mechanics', the bourgeoisie. Although the former is motivated by self-interest, deny the working class access to even the most basic needs, and utilize and organize nature's resources irrationally, they have transformed the productive face of the planet, thus immeasurably altering man's relation to nature, and 'put an end to all feudal, patriarchal, idyllic relations'[64] by creating an interdependent world market. In Marx's view, the civilizing mission of the bourgeoisie reiterates, but in a more substantial, lasting and empirically *real* way than Hegel's *Geist*-philosophy, the creative transformative power of human labour which emancipates men and women both from the inchoate power of nature and the obstinant dominion of human bondage.

Marx's recognition of a contradictory development of the modern age is now given a more thorough and systematic elaboration through the notion of labour. Labour becomes the focus for the analysis and resolution of the dialectic of the Enlightenment. Crude Communism, because its anthropology rests on moral virtue, envy and the equalization of needs, is an example of incomplete and incorrect resolution. It remains entrapped in private property precisely because it has not recognized private property's positive essence or understood the distinctly human (value) nature of need. Marx's response to both capitalism and Jacobinism stands within his phenomenologically materialist notion of the objectification of labour in its non-alienated form. The future of humankind can now be deduced from the concept of labour, once it is posited phenomenologically.

Marx envisages the practical resolution of the crisis-complex of capitalism through the overturning of alienated relations between individuals and society. Communism as a historical possibility signifies the complete and total reconciliation between human essence and individual existence.[65] It is transformed from the alienated loss of the working subject under capitalism into realized and objectified positive freedoms – a 'practical Utopia', practical because the antitheses of previous epochs are resolved by 'the practical energy of man'.[66] In this way, the notions of the richness and wealth of human needs are transformed from economized and impoverished forms under political economy to forms of sociability and the realization of human essence under communism.[67] Labour, as a 'materialized' version of Hegel's phenomenological *Geist*, becomes, through the category of need, both the real and ontological grounding of the communist *Sittlichkeit*. Certainly the strongest interpretation of this appears in Marx's 'Critique of the Gotha Programme' in 1875, where he states 'from each according to his ability, to each according to his needs'.[68] The emphasis is the same though; the complete satisfaction of needs takes place within a functionally harmonious and formally free society where these freedoms are expressed as a wealth of positive needs. Humankind takes sole self-conscious responsibility for its fate. In this way, the life-process of the human species, now understood through the anthropology of labour, becomes the repository of freedom and rationality. Put another way, freedom and rationality are derived from the anthropology of labour itself.

However, this phenomenology of labour as a species-essence ultimately proves to be, for Marx, methodologically crisis-ridden in two ways. Marx's attempt, throughout the *Manuscripts*, to generate a critical theory that both addresses and theoretically incorporates the working class through a materialist-phenomenological critique of Hegel, remains strained, even to their unfinished end. The two problem-complexes that confront Marx are first, the empirical working class and its plight in, yet exclusion from, the enclosed world of political economy, and secondly, the constituent features of human self-reproduction. These complexes constitute the strains and over-determining impulses in the *Manuscripts*, and like those of the 1843 period, revolve around the way in which the legacies of Kant's ethical injunction and Hegel's ontology appear in the *Manuscripts* themselves. Like the 1843 'Introduction' he collapses the problematics of emancipation and human self-production into one another. The two problem-complexes can be overcome, at least in Marx's eyes, once the legacy of universalism has been resolved in a dialectical *Aufhebung*. Ontology subsumes phenomenology.

The ontological strain of the *Manuscripts* is immediately visible in Marx's attempt to establish a link between the proletarianization of labouring activity and the emancipation of humanity itself. Marx's identification of the working class as the universal subject in the 1843 'Introduction' sets the scene for a continuation of Hegel's philosophy of identity in the 1844 *Manuscripts*. The working class is accorded a universal status since it is the class that labours under the regime of political economy. It is the representative of humankind's self-constitution and suffering. What occurs to it, occurs universally and self-constitutively to humankind in general. In this way, alienation is posited by Marx as a world-historical event that affects all of humanity because the working class consists of those who are dehumanized and estranged from the objects that they bring forth. In this respect, alienation ruptures the dialectic of recognition. Given 'that the relationship of man to himself becomes *objective* and *real* for him only through his relationship to other men', so Marx argues, then if the product of his labour stands alienated from him, 'his relationship to that object is such that another man – alien, hostile, powerful and independent of him – is his master.' [69] Because of this, humanity as a whole suffers.[70] The experience of alienation though, not only signifies this human suffering in a world made by humans, but also signifies that the suffering can be overcome. But how? Marx vacillates. On the one hand, and as Habermas comments, the over-coming of alienation belongs to a process of critical self-learning and self-transcendence by the subordinated social actors themselves.[71] However, on the other hand Marx not only positively assesses this Hegelian insight, absorbed from the later Kant, but also absorbs Hegel's own subsumption of reflection under ontological reconciliation. Kant's ethical injunction is interpreted through Hegel's holistic notion of humankind. For Marx, alienation – the phenomenological sign of a degenerated ethic – can only be overcome by a world-historical reconciliation of the polarized aspects of the human condition under-taken by the philosophically privileged proletariat. Like Hegel's world-historical subject, it is both the bearer of universal emancipatory consciousness and the guarantor of history's progressive path. This future-orientated project is, in essence, also an end of history – or more properly, a philosophy of history which is deduced from an ontolo-gization of labour. The path from religious consciousness to atheism to Communism is posited by Marx as a teleological self-realization of species-consciousness. This flight upon the wings of time is, for him, 'the positive significance of the negation which has reference to itself'.[72]

Marx's aporia surfaces. His teleo-ontological solution to the problem-atic of alienation circumvents his other demand, that philosophy be practical, that is, that critical insights attain practical efficacy precisely because humankind is practical. The teleologically posited emanci-pation of the working class (and thus humankind in general) denies to it (the working class) the principle of its own self-enlightenment and self-transcendence. The *Manuscripts* provide no clues as to the moti-vations and conscious intellectual, political preparation that the working class itself could articulate for its own emancipation. There is a gap, a yawning chasm, between the theory, even when disconnected from ontology and posited as a phenomeno-anthropologically situated critical *Bildungs prozess*, and the *Bildungs prozess* of the empirical addressee. As Markus points out,

> there seems to be no imaginable practico-political strategy able to bridge this gap and to render the actual contact between theory and practice, between the actual situation of the revolutionary subjects and the radical content of the theory, possible.[73]

In other words, Marx's phenomenological analysis of the working class, despite its insights but because of its lack of a practical dimension, is joined and bolstered by his ontologized response to the modern world. Each, either separately or together, circumscribes and curtails Marx's efforts to conceptualize the overcoming of alienation within a practical philosophy that locates the articulation and institutionalization of freedom in societal terms. In the 1844 *Manuscripts*, Marx deepens his recognition of the working class anthropologically. But the working class only exists; it does not yet act to oppose or contest the ravages of political economy.

5

The German Ideology
and the Paradigm of Production

MATERIALITY AND TOTALITY, FUNCTION AND POWER
A GENEALOGY

In *The German Ideology* Marx replaces the earlier version of critical theory (the philosophical criticism of ideologies) with another version: 'the fusion of philosophy and historico-social sciences'.[1] The validation of the philosophical categories is now open to 'testing' through the reconstruction of empirical history by the basic concepts of historical materialism. This is what marks it as an important work that should be retrieved from 'the gnawing criticism of the mice'[2] and placed centrally within any interpretative enterprise. It is here that Marx develops a supposedly unified theory based on materialist precepts, but in ways that force the text to move simultaneously in five directions that are either explicitly developed by him in subsequent works, or remain implicit throughout the *oeuvre* itself. Each direction is related to the underlying anthropological concerns of the 1844 *Manuscripts*, that is alienation and need, although in alternative ways that at times demolish the early ethical core. In other words, we suggest that *The German Ideology* is a formative and seminal, although transitional, work. It is unpredictably complex, a labyrinth for interpretation in which one finds formulations that are imprecise, unfinished and filled with conceptual ambiguity. This is so, not only because it is the first work in which Marx systematically introduces the notion of production, rendered as a paradigm through which the social totality of human life is constructed, but also because five subsequent directions stem from it. Three of the five formulations found nascently within it stem from Marx's paradigm of production; another opens onto the problem of class conflict, while one remains suppressed. Each is informed by his philosophical anthropology and his subsequent 'experiments' with its definitions.

If *The German Ideology* is examined closely, especially in the light of the *Grundrisse* and *Capital*, something interesting can be observed. Marx's attempts to generate a systematic framework to encompass all moments of human material activity under the rubric 'mode of production' are only partially successful. An inner tension is evident. He is concerned not only with the functional moments of production which have a 'syllogistic' relation with one another, but also to detail the anthropological core, or the anthropologically derived encompassing moments which make up the realm of production, the 'kingdom of humanity' itself. These encompassing moments – the productive forces, capital funds and forms of intercourse – denote the material totality of social life, and are for the first time formalized as a paradigm of production.[3] Moreover, the notion of the totality of production becomes the paradigmatic form through which the dialectic between the metabolism with nature and the historically constituted forms of co-operation is articulated in materialist terms. In other words, it denotes, for Marx, the complex organizational arrangements that human beings establish to enable them to sustain the means by which they create their material existence. It is the totality of the complex interactions between nature and society, nature and history and history and society.

However, our reading suggests that the encompassing moments do not necessarily have an equal status within the framework of totality that Marx develops. As mentioned there are five directions that stem from *The German Ideology* – three of these belong to the paradigm of production itself (although it will be argued that one of them implicitly goes beyond its boundaries). Each of the three competing models of the functional reproduction of society directly privilege, or at least favour, one encompassing moment against the other two.

The first direction and model more than any of the others, relies explicitly on the legacy of the early works in which anthropological holism and the sublation of alienation have their roots. The *Grundrisse* is the representative text. Termed by us *communal and autotelic totality*, it is an organic and holistic metaphor derived from an anthropological critique of capitalism that hovers between images of totality taken from either pre-capitalist or post-capitalist societies. For Marx, these societies subsume production to the needs of the community as well as provide the basis for the construction of human identities as a whole despite the pre-capitalist typologies of domination – self-enclosed parochialism, slavery and patriarchy, to name just three. The second direction generates a model which begins from the empirical world of capitalist relations: from the economization of labouring activity and its systematization into a societal type. However, it locates

political, symbolic, contemplative and critico-reflective practices outside the realm of materiality proper and thus denies them any position
of constitutive necessity. Primacy is awarded to one of the functional
units within the paradigm of production – the productive forces – to
help create the analytic distinction between the material contents and
the social forms. This distinction dictates the course of Marx's critique
of capitalism in *Capital*.

Moreover, in the context of these two directions Marx remains profoundly faithful to the underlying logic of both Hegel's formulations
of Objective Spirit and structure of argumentation, in spite of his own
theorizing which has become a project in its own right. The spirit of
Hegel, in particular the ontology of *The Logic*, reappears in the later
works of the *Grundrisse* and *Capital*. The Hegel which Marx 'redis-
covers' through *The Logic* is guided more by methodological concerns,
that is by preoccupations with the form of the argument and the
organization and ordering of concepts, than by the directly *political*
motivations that guided his earlier interrogation of Hegel. In the
Grundrisse Marx draws on the Hegelian movement of thought from
the abstract to the concrete in order to sustain an historical analysis of
capitalism through its own evolution and subsumption of prior
historical forms, or as Markus notes, to analyse the 'evolvement of a
single historical dynamism of a concrete content'.[4] In this formulation
of critique the real abstractions of capitalism are transformed into
concrete determinations, that is, abstract labour becomes the concrete
activity of scientized production. In *Capital*, alternatively, Marx
organizes his analysis according to the Hegelian principles of the
movement of thought from essence to appearance through which a
defetishizing critique is undertaken of political economy's value-form.
By investigating capitalism in this formal way Marx hoped to get
behind the antagonistic and contradictory pairing of opposites and
expose the distortions of the normative social form and the reification
of material contents.[5]

The third direction or model does not essentially develop a metatheory of society as such. Rather, it develops as another version of
Marx's critique of capitalism. This model is the subsumption of labour
under capital or what we prefer to term the capitalization of social
relations. Marx views capitalism in this version as an open-ended
system that incompletely imposes a value-identity upon the sections
of society that it reaches. This sense of incompleteness also means that
the capitalization process is immanently conflictual, and because of
this, presents the possibility of moving Marx's analysis outside the
paradigm of production. The subsumption model gives an alternative
formulation of the historical development of capitalism that is less

dependent on the underlying formal structure of historical materialism. The main text for this model is the so-called missing sixth chapter of *Capital*, 'The Results of the Immediate Process of Production'.

These three models which are generated from within the paradigm of production, do not exhaust *The German Ideology* itself. There is a different route that establishes another recognizably coherent paradigm. This emanates from another problem-complex and is the *paradigm of class action*. The opening line of *The Communist Manifesto* is indicative of this. In this pithy statement – 'the history of all hitherto existing society is the history of class struggle' [6] – Marx sets out the principle of a programmatic paradigm through which he interprets and reconstructs the specific conflicts of the modern, as well as the pre-modern, era. Moreover, the paradigm of class action immediately problematizes the basic conception and construction of the paradigm of production, particularly when it is placed in conjunction with what we shall call, following Castoriadis, Marx's 'hidden imaginary'.[7] This fifth direction stems from our interpretation of the aspects of the human condition that are systematically minimized in Marx's work. It suggests that another anthropological image to that of the predominant paradigm of production implicitly resides within his *oeuvre* that draws on Hegel's hermeneutically centred *historical dialectic*, which highlights the evolution and historical dynamics of social norms, and finds its way into the *Grundrisse*. It is here that the subsumption model is placed. Chapter 7 below, 'Marx against Marx', suggests that a society's self-understanding and self-criticism is objectified not only institutionally, but also as a co-determining cultural form. It is the latter configuration that is structured and contested by open-ended formations of classes and groups. It must be stressed, through, that the 'hidden imaginary' itself remains a suppressed and embryonic tendency that reappears in momentary fragments in various works after *The German Ideology*, specifically, the *Grundrisse* and 'The Results'.

The configuration of concepts that emerge from *The German Ideology*, though, centres predominantly on the paradigm of production. It is to this that we now turn.

THE PARADIGM OF PRODUCTION

The movement from nature to society, or more properly the meeting between society and nature, is conceptualized by Marx in terms of an initial development and subsequent growing sophistication of a double relation.

The production of life, both of one's own in labour and of fresh life in procreation, now appears as a double relationship: on the one hand as a natural, on the other hand as a social relationship. By social we understand the co-operation of several individuals no matter under what conditions, in what manner and to what end.[8]

The double relation that 'natural, sensuous labour' sets in motion establishes objective conditions of existence that take on an independent existence. Society is constituted, in Marx's view, as a natural material condition and result, comprising the sum of the productive forces and a historically created relation of individuals to nature and to one another – this latter relation is initially termed by Marx the 'social forms of intercourse' (*Verkehrsformen*).[9] Together they form the prescribed conditions of existence which social actors confront and inhabit in their everyday lives and into which each new generation is born. They form the totality and basis for their practical and conceptual relations to the world in general. It is, for Marx, 'the real basis of what the philosophers have conceived as "substance" and "essence of man" [and] shows that circumstances make men just as much as men make circumstances'.[10] The scattered remarks that conceptualize material totality as a triad including the encompassing moment of capital funds, basically disappear. The metabolism between man and nature and the social forms of co-operation becomes the basic configuration that emerges from *The German Ideology* and denotes the paradigm of production.

The notion of productive sociality, then, embodies for Marx the dialectic between subjectivity and objectivity. Marx is concerned not to transform the external conditions of existence, 'the definite material limits, presuppositions and conditions [that exist] independent of [people's] will',[11] into objectivistically conceived forms and structures that exist immutably beyond the life and actions of individual social actors. Alternatively, the world of subjectivity is no longer only the world of existential estrangement and suffering – it is the world of empirical 'practical activity, of the practical process of the development of men'.[12] The mediation between the objective world of social structures and the empirical world of the acting subject is established, for Marx, through the concept of labour. The antinomies with which Hegel's *Geist*-philosophy was also dealing (objectivity-subjectivity, materialism–spiritualism, activity–passivity), are resolved within the practical, *non-metaphysical* constituting activity of human life – through its labour. As early as 1844 this is for Marx the hidden message of Hegel's *Phenomenology*: Marx's reading gives labour a quasi-transcendental status through which the dialectic of human life is posited and constituted. To be sure, he had already established this in part by the end of 1843. The important point of the 1844 *Manuscripts*, the 1845 'Theses on Feuerbach' and *The German Ideology* is that labour has now been designated as the core element of the processes of objectification. In *The German Ideology* labour is not so much replaced by the notion of production; rather the quasi-paradigm of labour is expanded into the paradigm of production without a clear delimitation of the status of labour in production. While the paradigm of production is established through concepts that denote the systematization of the functional infrastructure of society through the division of labour (productive forces, forms of intercourse), these concepts themselves rely on premises grounded unreflectively in a praxistically orientated philosophical anthropology. This, too, locates the basic difference between the 1844 *Manuscripts* and *The German Ideology* – the construction of human identity is translated from the phenomenologically conceived and conceptualized self-transcendence of alienation, to formulations concerning the total self-production of the social conditions of existence by empirically existing human beings and within empirically designated parameters.

The 'first historical act' or the production of material life itself,[13] is set against two intertwined objective conditions – nature and history. In Marx's view all theoretical conceptions of human activity have to take account of the unassailed 'priority of external nature . . . the nature that preceded human history'.[14] Nature is the immediate and irreducible given that fissures Hegel's philosophy of identity. Marx not only posits nature as an autonomous realm that resists total absorption or colonization by a *Geist*-philosophy, but he also constructs it as the objective environment into which humankind is placed, and through which it produces its 'actual material life'. This actualization is grounded on the real, sensuous labour of the concrete species.[15] Though this activity, the multidimensionality of 'the first historical act' entails that this given externality of nature achieves an immediate fluidity that already places it within the bounds of history. More correctly, in Marx's view, the boundary between nature and human history, which Kant posited in transcendental terms and Hegel criticized and yet restated teleo-ontologically, is historically constructed through humankind's self-transforming efforts. Nature and history exist simultaneously and imply the conscious recognition of all relations of externality – of space, of time, of the other, in other words, of historicity. They are no longer evidence of *Geist's* laborious, crisis-ridden and estranging journey towards itself, but instead form the limited yet open-ended, 'natural' conditions through which the species evolves. In other words, for Marx, labour resides in both nature and history. Nature and history contextualize and relativize the problematic that Marx inherits from Kant's transcendental philosophy. One could suggest that Marx inadvertently continues and anthropologically radicalizes Kant's 'other Copernican Revolution' –the discourse with history that also finds its way into Hegel's formulation of *Geist*. By so doing he transposes the problematic of human self-creation into the 'natural history' of humankind. Humankind is conceptualized as having a reflexive relation to its external environment because labour activity also includes an objectivating consciousness.

Marx's conceptualization of the 'zoological' pre-conscious life of humankind is transformed 'empirically' in *The German Ideology* to include its own anthropological prehistory leading to hominization. In 1843 he had criticized 'zoological' pre-conscious life, and posited its transformation in Kantian terms as a process of radicalized enlightenment. In 1844, zoology is sublated ontologically. However, in *The German Ideology*, humankind steps from an entrapment in nature once it crosses an evolutionary threshold, develops beyond mere 'herd' consciousness and transforms instinct into conscious will. The 'first historical act' implies that humankind is not only a natural organism amongst other organisms, but also that it is the only species that creates self-consciously for itself. Through this the horizon of needs is inexhaustibly expanded; new needs are formed and the means for their satisfaction created. This too, for Marx, is part of the 'first historical act'. He had already established in the 1844 *Manuscripts* that the category of need mediates the structures of human action. This formulation of need absorbs the externality of nature and restates it in the context of the basic expression and historically transforming reproduction of human life in general, in Marx's view grounded on the notion of sensuous labour-activity.[16]

By being so absorbed or sublated, the developmental genesis of human life-needs also simultaneously articulates the social conditions that are, for Marx the formative 'modes' that envelop the species. Marx invokes the notion of the *division of labour* initially to denote the capacity of human beings to differentiate their labour activity and in so doing generate a complex of functional socially reproductive institutions. In other words, the notion of labour embodies both objectivity and subjectivity through the functional division of labour. It both determines and indicates, for Marx, the complexity of a society's self-reproduction, that is, the multiplication of productive forces and the forms of co-operation.[17] Marx can then argue that the double relation which the division of labour denotes establishes the *total* functional infrastructure of society. On the one hand, modes of production or productive forces are created that institutionalize the metabolism with nature and mark the major evolutionary thresholds of humankind (agriculture – the neolithic revolution, manufacturing – the industrial revolution). On the other hand, forms of intercourse or relations of production establish the institutional forms that mediate the modes of co-operation (the family, forms of ownership which themselves become identifiable as class forms, and the state).[18]

Totality emerges as the core concept that in fact stabilizes the paradigm of production from *The German Ideology* onwards, even though it is not fully conceptualized until the 1857 Introduction to the *Grundrisse*. In this light we shall treat *The German Ideology* and the notes on production, consumption, distribution and exchange that open the *Grundrisse*, as complementary sketches of a central idea. Markus gives us ample reasons for doing so when he points out that: 'from *The German Ideology* on . . . the notion of *social totality* understood as a system of dynamically changing social relationships constituted by interconnected, objectified and institutionalised human activities, stands at the centre of Marx's theory'.[19] It restates in a more cohesive and formalized way the conceptual framework that is already established by presenting production, the embodiment of the totality of social life, as a general human principle or determination that belongs to all epochs.[20] Like labour, which synthetically integrates the diverse elements of human action, production also emits its own synthesizing and integrating principle – totality. We will refer to a three-way distinction within this category, though. *Totality* refers to the construction of historical materialism in functional or systemic terms and denotes the general double-sided nature of production. *Communal and autotelic totality* refers to the construction of historical materialism and its critique of capitalism from the standpoint of anthropological holism whilst the notion *social totality* is located within the version of the primacy of the productive forces and is seen in the light of the base–superstructure model. The important point, though, is that 'socially determined individual production'[21] both contextualizes and conceptualizes the anthropology of labour more explicitly in systemic terms – the individuation of social actors occurs through the various branches or institutions of production within a given society.

Society is described by Marx as a configuration of interdependent elements. Marx presents the dialectic of the whole and the parts that informs Hegel's *Geist*-philosophy, as a general theoretical principle. The *logic* of Hegel's construction of a dialectical world-view remains forever present in Marx's work, absorbed irrevocably during his earlier ruminations. The formalization of the paradigm of production is evidence of this. Although mainly and explicitly developed in the 1857 'Introduction to the Critique of Political Economy', Marx invokes the organic metaphor imbedded in the notion of social totality even in *Capital* where the labour theory of value is described as a cell-form.[22] Production, as the systems category that portrays material life, encompasses 'the totality of branches of production'.[23] In this sense 'a regular syllogism' is formed between production (as the point of departure), distribution and exchange (as the middle), and consumption (as the end-point).[24] These portray the institutional parameters through which individuals both objectify their labour and articulate their needs as autonomous, yet interdependent subjects. This begins in the active transformation of nature into products, their proportionate sharing amongst the members of a society, mediated by exchange and the gratification of needs through the consumption of the object produced. Each particular moment cannot be treated independently, but must be seen in context with each of the other spheres. In this way, the 'syllogism' of production solves, for Marx, the conceptual problematic of functional integration, i.e. the relation between society as a complex of objective institutional structures which interact transformatively with nature and with each other, and with the individual as an autonomous person with needs.[25]

Moreover, by commencing with production as the general systemic category that fills out the anthropology of labour, Marx argues that he also solves the problem of historical continuity and social transformation within the context of a materio-practical philosophy. For, if production is seen to encompass the 'manufacture' of material objects, the forms of co-operation and the invocation of the types of need-systems which are developed and articulated, the

> real question of the relation between this production determining distribution and production belongs evidently within production itself . . . [which] above all reduce themselves in the last instance to the role played by general-historical relations in production, and their relation to the movement of history generally.[26]

The objective historical conditions and relations are the 'denaturalized constituted centres of subjective and objective social life in general, as well as the domain where the processes of modification occur between one generation and the next.[27] The processes of modification belong, in Marx's view, to the development of class societies based on property ownership. The emergence of class societies presupposes, so he argues, a certain complexity of social institutions and that likewise the complex social institutions become visible as being constituted through conflictually configured social groupings which set the parameters for societal conflict, rupture and change.[28] In other words, class also provides Marx with the key with which to unlock the problem of historical transformation. A historically sensitive concept of class based on the power imbedded in the monopolistic possession of the productive forces, complements for Marx the analysis of the specific functionally reproductive institutions of particular historical epochs. The notion of social conflict explains the way in which labour activity is socially institutionalized as a totality so that it not only expands society's metabolism with nature, but also is irrationally constituted and differentiated. In contemporary terms it denotes the distinction between system relations and networks of power.[29] The notion of power is implicitly generalized as a category that describes the relations of domination for societies in general.

However, this positive achievement is equally matched by a series of intertwined negative and reductionist strategies concerning the notions of materiality and emancipation. Marx's attempt to forge links between a practico-materialist anthropology, a theory of the functional totality of society and its social (class) practices of domination and a philosophy of emancipation that is guided by the central ethical maxim of freedom, leads to some ultimately self-defeating results.

In Marx's view, all forms of domination originate from the sphere of production itself. While starting with the unequal division of labour between the sexes, which is characterized in quasi-naturalistic terms,[30] Marx views the *social* division of labour as really beginning 'when a division of material and mental labour appears'.[31] The division of manual and mental labour is important, in Marx's view, because it draws together two of his basic anthropological precepts – holism and materialism. Marx had already absorbed Hegel's holistic image of humankind by the end of 1843, reconstituting it through the notion of labour in his 1844–5 critiques of Hegel and Feuerbach. The net result of this matrimony is that Marx can critically locate the historical process of societal differentiation in a fundamental separation of labouring activity which is structured into the institutional life of society.[32] This results in and manifests itself as a series of disconnected activities which compete or come into conflict with one another at all levels of society. Marx terms these structural conflicts and tensions contradictions, and thus links this systems-orientated notion derived from Hegel with the notion of class conflict within the paradigm of production. Contradiction comes to mean, for Marx, that the social totality is constituted through a series of necessary conflicts between unity and diversity, harmony and conflict, and domination and emancipation.[33] For Marx, the primary structural contradiction is located in and generalized from productive life – the contradiction between the productive forces and the relations of production. In later writings Marx

will term this the contradiction between the material content and the
social form. The series of contradictions between freedom and necessity,
subject and object, universality and particularity are dissolved in an imputed developmental logic of the productive forces. Although in
Capital vol.III, Marx separates the realm of freedom from the realm
of necessity, the movement of contradiction still continues to inform
the relation between and the evolution of, the societal subsystems.

Moreover, Marx's *inherited* philosphy is given an added impetus.
The problematic of emancipation is not only grounded on increasingly
impoverished versions of materialism, but also is addressed teleologically via the notion of holism. Marx sees the progress of human
history as being marked by stages in the overcoming of contradictorily
structured, alien natural orders in which the formation of class societies
is but an intermediary evolutionary step to a more complex and emancipatory social form. The notion of class, which quickly absorbs the
category and problematic of social action, links the *political* problem
of self-production to the Hegelian problematic of self-realization – a
problematic which has already been restated in Marx's already existing
philosophy of history and which ultimately helps to subsume and
paralyse Marx's notion of power.

These strategies, with their preoccupation with contradiction and
reconciliation, are played out within the two main versions of the
paradigm of production – communal and autotelic totality and the
model of the primacy of the productive forces.

CONTRADICTION AND RECONCILIATION
THE MATERIAL CONTENTS AND THE SOCIAL FORM

Communal and autotelic totality

Marx's attempt to melt the philosophies of the political economists
into the modern bourgeois world from which they originated, where
he watches them take root in the sphere of production,[34] is comple-
mented, or more correctly, overwhelmed by the legacy of the 1843
anthropological holism which is given paradigmatic voice in *The
German Ideology*. The latter (anthropological holism) is now posited
as the core critical component of this version of the paradigm of
production. The 'free development of individualities'[35] is envisaged
by Marx as 'the cultivation of all the qualities of the social human
beings, production in a form as rich as possible in needs'.[36] The use of
the word 'melt', with its allusion to *The Communist Manifesto*, is
deliberate. Marx wants to destroy bourgeois ideologies and the social
forms from which they originate, but not the human creativity that

capitalism itself unleashes. Rather, he argues that this can only be fulfilled in a radically transformed post-capitalist society, where the separation of work from all other aspects of labour activity (consumption and exchange) is replaced by 'the full development of activity itself'.[37] This is only achieved in its reunification.

Through the paradigm of production Marx can now view this anthropological holism in societal terms. What is termed *communal and autotelic totality*, is a reconstruction of Marx's transposition of anthropological holism from a formulation that in 1843 specifically addressed the nature of civil society, to one that attempts to establish in a socio-historical context the anthropological features of the logics of either domination or emancipation. In this way, too, the anthropological tone of this version is not, as far as Marx understands it, evidence of a latent and veiled return to the ontology of the 1844 *Manuscripts*. On the contrary, Marx's theory construction and his critique of capitalism is grounded on and generated from the general historical development of the material productive relations of social actors. This grounding and its critical intent has two points of reference, one situated in the past (pre-capitalism) and one located, as a Utopia, in the future. This enables Marx to refer on the one hand to the reality of pre-capitalist societies where, for him, the human ends of production are imbedded in the limited needs and aims of the community, in contrast to capitalism where production is an end in itself. On the other hand, Marx refers to the imaginary post-capitalist association of free producers where the unrestricted development of human capacities becomes the end in itself. Marx's critique of capitalism, in this version, then, depends on the interrelated criteria that he establishes from his assessment of pre- and post-capitalist societies: society's subordination of production to itself, and the reconstitution of labour as creative self-activity. To be sure, Marx had already expressed this latter current in *The German Ideology* where he states: 'Only [in post-capitalism] does self-activity coincide with material life, which corresponds to the development of individuals into complete individuals and the casting-off of all natural limitations.'[38]

As this quote from *The German Ideology* implies, this image of post-capitalist anthropological holism is grounded on the production of material life. This is the domain from which Marx also attempts to dismantle Hegel's 'idealist' strategy in which the formation of the (social) world is reconstructed through the categories of thought, specifically, *Geist*. Whilst accepting the Hegelian notion of totality Marx argues, in a manner similar to that in his 1843 'Critique', that Hegel incorrectly conceives 'the real as the product of thought concentrating itself'.[39] In one of his rare but ultimately self-defeating methodological reflections,[40] Marx links a now developed theory of historical materialism (in this context, one of the models from the paradigm of production) to the problematic of its epistemological representations. The notion of production, with its historicized anthropology, is the *concrete content* from which Marx proceeds and establishes this model of *communal and autotelic totality*. In the *Grundrisse*, the relation between social forms and material contents is interpreted as a *contradictory division* which can be overcome. Marx's construction of an anthropological holism, which is the way that he draws on the notion of totality in this particular version of critical theory, prescribes the historical analysis of capitalism and the direction of its potential supersession. Post-capitalist society overcomes the separation between form and content, and thus brings to concrete fruition the complex unity of modernity's anthropology which has its roots in archaic societies.

Marx has two interrelated notions of the concrete which denote the relation between reality and its reproduction in thought; on the one hand, 'a rich totality of many determinations and relations . . . hence unity of the diverse',[41] and on the other, the ground from which thought generates its categories. The concrete is both the point of departure, which the Humean break with metaphysics had already established, and the result of abstract thinking. Abstractions, in Marx's view, only reproduce conceptually the real concrete preconditions upon which they are based. This is not, however, a major concession to empiricism. On closer scrutiny one can see that Marx is arguing from within the logic of Hegel's own position. For Marx, it is not *Geist*, but labour-activity that is the concrete precondition with which thought begins, and which is its representational result. The problematic of conceptual representation, already present in the earlier works, is here placed firmly within the paradigm of production with its emphasis on materiality and totality. Beginning with labour as the most concrete objectification, and complementing it with the notion of totality, Marx can view it also as the most abstract form under which all other categories are drawn. It encompasses, organizes and synthesizes as a totality the diversity of thought-forms (categories, notions and styles) and the concrete social forms that are the real preconditions for representation. Society, as the total, material condition of the concrete, ensures that thought itself is not separated from its social conditions of existence. For Marx, 'the real act of production'[42] belongs to the real concrete totality itself, which maintains its autonomy against aesthetic, religious or philosophical interpretations. Conceptual or symbolic abstractions and representations of the world (both pertaining to nature and society) have only a *relative* authenticity, existing as '[a] *one-sided relation* within an already given, concrete living whole'.[43] However, Marx's half-hearted epistemological reflections concerning the relation between humankind's various forms of objectifying activity (labour, language and interpretation) in the 'Introduction' to the *Grundrisse* provide him with no guide-lines with which to fully investigate the problematic of consciousness.

Marx is, though, slightly more successful in his other dialogue with Hegel, a critique of Hegel's teleology, again through the notion of the concrete. In this context, it is Marx's notion of history, rather than material life as such, that ensures that the series of parallels that Hegel develops between being and thought, social forms and concepts – abstract/concrete, simple/complex – is broken. In an all too brief return to the *Philosophy of Right*, Marx criticizes Hegel for attributing to simple/complex categories a necessary relation to societal evolution in general. Whilst in specific historical circumstances simple categories may express less developed concrete social relations (or alternatively, complex categories may express more developed social relations),[44] the simple category also 'can achieve its full (intensive and extensive) development precisely in a combined form of society, while the more concrete category was more fully developed in a less developed form of society'.[45]

Marx's foreshortened historical investigations reconstruct the patterns of pre-modern complex communal totalities in both the occidental and non-European worlds. These play the role of critical yard sticks against which the modern capitalist world is judged. In this context, the Hegelian relation between simple and complex, abstract and concrete is uncoupled. The modern form of capitalist life both universalizes and *simplifies* the notion of labour. Capitalism treats labour abstractly and indifferently because it 'has ceased to be organically linked with particular individuals in any specific form'.[46] This simple, universalizing bourgeois category of labour is rendered under capitalism as only 'wealth-creating activity' (purposive-rational activity in another sociological tradition). It is counterposed (historically) by Marx, with complex, concrete 'autotelic' labour-activity.[47] Whilst initially this type of activity is located in pre-capitalist forms of property, it is, for Marx, to be reconstituted in a more complex form in post-capitalist society. In this way the complex concrete embodies the anthropological image of unification and encompasses diversity, identity and difference. The anthropological wholeness is, in his view, both a historical reality and a potentiality. Thus, on the one hand it is part of capitalism's prehistory, which it contradictorily absorbs and dissolves. On the other, it is viewed as a *potentiality* that can only be

realized in a post-capitalist society in which the qualitative development of an all-rounded subjectivity replaces relations based on the
instrumentalization and disembodiment of labouring activity.

Property is the socio-institutional form through which Marx analyses
the communal totality that embodies concrete human life. Marx now
approaches property within the paradigm of production, as a way out
of the cul-de-sac of the 1844 *Manuscripts* and now investigates its
pre-capitalist socio-historical form in an effort to contrast it to its
contemporary form as capital. This does two things. It not only continues to demarcate his critique of capitalism from that of the Jacobins
but also undermines the category of property from within by 'denatu-
ralizing' it in its bourgeois form. Taken together, these two aspects
give to property in a certain ambivalence that obscures Marx's reliance
on the modern definition of it, despite his historical investigations.

The pre-capitalist form of property is typified by Marx as 'co-operation in labour for the communal interests (imaginary and real), for
the upholding of the association inwardly and outwardly',[48] and is
represented for him by archaic, pre-state societies. This is contrasted
to the modern capitalist form that alienates, objectifies, dispossesses
and disembodies individuals and their labour-activity from their
objective conditions.[49] One can view Marx's discussion on property in
'The forms which precede capitalist production' in the *Grundrisse*
as an attempt to locate, both *empirically* and *philosophically*, the
anthropological basis for the communitarian model of social production
and its labour-activity. In this context, 'Marx's analysis deals with
three components of the original relation to the conditions of production: the appropriation of nature, the membership in a community,
and the relation of the individual to himself as a member of the
community.'[50] Each of these is presented by Marx as part of 'the
natural unity of labour with its material presuppositions'.[51] They
come together to form an objective existence which is not divorced
from the individual's specific labouring activity.

Nature is seen as the natural workshop, the basis of the community,
which is related to as the property of the community as a whole.
Through this, each community member relates to him- or herself as a
proprietor of this basic relation, hence 'as master of the conditions of
his reality',[52] and to others as co-proprietors. The important aspect, for
Marx, of the pre-capitalist sociality of labour is the form of co-operation
based on communal interest (real and imaginary) that upholds the
forms of associations that maintain both internal and external nature.
In this way the individual is firstly and foremostly a member of a
community. This is the basis of all relationships. The aim of labour is
not valorization – although surplus labour may be undertaken in order

to obtain surplus products in exchange – but rather to sustain the individual proprietor and family, as well as the total community. In these terms, property can only mean, as Marx interprets it,

> no more than a human being's relation to his natural conditions of production as belonging to him, as his, as presupposed along with his own being, relations to them as natural presuppositions of his self, which only form, so to speak his extended body. He actually does not relate to his conditions of production, but rather has a double existence, both subjectively as he himself, and objectively, in these natural non-organic conditions of his existence.[53]

As such, the commune as the extended form of archaic property relations is, for Marx, the original anthropological and autotelic totality. It is

> neither the substance of which the individual appears as a mere accident; nor is it a generality with a *being and a unity* as such . . . Rather, the commune, on the one side, is presupposed in-itself prior to the individual proprietors as a communality of language, blood etc., but it exists as a presence, on the other hand, only in its *real assembly* for communal purposes . . . [it is] really the common property of the individual proprietors, not of the union of these proprietors endowed with a separate existence from themselves.[54]

Against this image of anthropological holism Marx can, in a similar but more coherent way to that in *The German Ideology*, posit the structural or institutional features and historical processes that transform and alter its constitutent features. For him, there are two – the formation of the state (which itself has an ancient history) and the development of modern, capitalist bourgeois society. Each in its own way decomposes this initial unity. In a remarkable return to the problems addressed in 1843 the archaic communal form is counterpointed with the historical development of civil or civic society, the external form that houses and nourishes the state. The stable objective structures of civic institutions that denote urban political life (even in antiquity) portray, for Marx, a mere *being together, a diverse* economic totality that utilizes the politics of exclusion to form a 'unification made up of independent subjects, landed proprietors and not . . . a unity'.[55] The commune (at least for Marx in its Germanic form) rather has a *coming together*; it has no exterior or external 'existence for itself, except in the *assembly* of the commune members, their coming-together for common purposes'.[56] This is the political point of the imputed totality of the commune – it generates, from its productive soil, the participatory political formations that cannot stand apart from, or over, the communal membership.

Bourgeois society with its obsession with capital, also rends this original unity. It empties the human content of all previous communal societies, transforming their individual members into isolated wage-labourers. In Marx's view there are three historical conditions that must occur and converge before the individual is up against capital as a mere worker. First, the individual must no longer be a proprietor, that is, not relate to the community or to nature as an owner; secondly, the instruments of his or her labour are dispossessed, the possession of skill is no longer grounded on the 'secondary' guild community of craft work. Thirdly, the working individual has no immediate or communal relation to the necessities of life. These are, like the labour activity itself, mediated solely by exchange-value. In each instance he or she is simply a subject of proprietary relations.[57] For Marx, the contrast is clear:

> In [the] community the objective being of the individual as proprietor, say proprietor of land, is presupposed moreover, under certain conditions which chain him to the community, or rather form a link in his chain. In bourgeois society, the worker, e.g. stands there purely without objectivity, subjectivity; but the thing which *stands opposite* him has now become the *true community* [*Gemeinwesen*] – which he tries to make a meal of, and which makes a meal of him.[58]

Real communality in pre-capitalism ties the individual to the community, whereas under capitalism it rends him or her from it. It is not only the process of isolated independence that Marx has in mind; the individual in pre- (and more formally, demonstrably, in post-) capitalist society has a sovereign place within social life. In other words, in his view, the individual has the status of an autonomous and co-determining/participating member within the collectivity, even if this autonomy and participation is mediated (in pre-capitalism) by other forms of communally sanctioned domination. In this context, then, the term *Gemeinwesen* restates the critico-ethical problematic of sovereignty within the framework of Marx's argument. Moreover, it locates the essential shortcomings of this version of the paradigm of production.

Already present as an explicit theme in the 1843 'A contribution to the Critique of Hegel's *Philosophy of Right*', sovereignty or collective autonomy resides implicitly throughout all subsequent critical theories, however problematically. Marx's model of communal and autotelic totality, with its holistic anthropology, is a case in point. Taken from the standpoint of a transcendental critique addressed to social institutions in 1843, sovereignty is transformed by the end of *The German Ideology* period into a claim for general human emancipation from all conditions of domination. In the *Grundrisse*, this notion of freedom is interpreted explicitly through the holism inherent in Marx's philosophical anthropology. The great unfettering revolutions in industry and politics give vent to the creative potential of the human condition. Moreover, this creativity is, in Marx's positive assessment of it, a hallmark of a *potential* which restates the communal and autotelic totality of pre-capitalist life, but without its personal or institutional features of domination. Humankind emancipates itself from both tyrannous masters (real or imaginary) and a preoccupation with producing the necessities of life.[59]

In this context, capitalism is, for Marx, *progressive*. Marx can claim again in the *Grundrisse* that bourgeois society, despite its processes of dissolution, is 'the most developed and most complex historic organization of production'.[60] Its concrete complexity and hence its emancipatory potential, lies in the universalization of relations based on exchange and on the development of the productive forces. This does two things that herald the road to freedom. On the one hand, the money nexus and its corollary 'the individual pursuit of private interest',[61] inadvertently form a socially determined interest that dissolves local personal ties of dependence, thus creating the historical condition for individuality. Certainly, for Marx, this process of involuntary individuation is contradictory, antinomic. As Markus extrapolates:

> the historical process of individuation takes on the antagonistic form of the *depersonalization* of the individual . . . through the creation of a universal dependence of all individuals on objective–external conditions, which form a system sufficient unto itself, governed by laws of its own.[62]

On the other hand, capitalism's development of the productive forces sets the parameters for its own self-transcendence, as well as signalling humankind's movement away from a dependent preoccupation with necessity. Capitalism sows the seeds of its own demise by developing the productive forces beyond the application of direct human labour, through the rational and mechanical application of scientific and technological principles. In Marx's view, capitalism's rationalization of the working day (time) and mechanization of labour-activity, 'quite unintentionally – reduces human labour expenditure to a minimum. This will rebound to the benefit of emancipated labour, and is the condition of its emancipation.'[63]

By the end of the *Grundrisse* though, Marx is unable to generate a theoretical link between the dissolution of the money nexus and the development of the productive forces in a way that properly addresses the problem of autonomy in terms other than a techno-anthropological funcationalism or a philosophy of history. In arguing from the perspective of anthropological holism, Marx is not only concerned with the problem of the relation and distinction between simplicity and complexity, but also with the 'praxistic' constitution of reality as such. In this way, Marx's other notion of the concrete that denotes the groundedness of material production, comes directly into play through the idea of the contradiction between the material content and the social form.

For Marx, the realm of freedom is conceptualized through an holistic anthropology in which the development of the productive forces provides the impetus and basis for the development of the creative potential of all subjectivities and the reunification of self-activity with labour. The mechanisms of alienation, formally free pauperization and objective dependence reside, for Marx, not in the politico-normative composition of society, but rather in the institutional mechanisms of production itself, which Marx subordinates to the productive forces. Once the development of the productive forces makes the appropriation of alien labour superfluous, disposable time becomes a generalizable feature of modern life and the proper realm of freedom.

Marx's reliance on the productive forces, though, denotes a shift and a change of emphasis that has occurred between the *Grundrisse* and its predecessor, *The German Ideology*. In *The German Ideology*, to be sure, Marx had coupled the development of individual capacities with the development of the productive forces. This development, though, is matched by Marx's formulation of the working class's coming-to-consciousness of its denial of self-activity under capitalism. Post-capitalism is conceptualized, by Marx, as not only a universal appropriation of the productive forces, which denotes a liberation of human capacities, but also a participatory reorganization of the relations of production.[64] In the *Grundrisse*, this problematic (that is, under – or never theorized) formulation of the politics of material emancipation (as well as its class component) is not to be found. Its model of communal and autotelic totality relies on an image of the development of the productive forces that is 'beyond' the requirement of *direct* human intervention and control. Emancipation is dependent on the complete mechanization of the productive forces. This reduces the need for human intervention to a minimum, and signals a redefinition, by Marx, within the central category of freedom. It is no longer dependent upon the (under-formulated) notions of control and consciousness, but is conceptualized from the vantage point of *time*. In Marx's view, the 'indicator' of social wealth in post-capitalist society will not be labour-time, but free time. Freedom means

> the free development of individualities, and hence not the reduction of necessary labour time so as to posit surplus labour, but rather the general reduction of the necessary labour of society to a minimum, which then corresponds to the artistic, scientific etc. development of the individuals in the time set free, and with the means created, for all of them.[65]

And the reduction of labour-time, as the measure of exchange-value, occurs through, and is dependent on, 'the degree that large industry develops'.[66]

Marx's Gallic cock has certainly come home to roost. However, the nest is empty. Marx cannot address his conception of post-capitalist society in terms of a multidimensional sovereignty/autonomy that would encapsulate the dimension of the ethical norms and institutions that would structure it. This is because of, not only his disdain for politics (and particularly its bourgeois form) that is integrated into the paradigm of production, but also and more importantly, the priority that is given to the development of the productive forces as an emancipatory impulse. This impulse is the underlying tendency in the *Grundrisse*. However, as we shall see, it only attains full flight in the second direction emanating from *The German Ideology* – the model of the primacy of the productive forces. It is to this that we now turn.

THE PRIMACY OF THE PRODUCTIVE FORCES

The logic of primacy and historical materialism

The notion of the productive forces, as well as the primacy that is awarded to them is one of the most 'original', far-reaching, influential and disastrous ideas that Marx generates and develops systematically.

In the model of the primacy of the productive forces the internal relation between form and content is transformed. The notion of totality loses its anthropologically construed *holistic* hue; totality and anthropology are now interpreted as demarcated realms that denote a formal separation between form and content. The anthropological dimension is restricted to the notion of materiality (the material contents) while the image of totality pertains only to the systemic reproduction of society, grounded on the social relations of production (the social form). This categorial distinction, with its technicist reading of the material contents, becomes Marx's 'final' dialectical method, a method promised and prefigured as early as 1843, and formulated by Marx most clearly in the 1873 'Postface' to the second edition of *Capital* vol. I:

> My dialectical method is, in its foundations, not only different from the Hegelian, but exactly opposite to it. For Hegel, the process of thinking . . . is the creator of the real world . . . With me the reverse is true: the ideal is nothing but the material world reflected in the mind of man.[67]

The mystical shell is discarded, the rational kernel revealed.

Despite the notion of social totality that Marx develops in *The German Ideology*, in which the three encompassing moments of material/social life (productive forces, capital funds, forms of intercourse) are presented as forming an interrelated unity, there is, particularly towards the end of the first part of the work, a strain which subverts the sense of the unity that supposedly prevails. In an effort to establish the groundwork of a society's 'self-production', Marx tends to award primacy to the material contents through the productive forces, and present them as the constitutive moment. These form the parameters for the development of the forms of intercourse or relations of production which merely correspond to or develop the appropriate forms of 'structures of interaction' into which the social actor is born.

This categorial privileging of the productive forces only achieves mature and intended expression in Marx's 1859 'Preface' to *A Contribution to the Critique of Political Economy*. This is stated however, not as a systematic theory, but rather as a thesis. As G. A. Cohen rightly points out in his uncritical defence of this version of historical materialism, the preface not only defends the so-called base-superstructure model, but also categorically posits the ground from which the model itself is generated.[68] When Marx states that 'the mode of production of material life conditions the general process of social, political and intellectual life'[69] he is making a *basic categorial distinction between the material content and the social form of existence*. This is the thesis that is first explicitly established in the 1859 'Preface' and reiterated as the theoretical structure of historical materialism in *Capital*. Marx makes this clear when, in the first volume of *Capital*, he argues that the labour process which embodies 'the mode of production of material life', is

> the universal condition for the metabolic interaction between man and nature, the everlasting nature-imposed condition of human existence,

and it is therefore independent of every form of that existence, or rather, it is common to all forms of society in which human beings live. We [do] not, therefore, have to present the worker in his relationship with other workers; it [is] enough to present man and his labour on one side, nature and its materials on the other.[70]

This impetus within the paradigm of production, to be sure, has its roots in Marx's materialist transformation of Hegel's dialectic in both the 1844 *Manuscripts* and *The German Ideology*. In the 'Critique of Hegel's Dialectical and General Philosophy' in the 1844 *Manuscripts* Marx had already essentially outlined the materialist interpretation of the constitution of the human world in terms of the anthropology of labour. The tension of anthropological images, of labour, politics and cognition and their relation to the modern notions of freedom and rationality is 'resolved' in a conceptual slide; the political and symbolizing dimensions are incorporated into the realm of labour to save the primacy of the notion of 'material' self-activity. This means that Marx's theoretical structure is controlled by a systemics in which the more general problematic of intersubjectivity (which, for Marx, is the fundamental ground from which the problematics of politics and consciousness rise) is ultimately reduced to labour in general. Moreover, when Marx 'translates' the dialectic of labour into the fixed causal relation between the productive forces, the relations of production and capital funds, there is the implicit danger of a misinterpretation (or in Habermas' terms, 'a self-misunderstanding'[71]) that depicts the socio-historical dimension of social forms as a secondary and derivative feature. In other words, while the paradigm of production already absorbs and paralyses the dimension of politics, the movement towards primacy in this version alters the dynamics of an already problematic formulation by excluding the domain of intersubjectivity (the relations of production, forms of intercourse) from a constitutive role. This is what separates it from the previous model, even though the underlying problematic (historical materialism) is generated from the same categories – labour, totality, form and content. The notion of materiality now comes to mean the rational control over external environments. This denotes, for Marx, the final materiality of human self-production and thus becomes the basic framework through which all other analytic categories are generated and interpreted. Through this too, the division of labour (the relations of production) no longer mediates for Marx the dialectic of subjectivity and objectivity. Rather this dialectic is now mediated by *the technical mastering of nature through the application of purposive rules*. It captures and constitutes, in Marx's view, the inner dynamic or

dialectic of the material relation between societal self-reproduction
and individual activity. Both draw on the primal interaction with
nature as the forming, constituent moment of human life, analysed by
Marx either through the general institutionalized technologies that
denote a socio-historical epoch (the productive forces), or the production of artifacts by concrete labour. In other words, this technical
mastery of nature through the application of purposive rules encompasses both society's capacity to institutionally rationalize and
functionally integrate its husbandry of natural resources, and the
simultaneous activity of individual societal members who bring their
concrete labour to bear upon nature.

As such the formation of purposive rules is the only cognitive form
that Marx does not banish to the ethereal world of the superstructure
under the rubric of 'consciousness'. When he states that 'it is not the
consciousness of men that determines their existence, but their social
existence that determines their consciousness',[72] he has in mind the
legal, political, religious, artistic and philosophic conceptions of the
world which he terms 'ideologies'. However, it is another matter with
natural science. For Marx it is 'the general intellectual product of the
social process',[73] i.e. the cognitive form that is imbedded in and
expresses the fecund quality of the productive forces. As Wellmer
points out: 'natural science becomes the basic paradigm for what
theoretical knowledge can be, and the relation between science and
industry provides the normative model for the relation between theory
and practice and their possible unity.'[74]

Marx is a child of the rationalist spirit of the Enlightenment. This, to
be sure, had already been established in the 1844 *Manuscripts*, prior to
the systematic development of a paradigm of production. As early as
1844 Marx accepted the underlying reinterpretation of cognition in
terms of the emphatic deployment or expansion of purposive rationality
that occurred during the Enlightenment, and that was formalized in
Kant's *Critique of Pure Reason*. Marx's championship of purposive or
instrumental rationality is not brought about by a meta-epistem-
ological reflection concerning the veracity of modern scientific rationality. Rather, it stems from his own materialist transformation of
Hegel and has its roots in the deep tension within his project of
radicalizing the implicit philosophical anthropology of the Enlightenment.

The anthropology of labour and the notion of materiality that
informs it, retains a synthesizing quality that is inherent in Hegel's
reinterpretation of the Kantian regime of reason. All other categories
of human life are subsumed under it. Through this, Marx transposes
Hegel's implicit anthropology of labour, which pertains to the

reproduction of the realm of Objective Spirit (civil society), to the level of Absolute Spirit. It is the universal element of synthesis. This is the transcendental aspect that Habermas in his *Knowledge and Human Interests* recognizes in Marx's reconstruction of the dialectic of labour and the productive forces – the form that it takes once it is transposed and altered within the paradigm of production.[75] The synthetic quality of labour not only preserves the Kantian distinction between form and matter, but more importantly also identifies the deep structure which indicates the materiality of human life. The material praxis of human action can now be identified by Marx, according to Habermas, in two interrelated ways; through the invariant structures of 'instrumental action' and through the external existence which they take as the productive forces.[76] Marx marries the purposively derived concept of rationality that synthesizes the technically exploitable knowledge of the natural sciences, with the *practical* process of human production objectified through the productive forces. Both belong to the self-constitution of the species. In this sense, natural science signifies, for Marx, a metasocial and essentially neutral and progressive purposive rationality because:

> it has intervened and transformed human life all the more *practically* through industry and has prepared the conditions of human emancipation, however much the immediate effect was to complete the process of dehumanization. *Industry* is the *real* historical relationships of nature, and hence of natural science to man.[77]

For Marx, rationality is purposive precisely because it generates cognitive resources that enable humankind to control the natural environment, as well as organize society's productive capacity in an efficient manner.

The subjective side of the dialectic of the material contents takes place, so Marx argues, through the production or consumption of use-values. They mediate social individuals with their natural objective environment. Through purposeful labour (or with the instruments that conduct or extent that labour) individuals enter the 'neutral' domain of nature and transform it into domesticated and equally 'neutral' use-values. For Marx, the neutrality of use-values lies in an assumed direct utility of the object separable from the social form or the historical period in which it exists, or even from the *degree* of technological sophistication. The utility of the use-value is prescribed by the purposive rules through which it is created.[78] These rules lay down, as objectifications of the essential activity of humankind, the technical rules for their use and utility. As Markus points out, in his careful exposition of Marx's paradigm of production, 'the utilitarian rules of use define modes of human behaviour as senseful human practices, 'proper' ways of intentional activity in regard to some object of need; they have a constitutive–constructive character.'[79] It is of no consequence to Marx whether the objects are 'of nature' (for example, oats or corn) or are 'bathed in the fire of labour',[80] or under what conditions they are 'manufactured'. They are simply

> infused with vital energy for the performance of the functions appropriate to their concept and to their vocation in the process . . . The taste of the porridge does not tell us who grew the oats, and the process we have presented [the general metabolism with nature] does not reveal the conditions under which it takes place, whether it is happening under the slave-owner's brutal lash or the anxious eye of the capitalist.[81]

Their quality lies only in the service of fulfilling human needs. This, to be sure, is not to suggest that Marx views human needs as only deriving from physical sources. On the contrary, humankind's progressive dynamic (as he shows in *The Communist Manifesto* and the *Grundrisse*) stems from its capacity to infinitely increase its horizon of needs, whether or not they 'arise . . . from the stomach or the imagination'.[82] What is important, in Marx's view, is to confine the definition of the objects that are produced for the satisfaction of heterogeneous needs to their utility. This is their special *qualitative* aspect that links them to the material substrata of human self-creation. They are derived from nature, created only through specific purposive activity.

The development of the productive forces establishes for Marx, the identification of specific historical epochs and the mechanism for historical transformation. Marx argues that individual and societal development 'correspond at every stage with the simultaneous development of the productive forces, their history is at the same time the history of the evolving productive forces taken over by each new generation'.[83] For him, the identity of previous social formations is ultimately determined by the tools and implements of civilization. They are the 'fossils' that function as the hermeneutical key to past societal forms and thus enable a reconstruction of world history to take place.[84] The productive forces are 'the looking-glass' through which the past is unravelled because they constitute the material core of human life, as well as the repository of innovation in which the history of the (real, or technical/scientific) knowledge of humankind is accumulated. As such they also provide the impetus for social evolution by being expanded both qualitatively and quantitatively beyond the specific historical forms in which they are enveloped.[85]

History becomes for Marx, a real progression within the structure of purposive rationality, and the technics that are developed merely become the increasingly sophisticated instruments that mediate nature and need. Hence the material contents are the ground from which social life and its institutional forms develop and achieve systemic stability and change. The social *forms* – the institutional infrastructure that individuals inhabit, typified by the division of labour and the forms of ownership and earlier termed by Marx the relations of production – evolve around the productive forces.[86]

However, the notion of the social form itself is constructed with a series of concepts that are internal to this 'side' of historical materialism and rely on and absorb some of Marx's earlier formulations. The base-superstructure model, which itself gives priority to the economy, and is one of the lasting outcomes of Marx's first settling of accounts with Hegel, is systematically absorbed into this primacy version of historical materialism. What changes is not Marx's basic dual strategy (evident from the end of 1843) of viewing politics and forms of consciousness as 'superstructural' phenomena and linking this to the general idea that the material constituency of human life is the foundation-stone of civil society. Rather the base–superstructure model is adapted to the primacy thesis which itself indicated a fundamental formal alteration in the relation between the forming moments themselves. The base (the relations of production) is the social form which develops around the material contents or productive forces. Upon this base rest the superstructural phenomena of circulation and distribution (which can, institutionally, take the form of the state), and the world of ideological representations (forms of thought). This marks a distinct transformation in the arrangements between the 'interdependent elements' that figure in *The German Ideology* and the 1857 'Introduction' to the *Grundrisse* and hence in the notion of social totality. As has already been argued the notion of social totality has a crucial constituting status within the core unacknowledged presuppositions of Marx's theory. It is central to his idea of a self-reproducing society. Although it only achieves theoretical fruition within the paradigm of production it is related to the 'older' notion of anthropological holism which itself is related to the Hegelian version of civil society. This is where the legacy and the importance of Marx's first encounter with Hegel (1843) manifests itself, and where it helps to structure the object-domain of Marx's critical investigation. This first encounter becomes the edifice upon which he builds the paradigm of production as well as his late encounter with Hegel in *Capital*. In constructing his own critical anthropology Marx assumed with Hegel (and against Kant) that civil society was primarily the sphere of needs, and unlike Hegel (or Kant), that this constituted the reproductive centre of society as a whole.

In this way, the notion of social totality belongs constitutionally to the object-domain (society) that Marx is investigating. It constitutes the framework for the analysis of the sphere of the economy which in Marx's view constitutes the infrastructure of society. With this, the idea of totality becomes layered. Society is separated into either base and superstructure and the interrelated but not synonymous terms, 'phenomena' and 'deep structure'.

Marx is now furnished with an assumed integrated social theory that establishes not only the dynamics of humankind's self-production and socio-historical transformation, but also the framework through which social investigation and critique takes place. Social analysis of his object-domain, capitalism, is approached from each side of his theory.

Anthropology and totality – Marx's Capital

This impoverished materialism that emphasizes technics and utility as well as functional reproduction organized around the economy affects Marx's immanent critique of capitalism (the social form of modernity) through his analysis of the relation between use-value and exchange-value. Exchange-value is the manifestation of a social form which, for Marx, contains the social or productive relation of the domination by the capitalist of the wage-labourer. Capitalism, as it is depicted in *Capital*, is 'characterized as a distortion of a content',[88] the normative accent of which is still derived from an expanded notion of freedom as radical autonomy. However, the critical project is no longer marshalled from the aspect of anthropological holism, but from a defetishizing critique of the bourgeois form of the ownership of the 'free' labour of others. The idea of an active class domination re-enters Marx's critique, after its almost complete absence in the *Grundrisse*. In *Capital* vol. I – after the opening section on commodity production – Marx analyses the class relation. In so doing he intends to link the logic of reproduction of the modern social form to a specific type of class domination. The subject-matter of Marx's critique is the relation between the 'formal determinations' (*Formbestimmungen*) of a social form which presents itself as a totality and the particular social relations of domination.

This subject-matter, as it unfolds in *Capital*, contains two versions – the conventional and a metatheoretical upon which the conventional ultimately and problematically rests. The conventional reading is the one that is given the most conspicuous place by Marx in his *oeuvre* and is identified by his interpreters specifically with *Capital*. It typifies for a tradition a theory of domination and contestation *per se*. In this reading Marx depicts the modern world as one in which capital funds and socialized labour are increasingly centralized and monopolized by private owners who utilize and reproduce labour-power as a capital.[89] For Marx, capitalism possesses a logic, but it is only understandable in the context of a class relation between buyers and sellers of labour-power and the conflicts that ensue around this nexus. Hence, capitalism, as a specific socio-historical form, has two constitutive or forming features for Marx.

On the one hand, it is guided by the unmediated law of profit (or the production of surplus-value) which is, as he points out, no longer constrained by the traditional codes of conduct that pertained to the pre-capitalist worlds of antiquity or feudalism.[90] On the other hand, this aim presupposes a conflictually constituted class relation. The reorganization of work according to the constraints and prerogatives of the capitalist's voracious appetite for surplus-value is portrayed, by Marx, as an active engagement or relation between classes in their conflict over the control (and definition) of time. The capitalist's passionate interest only in surplus-value, the corollary of which is his merciless passionate disinterest in the life and well-being of his charge and real productive unit, is matched and contested by that unit – collective labour or the working class. As Marx states:

> There is here an antinomy, of right against right, both equally bearing the seal of the law of exchange. Between equal rights, force decides. Hence in the history of capitalist production, the establishment of a norm for the working day presents itself as a struggle over the limits of that day, a struggle between collective capital, i.e. the class of capitalists, and collective labour, i.e. the working class.[91]

Moreover, the essential precondition for the formation of the capitalist mode of production, the element that marks it, for Marx, as being constituted by or through a *modern* class formation, is the direct and unfettered use of and control over the labour-power of a work-force that is formally and structurally free. A work-force is free if it is not owned by, or has no obligatory relation to another (is not enslaved or enserfed) and hence has no institutional or communal ties. The worker is a free person in the formal/legal sense *and* an independent isolated producer.[92]

But Marx strenuously argues that the formal freedom and independence of the wage-labourer is illusory, a sham. The echoes of the ethical principle that informs Marx's 1843 'Introduction to "A Contribution to the Critique of Hegel's *Philosophy of Right*"' and 'On the Jewish Question' still reverberate throughout *Capital*, although from an altered and now systemized theoretical substructure, the

paradigm of production. Marx's view that modern freedom is a
contradictorily structured 'form of life', though, remains the same.
The relation between capitalist and wage-labourer is, for him, fundamentally one that disregards and circumvents the promise of practical
reason: that is, in its Kantian guise, the release from all forms of
tutelage and the development of critical enlightenment. Marx still
holds implicitly to the core of Kant's notion of enlightenment and
freedom whereby

> man is without qualification equal even to higher things in that none
> has the right to use him according to pleasure because of his reason –
> reason considered not insofar as it makes him an end in himself . . .
> and a being which no one might treat as mere means to ulterior
> ends.[93]

This right to freedom is, in Marx's view, systematically circumvented
by capitalism and redefined and narrowed by its ideologists, the
political economists:

> Factory work . . . confiscates every atom of freedom, both in bodily
> and intellectual activity . . . Every kind of capitalist production,
> insofar as it is . . . capital's process of valorization, has this in common
> . . . it is not the worker who employs the conditions of his work but
> rather the reverse, the conditions of work employ the worker.[94]

Capitalism actively replaces the authority of the lord and the structures
of his political legitimacy with a new typology of authoritarian
domination and hierarchicalization that emanates directly from the
sphere of production. Marx argues:

> If capitalist direction [or control of the labour process] is twofold in
> content, owing to the twofold nature of the process of production
> which has to be directed – on the one hand, a social labour process for
> the creation of a product, and on the other capital's process of valorization
> – *in form it is purely despotic*. As co-operation extends its scale, this
> despotism develops the forms that are peculiar to it. Just as at first the
> capitalist is relieved from actual labour as soon as his capital has
> reached a minimum amount with which capitalist production,
> properly speaking, first begins, so now he hands over the work of
> direct and constant supervision of the individual workers and groups
> of workers to a special kind of wage-labourer. An industrial army of
> workers under the command of a capitalist requires, like a real army,
> officers (managers) and NCO's (foremen and overseers), who com-
> mand during the labour process in the name of capital. The work of
> super vision becomes their established and exclusive function.[95]

The world of the factory is, for Marx, the microcosm of the modern world despotically controlled by the capitalist who imposes a restricted form of life, the value-form, on the hapless worker. In it – in front of the machine, on the factory floor and in units of time – the power imbedded in a class relation is played out. The salons and cafés of custom or freedom are left behind once the capitalist and the worker enter the factory, not on pleasure, but on business. The worker becomes a plaything of an alien power, an object of use, a tool to be guided and controlled by the ledger-fettered mind of the capitalist and the anxious eye of the manager.[96]

This conventional reading, though, can be reformulated to explicate four problems that, it is argued, Marx wishes to link up:

1   the formal determinations, that is, the institutional arrangements, of a society based on a particular social relation of production, that is, a relation of domination between social classes;
2   the logic of societal reproduction and whether this also constitutes the reproduction of the social relation of domination;
3   the class struggles that may occur, which contest the social relation of domination (and/or the logic of social reproduction);
4   the ethical dimension that informs the critique of domination.

There is also a fifth which Marx implicitly addresses yet theoretically circumvents: other components of domination that are not bound by a class form but belong to the logic of societal reproduction. Either together or separately this series of interconnected problems provides a vantage point through which the conventional reading of *Capital* can be connected to its metatheory. In this respect our reconstruction of Marx's critical theory follows in part, Jean Cohen's analysis in her book *Class and Civil Society*, particularly the chapter 'System and Class: The Subversion of Emancipation'. Her basic thesis is that Marx, in an effort to criticize capitalism, generates class as the key critical concept that links the analysis of the reproductive logic of the capitalist economy to the possibility of its transformation. In so doing, she argues, he fetishizes class by invoking the two-class model and transforming this into a systems-derived conception of societal repro-duction. While we agree with the basic thrust of this thesis, we wish to argue that Marx's analysis itself is also informed by his two other 'fetishes' derived from his metatheory – the anthropology of materiality and the social totality now made explicit in the paradigm of production. In contrast to Jean Cohen, who argues that in *Capital* 'the critique of political economy replaces the abstract forces/relations model with the detailed analysis of the wage-labour/capital relation',[97] we argue that

Marx utilizes the forces/relations of production categories in the context of the model of the primacy of the productive forces. This model establishes the investigative procedure which results in the notion of abstract labour and labour-power. Whilst this model, which the 1859 'Preface' introduces, gives no direct guide-lines as to the method of procedure for the immanent critique of the capitalist epoch, it suggests the causal relation between its subsystems and establishes the parameters for Marx's critique of capitalism in *Capital*. Materiality and totality make the system reduction of class understandable, and establish the correspondence between Marx's first and second encounters with Hegel. In this context an unlikely companion for Cohen's interpretation is found in Backhaus's interesting (although ultimately delimited and constrained) analysis of Marx's dialectic of the value-form.[98] Both Cohen and Backhaus address the central component of Marx's critical theory: his critique of capitalist social relations of production. It is precisely within this configuration of Marx's critique of the capitalist social relations of production, that the notions or 'fetishes' of anthropology and totality impinge upon his most famous critical theory.

Capitalism and, for Marx, its main representative object, the commodity, is approached by him from two interrelated sides. Each possesses an internal opposition in the light of the other. This supposedly uncovers the relation between irrationality and domination. On the one hand, Marx's analysis of capitalism is approached from the side of the *content* or anthropology that embodies the technical/material elements that constitute it – the labour-process and the productive forces. On the other hand, the commodity is also approached from the side of its *social form*. It is here that the notion of totality enters in a constitutive sense. Marx materialistically utilizes the 'insights contained in Hegel's *Logic* as the dialectical theory of *totality in process*'.[99] Marx's first reinterpretation of Hegel, and his subsequent process of self-clarification, hide a residual and unreflected absorption of, and reliance on, the *structure* and *movement* of Hegel's ontology, even if initially this is provided by the *Philosophy of Right* and the *Phenomenology of Spirit* and not the *Logic*. This reliance now surfaces explicitly as a constraining and mythologizing impulse and sets the scene for his later adventures with Hegel's dialectic. Marx's treatment of the *Logic* itself should be seen in the context of his 'search for a method' with which he can analyse the capitalist mode of production. There are two methods that appear alternatively in the *Grundrisse* and *Capital* and each uses different aspects of the *Logic*. In *Capital* Marx uses the notion of totality as a defetishizing critique based on the dialectic of identity with its movement of thought from essence to appearance. Marx becomes a 'friend of science'.[100] In so becoming, though, the critical *intent* of his use of 'totality' as the totalization of capitalist relations that establish the modern regime of unfreedom is ultimately undermined. Marx subordinates the dynamic, conflictual and constituting nature of the class relation to his analysis of the logic of capitalism's reproduction. Behind the 'far from innocent categories'[101] of capitalist/wage-labourer and capital/labour-power, there lurks Marx's notion of social totality with its assumption that 'the capitalist economy can be analysed as a self-sufficient, albeit contradictory system, with its own internal dynamics and reproductive mechanisms.'[102] The reason for this subordination is not only, as Jean Cohen rightly argues, Marx's formalistic analysis of class which is constructed as a two-class model, and which conflates the social actor within the logic of capitalism's self-reproduction, that is, the production of surplus-value through valorization (despite the constitutive role of the class form itself). This separation also occurs, as is already implied (an implication which Jean Cohen recognizes but does not explore),[103] because of Marx's impoverished materialism and his residual appropriation and use of the structure of Hegel's thought. This pertains to the constitutive notion of totality as well as the already established distinction between the material content and the social form.

Marx moves from, or more accurately between, anthropology and totality, and to totality's world of appearances (the value-form) and an essence underlying it (the class relation of capitalist and wage-labour). In this way, the movement that has been described as an inexplicable, 'unmediated jump . . . from "the substance to the form of appearance"'[104] becomes explicable. Marx proceeds, from an analysis that establishes (in the first two sections of chapter 1) the material content of the commodity, to an analysis (in the third section) of its 'other' – its social form. In order to uncover the problematic nature of the relation between anthropology and totality as well as the problematic nature of the concepts themselves, we shall begin, though, with capitalism's 'forms(s) of appearance', the value-form.

According to Marx, the value-form or commodity-form is the configuration through which the reproduction of capitalism and its class relation, in its manifold complexity, is represented and can be analysed. It is 'the economic cell-form'[105] through which the functional reproduction of the modern social system can be analysed. However, it is not the determining, forming moment of modern society. It is only a 'form of appearance' of a 'formal determination' yet to be uncovered. Exchange between commodities only portrays the world of the taken-for-granted bourgeois reality that constitutes its own self-understanding, a self-understanding that Marx essentially accepts. Marx assumes that capitalism's reproduction as a class-form can be analysed as a totality through what is seen to be its basic categorial (and real) representative – the commodity. This is not only because the commodity represents the economy as such – the constitutive sphere of life that is presented metatheoretically within the paradigm of production – but also because Marx assumes that the economy, like Hegel's corporatistically conceived society, functions like an organism. The structures and institutions are organically interconnected to one another and, because of this, the categories of class action (capital/wage-labour) are interpreted by Marx as synonymous with their functional and reproductive position within the totality itself. As he states: 'Individuals are dealt with here [in *Capital*] only in so far as they are the personifications of economic categories, the bearers of particular class-relations and interests.' [106]

The notion of the cell-form (which represents a functionally integrated totality) entails that the movement of thought itself proceeds in a manner different from that of his previous critical theories. There is, as Markus has pointed out, a change in the movement of thought from the abstract to the concrete (as in the *Grundrisse*), to the movement of thought from essence to appearance. [107] Marx adopts a specific part of Hegel's *Geist*-philosophy, as it appears in book two of the *Logic*, 'The Doctrine of Essence'. It is argued that this is for Marx, a more appropriate methodological form through which to uncover the logic (rather than the historical development) of capitalism's self-reproduction as a class-form. However, it is more than this. Between the 1857-8 *Grundrisse* and the publication of *Capital* vol. I in 1867, Marx had, as we have already argued, established the metatheoretical structure of what is considered to be the coventional reading of historical materialism – the model of the primacy of the productive forces which contains the formalized base–superstructure model. Given this, Marx absorbs the *language* of Hegel's *Logic* (the assumed movement of thought) into the structure of the paradigm of production with its categorial distinction between material content and social form. The notion of social form itself is interpreted as a social totality, the basic reproductive mechanisms of which reside in the economy, and upon which stand the array of the superstructures. Having anthropologically reinterpreted Hegel through the notion of the *material content* (the labour-process and the productive forces) and accepting the basic Hegelian conception of civil society, Marx also proceeds sociologically with a structural and functional bifurcation between base and superstructure, and in so doing categorially utilizes a language that 'reflects' the structure of his paradigm. [108] He finds this in the movement of thought from essence to appearance. In this sense, this movement of thought is important *only* in as much as it structures, *metaphorically* (rather than as a dialectical movement in the strict sense)[109] Marx's investigation of the totality and hence the paradigm of production, or at least this version of it.

Thus structured, Marx's value-form analysis and his critique of the fetishistic nature of commodity production does two things. It first inaugurates his critique of capitalism, and secondly, connects this to his underlying social theory. In other words, it enables Marx first to solve the problem of 'why and to what extent can the "relation of things" only be conceived as a "mere form of appearance, external to the relation of human relations hidden behind it".'[110] Secondly, it enables him to ground this in the conceptual organization of the theory itself. According to Marx the 'appearance of value' is *represented* in two interrelated ways; as a 'form of thought' (the doctrine of political economy)[111] and as a symbol (money or the price-form).[112] They are interrelated because each provides the set of objective categories, forms or mechanisms that represent the world of commodity production *outside* the sphere of production itself – either in the sphere of circulation, or in the ethereal realm of the imagination. They are, for Marx, the necessary but nonetheless illusory or derivative forms that capitalism creates to conceal the process which realizes commodity production – a class relation.

Political economy's presentation of the value-form is, then, the *'post-festa'* representation of capitalism's stabilization into a singular and historically identifiable mode of production. It is an ideology, a 'form of appearance', its own form of self-deception that both projects and mystifies capitalism as a natural, immutable law, and glorifies, universalizes, yet reduces human labour to mere abstract labour-power (time) without recourse to its relation to need.[113] Moreover, it simultaneously presents commodity exchange as a mere exchange of use-values in the market-place. This conception is 'mysterious', that is, fetishistic; it appears as 'a relation between things' signified by the money-form.[114] Despite, in Marx's view, the positive historical 'rationalization' of commodity exchanges through an equivalent form, the commodity-form under capitalism is inherently contradictory and antagonistic, alienating and reifying. This money-form conceals (while political economy fails to comprehend) the inner connections between exchange-value, labour and the class-imposed relation between commodity producers. In uncovering these inner contradictorily constituted connections Marx moves from the sphere of circulation to its 'material ground', the realm of production.

During the process of circulation under capitalism, the commodity changes from its identity as an object of use to become something else

– a possessor of value, which is expressed through money. Unlike the critique generated from 'communal and autotelic totality' in which Marx argues that capitalism essentially *dissolves* an identity based on a holistic determination, the critique of capitalism in this version holds to an antagonistic opposition between form and content itself. Marx puts it thus:

> Exchange produces a differentiation of the commodity into two elements, commodity and money, an external opposition which expresses the opposition between use-value and exchange-value . . . These antagonistic forms are the real forms of motion of the process of exchange.[115]

Instead of drawing on the anthropological translation of Hegelian holism, Marx now draws on the structure of the dialectical form through the principle of identity that appears in the *Logic*: the opposition, yet unity, of being and non-being. The commodity/ money equation is the internally antagonistic 'form of appearance' that is depicted by Marx in the sphere of circulation. This is, as Marx points out, 'the first peculiarity that strikes us when we reflect on the equivalent form . . . that use-value becomes the form of appearance of its opposite, value'.[116]

However, for Marx, there is by definition and through the formal structure of his theory another analogous process of identity-formation and equivalence that establishes the commodity relation. This takes place in a different realm – the sphere of production. This is the material 'ground' upon which value ultimately rests. Marx's procedure of critique here is the same. Money is no longer the *real* equivalent form, but, according to him, is reliant upon and expresses another contradictory and antagonistic 'peculiarity' that resides within each commodity – the opposition between concrete labour and abstract labour. As he states, 'the equivalent form . . . possesses a second peculiarity: in it, concrete labour becomes the form of manifestation of its opposite, abstract human labour.'[117] At this level then (that is, at the level of the anthropologically grounded realm of production), Marx argues that the commodity is the recipient of another (and more real) doubling effect; on the one hand, of concrete labour and on the other, of the labour-power that is abstracted from it in the particular form under which it is manufactured. The internal opposition between use-value and exchange-value is played out at the level of its material content or substance: the labour-process (leaving aside for the moment, the substance's or content's relation to the social form or social relation that encapsulates it). For Marx, use-values, as man-made objects, are already united at the level of anthropology by virtue of the fact that they are products of heterogeneous forms of 'specific and useful concrete labour'.[118] However, under generalized commodity production this implicit recognition becomes explicit, but explicit in a specific sense. The commodities become united by the labour that is abstracted from them as homogeneous, quantifiable units.[119] This general process of homogenization and quantification in terms of time, constitutes for Marx both the mystery of the *expression of value* (which could only become evident, according to him, in his overly historicized and production-centred interpretation of Aristotle)[120] and the secret of the *process of valorization itself*. Abstract labour is the identity-forming 'thing' that unites the diversity of commodities (as values) because it too is commodified – albeit *in potentia* rather than *in actu*. In other words, it is – from different sides of the same coin – both the universal component that resides within each commodity, and the 'thing' that is bought and sold as if it were a commodity in order to activate the production of commodities.

The dual process of the commodification of labour and its valorization brings Marx to the real object and realm of his analysis – production – both as the real place of human self-reproduction, and as a social relation. As the latter, it is a class relation between buyers and sellers of labour-power. This establishes general commodity production. Hence while Marx grants the representational forms (political economy and the equivalent form) a place within the social world, they are interpreted by him as ideological, superstructural and masking devices, rather than as constitutive elements. Marx argues that the world of political economy and 'the finished form of the world of commodities' need to be punctured.[121] Criticism needs to 'get behind the secret of [capitalism's] own social product'[122] to reveal precisely what it is: a class (power) relation which is formed and constituted within the sphere of production itself. This is Marx's 'hidden reason'[123] for the 'pseudo-dialectics' of the value-form. Its internal contradiction or opposition, played out in the phenomenal and superstructural realms, is both formatively and ultimately played out in the sphere of production. And, for Marx, the basic contradiction is that between private and social labour. For him, the equivalent form denotes a third and final peculiarity: 'private labour takes the form of its opposite, namely labour in its actual social form.'[124] This is established at the level of *organization* within the sphere of production, that is, of labour-activity itself, whereby 'the process of production has mastery over man, instead of the opposite.'[125] The antagonistic, contradictory way in which the commodity 'doubles' into commodity and money (which is expressed as a relation between things) is unravelled and revealed as a similarly antagonistically structured power relation between people. This relation is, for Marx, the 'essence' of the 'pseudo-dialectical' unfolding of the categories. Although he does not use the term 'essence' in *Capital* vol. I, its precise meaning is clear to us from his sixth thesis on Feuerbach and *The German Ideology*. Marx's critique of Feuerbach centres on the meaning of essence itself. He argues that Feuerbach's anthropological critique of Hegel merely resolves religious, external essence into human essence, and that, rather, the notion of essence requires further anthropological radicalization and elaboration. For Marx, 'human essence is no abstraction inherent in each single individual. *In its reality it is the ensemble of social relations.*' [126] This ensemble is now, for Marx, the base of the social form of the paradigm of production – the social relations of production.

The movement, then, from 'the forms of appearance' to the basis of generalized commodity production involves the analysis, by Marx, of the internal structure of the social form of capitalist society and its relation to the material content.

A tension, however, appears in *Capital* within Marx's construction of the dialectic of the value-form. The tension is between the notions of substance and essence, each of which offers an alternative and ultimately competing ground from which Marx generates his critical theory. Each of these notions within *Capital* has a key category through which Marx analyses modern society, and which returns him to the two central conceptual complexes of historical materialism: anthropology centring on material content, and totality centring on the social form. Whilst each involves Marx's attempt to address his object of enquiry in terms of the ethical maxim of freedom that he builds into his critique, they develop either into a one-dimensional theory and a philosophy of history (on the side of the content), or into a functional and economized notion of class composition and conflict (on the side of the form). In each case the relation between anthropology and totality alters, although they still remain to buttress each other. In the former, social conflict and subjectivity succumb to a combination of objectivism and teleology; in the latter the parameters of social conflict are determined and delimited by the notion of functional totality and the two-class model. Either way, the Kantian-derived ethical maxim of freedom collapses. [127]

To take the latter first, Marx assumes that he analyses the class structure of capitalism primarily in terms of a power relation of domination and subordination that exists within the sphere of production itself, rather than in terms of the mechanisms of reproduction. In this context, the chapter in *Capital* vol. I where this occurs – 'The

Working Day' – is both conspicuous by its presence and significant through the way in which the analysis proceeds.

Surrounded on one side by Marx's reconstruction of the logic of the production of surplus-value, and on the other by his analysis of the technical/material requirements for such a production, what we could term Marx's 'class chapter' concerns the struggles over 'the establishment of a norm of the working day'.[128] Having isolated one of the main organizing principles of modern society – time – Marx turns his attention to investigate the coercive way in which capitalism imposed its definition of this principle in 'those houses of terror' the factories.[129] Marx analyses the nature of the conflict between capitalists and wage-labourers in terms of a new form of power relation that constitutes the anti-emancipatory side of modernity. For our purposes the dates and details of revolts, strikes, meetings and reports are important only inasmuch as they enable the reader to watch the way in which Marx highlights certain actors and classes, whilst precluding an analysis of other actors and classes.

The struggles over the series of Factory Acts concerning not only health, safety and sanitation, but also the limitation of the working day is portrayed by him as a 'protracted and more or less concealed civil war between the capitalist class and the working class'.[130] Each attempt by the working class to shorten the working day and, in Marx's view, retrieve a portion of its life from the prerogative of surplus-value, is countered by an equally tenacious, yet vicious and cynical reply by the capitalists, or more specifically the manufacturers and their parliamentary or legal/judicial representatives. This in turn is challenged either through strikes or other agitation by the working class until 'the principle [the formal and legislative shortening of the working day] had triumphed with its victory in those great branches of industry which form the most characteristic creation of the modern mode of production.'[131] With this, the capitalist unwillingly accepts this 'new "extravagance"'.[132] This results, according to Marx, in the gradual weakening of the power of the capitalist, and the concurrent strengthening of the power of the working class. Because of this, the English factory-workers, in Marx's view, 'are the champions, not only of the English working class, but of the modern working class in general'.[133]

However, Marx is not only portraying an 'active' class history but is also constructing a mythology that concerns the notion and nature of class conflict and social action. Marx takes two interconnected notions that belong to his definition of the social form as the starting-point for his analysis of the working day. They are, on the one hand, that capitalism can be analysed as a self-producing functional totality, and on the other, that this totality is composed of two main classes. The two-class model of social conflict, which is basically developed in *The Communist Manifesto*, becomes the converse of Marx's notion of totality. From within this model Marx argues that there are only two groupings that are the major and constitutive classes in modern society. Prior to 'The Working Day' they are introduced, constituted and analysed according to the categories of capital and wage-labour. As functionally defined and located 'units' of social action, the classes in *Capital* are described as homogeneous entities with clearly defined and understood interests that stem directly from their respective dominant or subordinate places in the production process.

However, this interpretation of the conflicts of modern capitalism from within the paradigmatic structure of the two-class model misrepresents the composition of the players who participate in the pages of 'The Working Day', as well as the way in which the working day itself was shortened. A brief yet salutary glance indicates that bureaucrats (commissioners, health inspectors), parliamentarians, journalists, medical practitioners and clerics also participated in the struggles that resulted in factory-reform legislation encompassing health, safety and restrictions on the numbers of hours worked. Moreover, they participated in the spheres of the state and the public. Marx, though, is not interested in all of this. Marx's exclusion of those people from the two-class model means that he does not have to reflect upon the nature of reform as such, nor upon whether the participants could possibly be an early version of the technocratic welfare worker. The shortening of the working day was also achieved through the moral interdictions placed on the labour of women and children, which to be sure Marx notices. The point is that he attributes the victories to a working-class revolutionary consciousness (that is, to universality) rather than to a particularity that draws its values for conflict in places located outside the sphere of production. Furthermore he does not need to reflect upon the fact that conflict takes place in the domain of the state. Conflict in the sphere of the political is replicated in Marx's view according to the same logic as that in the economic sphere.

To be sure, what the chapter on the working day accounts for is the development of a contestatory working class and its trade unions. However, it accounts for them in terms that posit the constitution of the totality as an agglomeration of functional groupings only, and not as containing both other actors and groupings that are not functionally located in the productive sphere and claims that may be outside the production paradigm i.e. their value-relations. These other actors and claims are just part of the accumulated 'necessary appearances'. In his move from historiography to theory he leaves them behind. The nature of the essence belongs to the relations of production which, in the final analysis for Marx, are conceptualized as an institutional infrastructure that produces surplus-value in a specific way. This is where his critique both departs and returns to the anthropological formulation of his metatheory.

The specific nature of surplus-value, according to Marx, is that it relies on abstract, quantified labour to produce it. It relies on the exploitation of labour through time, which is a dispossession or alienation of a determinant of activity that belongs to the worker. Hence, in Marx's view, what the trade unions grasp in their hands (in the form of the Ten Hours Bill) is 'the modest Magna Carta of the legally limited working day, which at last makes clear when the time which the worker sells is ended, and when his own begins'.[134] Labour-power, though, (not labour as all-rounded activity) is conceptualized by Marx as a resource that constitutes 'the absolute extent of his labour-time, that is the working day'.[135] It is the ultimate source of value:

> In order to extract value out of the consumption of a commodity, our friend the money-owner must be lucky enough to find within the sphere of circulation, on the market, a commodity whose use-value possesses the peculiar property of being a source of value, whose actual consumption is therefore an objectification of labour, hence a creation of value. The possessor of money does find such a special commodity on the market: the capacity for labour, in other words labour-power. We mean by labour-power, or labour capacity, the aggregate of those mental and physical capabilities existing in the physical form, the living personality, of a human being, capabilities which he sets in motion whenever he produces a use-value of any kind.[136]

However, this anthropological formulation of the substance of value transforms Marx's argumentation concerning the nature of power. The insight about power that Marx has into the kingdom of the factory, that:

> the capitalist formulates his autocratic power over his workers like a private legislator, and purely as an emanation of his own will, unaccompanied by either the division of responsibility otherwise so much approved of by the bourgeoisie, or the still more approved representative system,[137]

is circumvented. It cannot be brought into play, that is, developed into an analysis of power relations as determinative of the value-form.

Rather, Marx's formulation of labour-power indicates that legitimate contestatory action revolves around wage-rates. His concentration on the struggles over time and wages in *Capital* brings to light Marx's inability to confront the nature of the capitalist form of authority as a normative complex even though it is functionally located, and thus the paralysing of his own ethical stance. It also brings to light his underlying reliance on the material content rather than the social form for explanatory force. The existence of a conflict over *something* between *acting* classes basically disappears after the chapter, 'The Working Day'. The stake of the struggle, that is wages, is reduced to the appearance of an underlying essence that is ultimately defined in terms of a metasocial substance. The struggle itself is either devalued,[138] or as we shall see, redefined.

Marx's analysis of the social form is ultimately subordinated to his criterion of material life, that is, to the material content of the commodity. In this way, the notion of labour-power is itself subjected to a naturalistic interpretation that essentially bypasses rather than merely minimizes the problematic of the class constitution of society and the conflicts that this constitution engenders. This bypassing and subordination is most evident if we move from Marx's analysis of the working day to his analysis of commodity fetishism.

Marx's analysis of commodity fetishism is the other critical impulse that emerges, at first sight as a *companion* to, but at the level of metatheory in *contradistinction* to, his analysis of the struggles over the working day. The equivalent form of the commodity (the form that is directly exchangeable with other commodities) to be sure, conceals a social relation between the producers of the commodities themselves. Marx argues:

> Fetishism . . . arises from the peculiar social character of the labour which produces them . . . [when] objects of utility become commodities only because they are the products of the labour of the private individuals who work independently of each other . . . Since the producers do not come into social contact until they exchange the products of their labour, *the specific social characterisitcs of their private labours appear only within this exchange.*[139]

The act of exchange between commodities replaces the direct social exchanges and social labours of pre-capitalist societies.[140] For Marx, commodity production transforms personal relations into material relations and social relations into relations between things. Labour activity is disconnected from the social producer during production, and she or he only relates to it as one object to another, that is, in a completely indifferent and fetishized way. The fetishistic relation affects the whole range of social life including the forms of inter-course.[141]

Yet Marx traces commodity fetishism back to the process of production, although not as a class-form, but as labour as a resource that is imbedded in the commodity. From this he can argue that value is abstracted from this resource once it is activated by capital. The discovery of abstract labour as the hidden substance of value (leaving aside for the moment the question of whether it is socially constituted or only socially utilized), enables Marx to argue that it is labour-power as such that is bought and sold as a commodity, and not 'living labour'. As a reproducible resource, labour-power has value, although it differs from other resources in being incarnated in a concrete subject; it produces value in its active manifestation through time. Marx argues that since the value-producing activity is separated from the concrete subjectivity of the producers, it is alienated labour (in the sense defined already in the 1844 *Manuscripts*).[142]

However, the value-producing activity is, according to Marx at the beginning of *Capital* vol. I, identical with the most elementary (and infrasocial) structure of human action, that is, the expenditure of time and energy. By being thus identified, the process of alienation is simultaneously totalized and naturalized – it swallows the subject whole, and for that very reason, it can no longer be diagnosed as alienation. Rather, for Marx, the result of commodity production is now a complete reification of the act of production, an inversion of subject and object. Accordingly, fetishism 'is nothing but the definite social relation between things'.[143] This means that within Marx's own metatheory subjectivity also becomes disembodied. This is because the critique is now generated, not so much from the vantage point of an essence of the social totality, but rather from the domain of the reduc-tively construed material content.

In assuming that abstract labour as the common denominator of human activity is completely commodified and reified, Marx's analysis of what he terms commodity fetishism leads inevitably to a one-dimen-sional theory that annihilates human subjectivity. Commodification and reification take place in the extraction and the complete expenditure of labour-power during the valorization process. Time, the external empirical manifestation of labour-power is completely exhausted: so too is the worker.[144] It is as if the worker find him- or herself in the pages of the first chapter of *Capital* vol. I on the shelf – another commodity among the boots and shirts, beds and sheets which Marx discusses.

However, the economization of class conflict and the complete reification of the producer, is not what Marx is really after. The logic and practice of emancipation is not, for him, found ultimately in the continuation of indeterminate struggles over 'rates of participation', or a continuing exhaustion of labour-powers. Emancipation is found in the overcoming of the crisis-complex of *production* under capitalism. For Marx, all of this is located in the sphere of material life itself (the sphere of production), that is, in the basic contradiction between the material content and the social form. As Marx says:

> There is an antithesis, immanent in the commodity, between use-value and value, between private labour which must simultaneously manifest itself as directly social labour, and a particular concrete kind of labour which simultaneously counts as merely abstract universal labour, between the *personification of things and reification of persons*.[145]

Reification, in this context, then, is essentially the concrete fusion and inversion (within the social form of capitalism) of the social mechanisms that *dictate* the estranged aims of production, with the rational functionality of the material–technical productive forces. Its existence is, for Marx, an indication that the *material* production of life under capitalism is basically irrational. Hence the world of the factory – of overwork, of physical degeneration and degradation – is judged within a criterion of rationality which points to the irrationality of the social aims that prescribe the productive process under capitalism. A theoretical analysis of the emergence of power relations in the factory which Marx uncovers empirically,[146] is left untouched because such an analysis is circumscribed by the paradigm of production and a concentration on the irrational logic of valorization. The crisis-complex of productive life under capitalism is overcome, and hence emancipation brought forward, in *Capital*, not by acting subjects, but by a separation of the material content from the social form, that is, a separation of the realm of necessity from the realm of freedom. Marx argues that:

> the realm of freedom actually begins only where labour which is determined by necessity and mundane considerations ceases; thus in the very nature of things it lies beyond the sphere of actual material production . . . Beyond it [the realm of necessity] begins that development of human energy which is an end in itself, the true realm of freedom, which, however, can blossom forth only with this realm of necessity as its basis. *The shortening of the working day is its basic prerequisite*.[147]

Time is the element that Marx isolates in his discourse concerning emancipation. The impetus for both this separation and the development of a fully-fledged realm of freedom comes from, according to him, the development of the productive forces.[148] Emancipation is grounded in the rational utilization of nature's resources, a rational utilization that overcomes the processes of reification. The notion of conflict is absorbed into Marx's philosophy of history, which enters under the guise of the contradiction between the material content and the social form, and thus fills the gap left after the annihilation of the subject.

Marx's resolution of the crisis-complex of capitalism points to the internal limits of his theorizing. These limits concern his anthropological formulation of labour and his notion of freedom.

Marx's specific conception of the relation between the anthropological foundations and the social totality, as a contradiction between the material contents and the social form, as well as his conceptualization of each of those domains, determines the outcome of his critique of capitalism. The critique is guided by the above two currents; one concerning the developmental tendency and potential (logic) of the productive forces, which rides in tandem with the other, the notion of society as a self-reproducing totality. These currents conceptualize the challenge to, and overturning of, the despotic relation of capital to wage-labour either through the disappearance of the acting subject and the development of a one-dimensional theory which places the 'promise' of emancipation in a teleologically imputed development of the productive forces, or through struggles over wages which accounts only for the development of trade unions and can lead to social democratic or corporatist political forms. Each circumscribes the problematics of the logic of and struggles for democracy and leads to impoverished versions of socialism. On the one hand, the Jacobin-authoritarian socialists absorbed Marx's philosophy of history as a self-legitimizing pseudo-science, while simultaneously creating the political form of the Bolshevik Party. On the other, social democratic parties were formed that continued to view conflict economistically and developed a technocratic vision of social reform. In each case, the libertarian current that drew its strength from a notion of extended democratization is circumvented.[149]

However, as we have argued, there are some indications in Marx's own work of a competing paradigm and a subterranean current that involve a rupture of the basic conceptual framework of historical materialism. This occurs first in the development of a paradigm of class action that fissures the notion of totality and the two-class model that resides within it. Secondly, there is a subterranean current that implicitly reflects upon the problematic of consciousness. It is to these that we now turn, only to see them paralysed and suppressed, while they problematicize the conceptual edifice of historical materialism.

6

The Paradigm of Class Action

It is hardly surprising that given the logics of *Capital* Marx never finishes the all too brief remarks on class that constitute the final chapter of volume III.[1] As this chapter has been analysed by Jean Cohen, mainly in relation to Marx's restrictive categorization of classes,[2] a recapitulation and critique will not be undertaken here. One should say, though, that Marx in response to his own question 'What constitutes a class?',[3] confronts immediately the limits of a construction constrained by the paradigm of production. Instead of focusing on Marx's question (which may well be misconstrued, but has underscored much contemporary literature on class analysis) another will be asked in its place; 'How do classes act?'.[4]

This question introduces the basic theme of this chapter. It is suggested that Marx's stilted and ultimately self-defeating analysis of class relations (in terms of a one-dimensionality and the circumscription of the ethical maxims of autonomy and freedom) is not the end of the story on class in his *oeuvre*, and that he generates an *alternative and competing paradigm*: *the paradigm of class action*. This is not to be found in the later works on critical economy that constitute the fourth and fifth critical theories, but rather in the more directly politico-historical writings: 'The Class Struggles in France', 'The Eighteenth Brumaire of Louis Bonaparte', and 'The Civil War in France', even though it is introduced as a thesis in the opening lines of *The Communist Manifesto*.

Marx opens *The Communist Manifesto* by stating: 'The history of all hitherto existing society is the history of class struggle.'[5] In this short pithy sentence Marx captures the alternative and competing starting-point for his critical theories, the outplay of social relations that are conflictually constituted.[6] However, the seed of the paradigm of class action is sown in *The German Ideology*. This construction of class stems from one of Marx's constituting 'conditions of life' that he establishes as the cornerstones for his theory of historical materialism –

the social forms of intercourse. The notion 'forms of intercourse' is vague and elusive, like *The German Ideology* itself. Without pre-empting the further discussion of it in 'The Hidden Imaginary', it can be asserted that from it stem two interrelated directions; the problem-atic of the ensemble of social relations and the problematic of consciousness. Marx is concerned to address the nature of societal control and transformation. As he says at the end of the first part of *The German Ideology*: 'The conditions under which definite produc-tive forces can be applied are the conditions of the rule of a definite class of society . . . therefore, every revolutionary struggle is directed against a class, which till then has been in power'.[7] This suggests that, notwithstanding the teleology that is imputed to the notion of the productive forces and which surrounds that particular quotation, Marx confronts the problem of classes in their right, in their own making, and in relation to other classes. In this way, and through the multi-layered notion of the forms of intercourse, Marx suggests that the stabilization of social forms takes place in part by one class taking control over both a society's productive functioning and its cognitive capacity against other classes and groups, as well as imposing and institutionalizing its identity over society as a whole. Marx states this clearly in *The German Ideology*: 'The ideas of the ruling class are in every epoch the ruling ideas i.e. the class which is the ruling *material* force of society, is at the same time its ruling *intellectual* force.'[8] The critical 'destabilization' of society comes about in two ways, through the growth and sophistication of material activity and through new cognitive approaches which challenge the homogeneity of the domi-nant conceptions. It is through this sense of conflicting 'otherness' that classes construct their self- and societal definitions. Thus, according to Marx, in the event of a social transformation, a new ruling class must present its own ideas and interests 'as the interests of all members of society . . . it has to give its ideas the form of uni-versality and represent them as the only rational, universally valid ones'.[9] In this way, ideas are linked to the critico-practical project of class struggle. The opposing class must become significant, it must symbolize the interests of all oppressed classes and, hence, become ideologically universalizing. Moreover, this specific form of oppo-sitional universalization undermines the nature-like basis of those ideas which have current hegemony – its real challenge is to represent the ruling ideas as particular ideas.

In this context, though, Jean Cohen's critique of Marx's notion of class cannot be dismissed. There is no doubt, as she has shown, that Marx's writings that deal with class generally,[10] and his so-called historical writings, remain dependent on the core notions of his mythological construction of the notion of class. These notions are an economized version which derive the notion of class interest from its respective dominant or subordinate position in Marx's assumed socially constituting sphere of production and the two-class model with its 'paradigm of class rule'. Each of these interpretations, as she constantly reminds her audience, is intersected and formed by his philosophy of history:

> For Marx . . . the concept of class retains its socio-economic determination and is projected backward (along with the concept of mode of production) as the motor of all history and the key to the understanding of relations of domination and struggle for emancipation in dynamic societies. Accordingly, all societies are leveled to the same plane of production relations and are fraught with the same kind of internal antagonisms . . . The apparent opposition between the *evolutionary* forces/relations model and the *revolutionary* theory of class struggles is resolved by attributing to the revolutionary classes the role of *representing* progress in the further development of the forces of production.[11]

While in agreement with Jean Cohen's argument in general, especially concerning Marx's philosophy of history, there is a tendency for her to conflate the problematic of historical materialism with it. For her, these constructions are *essentially* the same. However, this conflation means that the specific problematic of historical materialism eludes her. This concerns the anthropologically conceived constitutional determinants of human life and society, and as a project is theoretically configured by Marx through the internally differentiated paradigm of production. This, too, transforms the notion of class relations especially within the formative argument of *The German Ideology* and the subsequent productionist models that spring from it.

'Forms of intercourse' is transposed by Marx, into the shorthand expression 'relations of production'. This refers to the institutional infrastructure of the division of labour, that is the separation of tasks into functionally demarcated spheres. This functional demarcation also refers to, or more correctly, is constituted through the various forms of ownership in Marx's view. As he states: 'The various stages of development in the division of labour are just so many different forms of ownership . . . [that] . . . determines the relations of individuals to one another with reference to the material, instrument, and product of labour.'[12] The notion of the relations of production simply refers to the classes and groups that inhabit the institutional infrastructure of the division of labour. The problem of class relations, then, becomes too over-burdened by the paradigm of production for it to emerge from the more theoretical texts with any independence force as an alternative paradigm.

The presence of such a paradigm is the beauty of the politico-historical writings. It is in these specifically, rather than in *The Communist Manifesto*, that the problem of class relations is explored with some unexpected results. In them, the paradigm of class action comes into its own. Here, the emphasis changes from the notion of relations of production to its more flexible 'sister' notion of 'an ensemble of social relations'. Although at times constrained by the languages of production and teleology, the paradigm of class action introduces the notion of class relations (or ensemble of social relations) in a way that enables classes to form and act in their own terms, and in a different terrain from the sphere of production, in particular in the domain of the state. This means that the notion of a structurally or systemically determined class location which resides within the paradigm of production is implicitly displaced by Marx by a conception of an open-ended formation and contestation of class identities. Moreover, Marx's paradigm of class action not only generates a dynamic topography of class formation and class conflict, but also connects him directly with the tensions of his 1843 critique of Hegel, that is his debt to both Kant and Hegel, and his conception of politics. In other words, although expressed, as we have already mentioned, as a thesis in the 1845 critique of Feuerbach, this construction (of the ensemble of social relations) is reminiscent of his earlier critique of the logic of Hegel's corporatism, and Marx's own lost political anthropology.

Our task, then, is slightly different from that of plotting the constraining elements that are either internal to Marx's notion of class (two-class model, economized notion of class interest), or external yet related to it (philosophy of history, paradigm of production). Not only will Marx's 'critical sociology of class'[13] be investigated to open an untheorized argument concerning the multidimensional 'logics' of the modern world, but also this will establish the images that emerge as well as their implications for a social theory that goes beyond the restrictive anthropological metatheory of the paradigm of production. The so-called historico-political writings, then, will be approached in two interrelated ways. The first concerns the way in which Marx reconstructs the conflicts of the modern era. Marx fractures the economically circumscribed and fractionally articulated two-class model, and analyses class in terms of fractions, politics and power. The second concerns the way in which Marx constitutes the notion of class action itself. The paradigm of class action that is uncovered in the historico-political writings implicitly generates a philosophical anthropology that necessarily addresses the political, normative, interpretative and symbolic dimensions in terms other than those derived from the notions of labour and production.

FRACTIONS, POLITICS AND POWER

Jean Cohen suggests that in 'The Class Struggles in France' and 'The Eighteenth Brumaire of Louis Bonaparte' Marx puts forward a five-class model of class relations.[14] It is the model that implicitly resides within *The Communist Manifesto*, but is subsumed under the two-class model, which itself is anticipated in the 1843 'A Contribution to the Critique of Hegel's *Philosophy of Right* Introduction'. The five classes are the bourgeoisie, the petit-bourgeoisie, the proletariat, the lumpenproletariat and the peasantry. But, as her commentary throughout this chapter in her book makes clear, the situation is more complex than this – Marx generates a six-class model, the sixth being the 'caste' of state officials, together with a possible differentiation within each class.

The inclusion of the sixth grouping suggests that Marx is utilizing the notion of class in two ways that separate it from its determination under the paradigm of production. First, Marx wants to detail all social actors and groups who participated in the political turmoil of the 1848 Revolutions. This means that the notion of class itself must attain a fluidity or flexibility if it is to absorb all participants and thus function as a viable and representative critical sociology. Secondly, this flexibility indicates an implicit movement away from the notion of production as a total and/or basic form of/for social action. For Marx, under the production version, the bourgeoisie and the proletariat are the major and real classes of modern society, because they constitute its functional and reproductive units. However, in the class-action version, he includes other groups that notably are neither functionally necessary, nor reproduce the logic of capitalist relations. In this way, they do not derive their social location or social definition from the capitalist mode of production. These groups or classes are the peasantry, the 'caste' of state officials (including the military), and the lumpenproletariat. This suggests that conflict is not only generated according to different principles, as well as being located in a realm different from the one indicated by the paradigm of production, but also that the conception of society is different from that of a functionally integrated unit. Society in this version of class action is conceptualized implicitly by Marx as a series of centres of power.

Moreover, this fluidity enables each class to be viewed as a configuration of different elements that combine or coalesce to form a homogeneously identifiable class. To quote slightly out of context,

Marx posits that classes are 'a combination of heterogeneous social substances'.[15] Marx now speaks of *class fractions* which, although located within the general domain of a particular class, may pursue courses and possess identities different from those of their cohabitors. This is not so much a device that enables Marx to establish the structural location and composition of each class, but rather a way in which he can bring to bear the notion of conflict within each class itself, as well as within society. He presents a critical sociology of class that plots not only the external relations between classes, but also their internal relations. Marx, then, pinpoints a tension between three things: heterogeneity, homogeneity and dramaturgy which can be transposed sociologically into a tension between class formation, class identity and class action.

On first sight, the introduction of a notion of dramaturgy is perhaps curious. However, it is introduced as a hermeneutical key with which to unlock Marx's images of politics and society that emerge from within the paradigm of class action. One of the striking features of these works is the way in which Marx constantly invokes the image of drama, of theatre, as a metaphor for political activity. Marx presents the classes as they strut and stomp upon the (French) political stage, more or less on cue, deliver their silver-tongued speeches, their rude dialects, bow and leave. Scenes change; so too do 'costumes, language, actors, supernumeraries, extras, promptors, the position of the parties, and dramatic motifs, the nature of the conflict'.[16].

This notion of dramaturgy, with its flourishes of ceaseless activity, operates on two levels. On the first, Marx reconstructs a mythic grand plot with its heroes and villains. It is mythic in the sense that the grand plot of the two-class model, with its teleological component, becomes the paradigmatic form through which all elements are interpreted. On the second level, the ceaseless dramaturgical activity challenges this mythic construction; the stage, now fully lit, is larger than that which the spotlit mythology indicated. Scenes become nuanced, the cast is larger and the dialogue more complex, unfinished and not as well defined, like modernity itself. The two levels of dramaturgy capture the relation between Marx's analysis of (political) class action as *style* and his judgement of its content, the relation between his aesthetics and his ethics. Through this, the tensions of Marx's earliest 1843 critique of Hegel re-emerge, a re-emergence that is both tragic and farcical, to borrow from Marx's own opening remarks to 'The Eighteenth Brumaire'. These tensions between a Kantian quasi-transcendentalism and a Hegelian universalism imputed to the proletariat, emerge in Marx's analyses of the overthrow of Louis Philippe in 1848, Bonaparte's *coup d'état* in 1851 and the formation and defeat of the

1871 Paris Commune. Emerging from the overall composition of these works is a complex picture of the tension between a class and its factions, its identity, and the way in which it acts on the political stage (to use Marx's language) against the power of the other for both political and economic control. It is in this sense of conflict that Marx's notions of class identity and class interest become highly ambiguous. However, it cannot be stressed enough that this complex picture is simultaneously overlaid, and thus has its critico-analytical potential circumvented, by the mythological currents that constitute Marx's philosophy of history as well as by the language of production.

Marx works with three combinations of heterogeneity and homogeneity. The first combination consists of the homogeneous classes with single identity (the proletariat and the 'caste' of state officials);[17] the second, the heterogeneous class with polymorphic identity (the petty bourgeoisie);[18] and the third, heterogeneous classes with a single identity (the bourgeoisie and the lumpenproletariat).[19]

Notably, the peasantry has been excluded from these series of categorizations; this returns us to the opening question of this section – how do classes act? We are now in a position to answer this tentatively at least in the sense of what Marx could mean by it. What we can interpret to be Marx's self-understanding of class comes from his analysis of the peasantry and his dismissal of it as a pre-modern psuedo-class in 'The Eighteenth Brumaire'. His sardonic and scornful remarks concerning this grouping act as a counterpoint against which we can establish his definition of a *positive* class. The peasantry, the proprietors of small, rude holdings, in Marx's view forms no real class because of its isolated, self-sufficient existence. It is worth quoting Marx at some length on this.

> The small peasant proprietors form an immense mass, the members of which live in the same situation but do not enter into manifold relationships with each other. Their mode of operation isolates them instead of bringing them into mutual intercourse. This isolation is strengthened by the wretched state of France's means of communication and by the poverty of the peasants. Their place of operation, the smallholding, permits no division of labour in its cultivation, no application of science and therefore no diversity of development, variety of talent, or wealth of social relationships. Each individual peasant family is almost self-sufficient; it directly produces the greater part of its own consumption and therefore obtains its means of life more through exchange with nature than through intercourse with society. The smallholding, the peasant, and the family; next door, another smallholding, another peasant, and another family. A bunch

of these makes up a village, and a bunch of villages makes up a department. Thus the great mass of the French nation is formed by the simple addition of isomorphous magnitudes, much as potatoes in a sack form a sack of potatoes. In so far as millions of families live under economic conditions of existence that separate their mode of life, their interests and their cultural formation from those of the other classes and bring them into conflict with those classes, they form a class. In so far as these small peasant proprietors are merely connected on a local basis, and the identity of their interests fails to produce a feeling of community, national links, or a political organization, they do not form a class. They are therefore incapable of asserting their class interest in their own name, whether through a parliament or through a convention. They cannot represent themselves; they must be represented. Their representative must appear simultaneously as their master, as an authority over them, an unrestricted governmental power that protects them from the other classes and sends them rain and sunshine from above. The political influence of the small peasant proprietors is therefore ultimately expressed in the executive subordinating society to itself.[20]

Marx's concept of a self-constituting class, then, must involve the following characteristics if it is to be identified as such. First, those who form the class must have 'manifold relations' with one another, secondly, they must have a separate mode of life and a cultural formation that brings them into conflict with other classes and, thirdly, they must represent themselves in the sphere of politics, speak in their own name, assess their own interests and needs.[21] In other words, the isolated existence of the small peasant proprietors entails, for Marx, that they form no real community, no external relations with an 'other' or 'others' and, hence, establish no *identity*. This is the important point: Marx's assessment divides the classes along the lines of *conscious recognition*, of *enlightenment*, into those belonging to the modern world (civilization) and the pre-modern one (barbarism).[22] Real classes act, then, according to Marx, in terms of a consciously perceived interest or intention. This, in Marx's terms, transforms a class-in-itself into a class-for-itself (although it was Lukács who later articulated this transformation *theoretically* and thus recognized the voluntarist component of this configuration).[23] The notion of conscious rational interest belongs to the lexicon of political economy (counterposed as it was to the notion of passion).[24] Marx, too, understands it in this way, although he adds a Hegelianized materialism to it. Classes are critically enlightened if they act according to their economic interests and thus manifest their 'world spirit'.

This formulation of class-consciousness means that Marx's overt commitment to the principle of enlightenment (a commitment which continues to contain an oblique Kantianism), is ultimately tied to the mythological structure of his philosophy of history. This absorbs the dialectic of struggle through the equally mythological two-class model which entrenches his socio-class analysis in the realm of production. However although Marx ties his class analysis together through the notion of true class-consciousness (class-for-itself) this formulation competes with another at the level of Marx's substantive analysis, within the dramaturgical interpretation that he gives to the century of French class struggles from the Revolution to the Paris Commune.

MYTH AND CLASS –
RECONSTRUCTION OF THE FRENCH REVOLUTIONS

On the level of myth, class conflict and class action are related for Marx (as we have already indicated),[25] to what is for him the great and truly authentic Revolution, that of 1789 and the role of the main protagonists within it. As Fehér points out, this authenticity and greatness, this larger-than-life Hegelian world play, is the criterion against which all other revolutions are judged by Marx.[26] Translated directly into the language of drama, specifically into the world of Shakespearean drama to which Marx was constantly drawn,[27] the 1848 Revolutions can be characterized tentatively as the Malvolio[28] of bourgeois society – egoistic and ineffectual – and the 1871 Commune as the Hamlet of proletarian revolutions – great and authentic. The outcome of each can also be characterized in theatrical terms: Marx saw the former as farcical (although ultimately monstrous – a Caliban in disguise)[29] and the latter as wholly tragic.[30] Marx dramatically assembles the protagonists of the 1848 Revolutions; one by one he identifies them. The bourgeoisie relive glorious memories while enacting them ingloriously.[31] The Bonapartists parade in red breeches and gold braid with which the oafish, earthy peasantry identify in a piece of pathetic burlesque that pinpoints them as transitional and ultimately irrelevant.[32] The revolutionary proletarians and their allies diffidently and boyishly doff their Phrygian caps, too immature to seize the moment and raise their red flag above the tricolour.[33] The petit-bourgeoisie of the new *Montagne* bask momentarily in a half-light whilst uttering hollow democratic speeches. On this mythological level, the proletariat is defeated and the bourgeoisie trade the comfortable, convenient prop of democracy for naked self-interest and turn over the state to Bonaparte and his lumpenproletarians, who manage it on their behalf, crudely and ill-rehearsed, yet not without self-assuredness, like the plebeian players in *A Midsummer Night's Dream*. Bonaparte's rule is portrayed as a grotesque–comic play that transforms men into beasts. Marx puts it thus:

> An old cunning roué [Bonaparte] conceives the historical life of nations and their state proceedings as comedy in the most vulgar sense, in a masquerade in which the grand costumes, words and postures merely serve as a cover for the most petty trickery . . . In his Society of 10 December he assembled ten thousand rogues, who were supposed to represent the people in the way that Snug the joiner represented the lion. At a time when the bourgeoisie was playing the most complete comedy, but in the most serious manner in the world, without infringing any of the pedantic requirements of French dramatic etiquette, and was itself half duped and half convinced of the serious character of its own stale proceedings, the adventurer had to win, because he treated the comedy simply as a comedy. Only now that he has removed his solemn opponent, now that he himself takes his imperial role seriously and imagines that the Napoleonic mask represents the real Napoleon, does he become the victim of his own conception of the world, the serious clown who no longer sees world history as a comedy but his comedy as world history.[34]

Hence, this Bonapartist play is itself a play within a larger play of dominant-class power and interest. In Marx's view, the bourgeoisie merely gives up its general, that is, political interests to the buffoonery of Napoleon the nephew, for its 'sordid interests'. It thus arranges the form of state rule most appropriate for its material livelihood. 'The French bourgeoisie revolted at the prospect of the rule of the labouring proletariat; it has brought the lumpenproletariat into power . . . Their solution is the Cossack republic.'[35]

Interestingly, the class fraction that Marx takes as his model for an imputed and invariable connection between economic interest and political action is the financial bourgeoisie. In all the other major works though, the industrial bourgeoisie is the primary fraction. It is this class that enacts, for Marx, the progressive industrialization of the world, as well as simplifies the class conflicts that is constitutive for capitalism and its demise. In this respect only, Marx's reconstruction has elements that implicitly break out of its mythological encasement. The financial fraction competes with the industrial bourgeoisie, not for teleological supremacy, but on the grounds of its historical development, self-perception and self-representation. This suggests, then, that another reading of class emerges from these works that draws on the other notion of dramaturgy.

THE DRAMAS OF THE MODERN WORLD

This other level of dramaturgy which, we argue, is present in these writings, portrays relations between all of the six classes that draw explicitly on culturally determining forms for their orientation and self-understanding in the context of the specific nature of power in the modern world. In this light, action may never be wholly conscious, nor rational, let alone economically motivated. It is precisely in this gap between action and consciousness, action and purposiveness that Marx's 'critical sociology of class' with this second level of dramaturgy, comes to life.

This other level of dramaturgy becomes the focus through which Marx addresses and attempts to conceptualize the complex nature of the conflicts of the modern age, not as the necessary but derivative components of a contradictorily constituted totality, but as a series of open-ended and competing struggles over the centre of power. This formulation it can be argued, emerges as the unacknowledged central pivot around which Marx's critique of the period 1848-51 revolves. It takes the form of an analysis of either the decentring and pluralization of power centres which Marx always saw as a positive achievement of the modern age or the processes through which power is reconstituted and centralized. This occurs in both the 'old' and 'new' areas of society, the 'old' being the state and the church, the 'new', and most important for Marx, being the economy with its subordination to the demands of capital.

In other words, the post-absolutist (1789) world is typified, by Marx, as a tension-ridden, simultaneous decentring and centralization of power relations. Whilst, for him, the French Revolutions unfold as bourgeois dramas, they are nonetheless dramas concerning the conquest and maintenance of power. This aspect which remains untheorized by Marx, and despite the central role of the notion of the bourgeois drama which precludes a closer analysis of power, means that a more differentiated story emerges from the pages of 'The Class Struggles in France' and 'The Eighteenth Brumaire of Louis Bonaparte'. They portray a drama composed of other scenes in which other characters besides the bourgeoisie and the proletariat play more central roles and generate competing claims and demands. The competition for power, and the contestation against both the old and new power centres, occurs, in these dramas scripted by Marx, by the heteromorphology of classes that have experienced and realized the tensions between the decentring and centralization of power.

After the brutal defeat of the proletariat in June 1848, it essentially disappears from the stage. The play, however, goes on. Despite Marx's burning conviction that the 22 June insurrection was potentially an authentic proletarian revolution denied fruition because of its imputed immaturity, and which gave way to a farcical, frozen bourgeois reaction, Marx's analysis of the post-insurrectionist period and the Bonapartist state points beyond the paradigm of class rule and its companion, the paradigm of production. In the light of the current debates concerning the genesis and notion of modernity it can be argued that Marx's analysis of the struggles between classes can be related to the different *logics* of development by which this historico-theoretical notion is typified. While for Marx there really is only one logic of modernity, namely capitalism which is ultimately absorbed into the meta-logic of humankind's productive metabolism with nature, a charitable reading of these works suggests that two other logics are present and fought over. They are, on the one hand, the logic of democracy, and on the other, the logic of modern statism. 'The Class Struggles' and 'The Eighteenth Brumaire' implicitly pinpoint a tension, an interpenetration, between these three autonomous and non-derivative logics.

In this context, the so-called minor classes, with their bit parts, become significant, in particular the petit-bourgeoisie and the peasantry. They not only fracture Marx's two-class model, but also suggest a divergent analysis that is extraneous to the one developed in the light of the paradigm of production. In other words, their presence is significant in two crucial ways. First, in directly political terms Marx generates an analysis of the new typology of conflict. That is of the struggle between the process of political democratization and pluralization and the modern bureaucratic state particularly when it is transformed into a 'praetorian', militarist, proto-fascist state. Secondly, the classes invoke the role of traditions and symbols in their conflicts, that is, the whole range of 'theatrical garb' that becomes more than a mere prop. Rather, it becomes or is part of a cultural nexus which co-constitutes social action, and mediates it with the societal insti-tutional infrastructures. In other words, Marx's analysis of the central-ization/decentralization of power is, in part, based on the recognition of democracy's emancipatory content and stance, which is conceptual-ized in his early (1843) work in quasi-transcendental terms, 'beyond class'. It is also based on and overlaid by a class analysis from which stem two countervailing tendencies. On the one hand, there is the critical sociology that analyses the way in which the various classes act around, and in between, the forms of modernity and utilize symbols to express their definition of, and relation to, these forms. On the other hand, the mythological, identitarian notion of class, which also stems from the 1843 period, also continues to be present, and pushes

the analysis back to the sphere of production from which Marx
generates the logic of class conflict.

Abstracting momentarily from the specific class component that
Marx attributes to the configuration and contestation of power centres
it can be argued that Marx concentrates, at least in 'The Class Struggles
in France', on two phenomena. Dramaturgically, symbolically, they
are organized around the images of anarchy and order. Each is marshalled in a particular way. Each tells its own story. On the one hand,
Marx draws on the image of anarchy which is constructed by the
bourgeoisie in its efforts to discredit its social democratic opponents,
and which he also utilizes as a caricature to lampoon the social
democrats and to denote the alternative centres of power to the state
and capital.[36] On the other hand, the image of order is used to signify
the various strategies of closure that the state and capital can utilize to
obstruct or terminate the alternative centres of power either abruptly
or gradually. It also signifies the ability of the state to function as a
domain of power and authority in its own right.

To take the former first, Marx's analysis of the decentralization and
pluralization of power can be established first of all through his assessment of the September/October Constitution:

> The most comprehensive contradiction of the Constitution consists of
> the fact that it gives political power to the classes whose social slavery it
> is intended to perpetrate: proletariat, peasants and petit-bourgeoisie.
> And it deprives the bourgeoisie, the class whose old social power it
> sanctions, of the political guarantees of this power. It imposes on the
> political rule of the bourgeoisie democratic conditions which constantly
> help its enemies towards victory and endanger the very basis of
> bourgeois society. It demands from the one that it should not proceed
> from political emancipation to social emancipation and from the other
> that it should not regress from social restoration to political restor-
> ation.[37]

Thematically, the contradiction first addresses the problematic of
political power in terms of the formal nature of democracy, the
universal right to political participation and self-sovereignty/autonomy.
This element, left dangling after Marx's unfinished treatment of it in
the 1843 'Critique of Hegel's Doctrine of the State', re-emerges
around the claim for universal suffrage. While Marx views universal
suffrage as the culmination of bourgeois political philosophy, it is
nonetheless, for him, a constituting feature of civil society's sovereignty
over the state, as well as the means for the inclusion of all actors and
classes into the world of politics. It is in this context that the image of

anarchy becomes important. Marx turns it against its own bourgeois inventors as a weapon. The ammunition is universal suffrage:

> But does the Constitution still have any meaning the moment that the content of this suffrage, this sovereign will, is no longer bourgeois rule? Is it not the duty of the bourgeoisie to regulate the franchise so that it demands what is reasonable, *its* rule? By repeatedly terminating the existing state power and by creating it anew from itself does not universal suffrage destroy all stability; does it not perpetually call all existing powers into question; does it not destroy authority; does it not threaten to elevate anarchy itself to the level of authority?[38]

But Marx's ambivalence towards suffrage is of note here. On the one hand, suffrage is a stage and even a means towards achieving a post-capitalist society and a necessary component of a democratized political life.[39] On the other hand, as a part of democracy in general, it is a partial measure that conceals the real origins of power – the control over the economy. It is the re-entry of this second element that transforms the first substantively in a radicalized Kantian direction, at least initially, but ultimately in a way that circumvents this radicalization.

In the first instance, the problematic of civil and personal sovereignty (which is still counterposed by Marx to the 'zoology' of pre-modern forms) is absorbed by him under the more extensive problematic of humankind's generalized emancipation from all forms of tutelage. The model for this emancipation, that is, the form that it should take, remains for him in these works at least, the radical potential imbedded in the democratic organization of political life, rather than either its containment within parliamentarianism and the strategies of party politics, or its curtailment by the state. This, then, is the significance for Marx, of the emergent critically orientated *public* spaces and institutions such as the press, the clubs (despite his recognition of their double-edged existence as both venues of conspiratorial Jacobinism and as public constituent assemblies guaranteed through the constitutional right of association, which of course may not protect them from the ideological imperatives of Jacobinism), the National Assembly, the worker's committees and associations that were formed during the period of the Paris Commune and the streets.[40] This pluralization is evidence for him of a potential radical democratization, because each is seen by him as a challenge to the monopoly of executive state power, as well as the control of capital over the workplace and economy. This is also the basis of Marx's positive assessment of the 1871 Commune – the processes of political pluralization both generate their own areas for political life and transform existing institutions (for example the state and the factory) once they are grounded on the organizing principle of democracy. Marx sees the Commune as decomposing the monopolies of state power and capital by reorganizing four main domains of socio-political life. These domains are:

1 The reintroduction of universal suffrage as the means for electoral decision making;
2 the reconstitution of civil society over the state whereby public servants and the judiciary are elected on a short-term revocable basis;
3 the decentralization of all power and decision-making to the districts, regions and towns, thus establishing a federation of autonomous units;
4 self-managing economic enterprises.[41]

Moreover, in Marx's view these can only be constituted through, and thus accompanied by, self-enlightenment of the actors, classes and groups:

> They know that in order to work out their own emanicipation, and along with it that higher form to which present society is irresistably tending by its own economical agencies, they will have to pass through long struggles, through a series of historic processes, transforming circumstances and men.[42]

This notion of decentralization implicitly problematizes Marx's view of the state as a superstructural phenomenon representing a specific class that is located in and grounded on the sphere of production. Rather, the notion of decentralization indicates that the state too, organizes itself according to a principle and logic. This we suggest, is the significance of the image of order for Marx. Through this, Marx reconstructs the principle of executive power; the logic of centralization.

In both 'The Eighteenth Brumaire' and 'The Civil War in France' one finds an analysis that suggests that the modern state stands outside the 'paradigm of class rule'. Under the regime of Louis Bonaparte it follows its own logic of non-capitalist development through the expansion of the bureaucratic form, either in terms of modern principles or the pre-modern typologies of patronage and patrimonialism. Marx's analysis is incisive; the state's omnipresent quickening on French soil resulted from executive incursions into all spheres of life, reorganized around three modern features. These are the principle of rational centralist organization that enables the absorption of all areas of life under the auspices of the efficient functioning of the state; the emergence of a specific class or group to effect this (the 'caste' of state officials); and the development of generalized forms of taxation.[43] The pre- and anti-modern typologies also become important: Bonaparte, 'the patriarchical benefactor', effects an inverted Copernican Revolution – the world revolves around him instead of around the sun, society. By so doing he draws upon a personalized form of politics through which he creates new sinecures and a private army based on personal loyalty.[44] Each of these enables a renewed investiture into the notion of order on the state's terms. Scenes and locations of decentred power, debate and opinion are suppressed, the public is dissolved, universal suffrage abolished. Through Bonaparte the state creates its own panoptic society of surveillance.[45] The 'Cossack republic' rules on its own: before it 'all classes fall on their knees, equally mute and equally impotent before the rifle butt.'[46] Marx insightfully views the Bonapartist state as a hybrid of modern and pre/anti-modern features, which arises from crises imbedded within the tensions between the other logics of modernity.[47]

The reconstruction of these works, through the notions of anarchy and order, suggests that it is not necessarily the greatness and authenticity of the class or the group that matters (despite Marx's championship of the working class) but rather the presence of competing normative complexes. Addressing this in sociological terms, the presence of these competing, normative complexes means that Marx implicitly transfers his analysis from a location-determined nexus, to struggles concerning norms, symbols and values. In the context of the modern age, the struggles are over either the quasi-transcendental universalism of the nascent democratic norms, or the strategies and logic of the modern state. Moreover, Marx's class analysis addresses the way in which the various classes constitute themselves through these culturally situated significations. It is in this sense that we can now reintroduce the notion of class action and the second level of dramaturgy. The so-called minor classes, with their hopes and fears, memories and myths, and Marx's analysis of them, now become significant.

The classes that marshal or are represented under the explicit banner of democracy are the petty bourgeoisie and the proletariat.[48] Given that Marx consistently assigns the proletariat to a specific place on the world-historical stage, the role of the petty bourgeoisie becomes important for the constitution of critical class analysis. A gap, or specifically a break, emerges in Marx's presentation between the notion of economic interest and political interaction, that is between class formation and class identity, and hence its actions. As J. Cohen points out, 'Marx grasps the importance of the symbolic power of apparently dead tradition in guiding the action of social classes, evidenced in this case by the selection of the name of the *Montagne* by the representatives of the petty bourgeoisie'.[49] Hence, neither the class identity of the petty bourgeoisie, nor the characteristics of its representatives that constitute the *Montagne* is understandable in terms of economic interest. Rather, their identity and actions are forged though a common perception, a common model of action and a common definition concerning the notion of society. For Marx,

> the peculiar characteristic of social-democracy can be summed up in the following way . . . [Its] context is the reformation of society by democratic means, but a reformation within the boundaries set by the petty bourgeoisie . . . Nor indeed must one imagine that the democratic representatives are all *shopkeepers*, or their enthusiastic supporters. They may well be poles apart from them in their education and their individual situation. What makes them representatives of the petty bourgeoisie is the fact that their minds are restricted by the same barriers which the petty bourgeoisie fails to overcome in real life, and that they are therefore driven in theory to the same problems and solutions to which material interest and social situation drive the latter in practice. This is the general relationship between the *political and literary representatives* of a class and the class which they represent.[50]

Unity, identity and action, then, are not guided by socio-economic interest, but perceptions and models that help establish and frame a vague and illusory allegiance to a normative complex that is part both of the French revolutionary past and of its unfinished present.

In this context of an unfinished historicity, the *Montagne's* political responses, failures and retreats also become comprehensible. Their 'insurrection within the limits of pure reason'[51] as Marx puts it facetiously, and their constitutional legalism in the face of electoral closure by the Bonapartist executive,[52] contains a logic, which to be sure, for Marx, is illusory and pretentious, but one that is formed through, and counterpointed by, the banquet questions of universal suffrage,[53] that is by a normative complex, the definition of which they claim as their heritage.

A similar pattern of analysis unfolds in Marx's analysis of the peasantry. Whilst Marx views the peasantry as structurally destined for pauperization and proletarianization (which would hold the key to its emergence as a *real* class, a class-for-itself) at the hands of urban capitalist creditors and land-sharks, its categorization as a pseudo-class contains an insight into its processes of self-identity that take the form of defensive and delegated action, either by giving Bonaparte electoral support in the heady days of universal suffrage or by serving in his armed force.[54] The peasantry's processes of externalization, that is its relations with the world at large, follow a traditional route of *mediated representation*, on the one hand through a heavenly God and its earthly institution, the Catholic Church, and on the other, the earthly duality (the two Bonapartes) in their 'heavenly' kingdom, the executive state. As Marx states incisively:

> Historical tradition produced the French peasant's belief that a miracle would occur, that a man called Napoleon would restore their glory. And an individual turned up who pretended to be that man, because he bore the name Napoleon, thanks to the stipulations of the Code Napoleon that *'La recherche de la paternité est interdite.'* [55]

To comprehend the peasant's allegiance to Louis Bonaparte, Marx displaces his mythological dramaturgy with this other version that derives its critical value from the *power* of tradition and symbol. Despite heavy taxation and a betrayal of interests by this Bonaparte, Marx, as J. Cohen again points out,

> demonstrates that it was above all the tradition of Napoleon I that secured peasant property, glorified the peasant in uniform, ennobled the desire for land through the concepts of nation, patriotism and empire, and through a strong centralized government, provided the security which economic activity of the smallholder could never produce.[56]

In this way, an 'elective affinity' rather than a causal nexus between a form of property ownership and a 'superstructural' phenomenon, is established between the peasantry and the Bonapartist state. A reading of 'The Eighteenth Brumaire' with one eye on Weber as well as Marx, suggests that the state does not require a class basis for its existence. Its existence is rather conditioned by a notion of legitimacy that contains two components. On the one hand, the state can claim legitimacy on the basis of authority with the sanction of *force* residing permanently in the background. On the other hand, it can draw upon the symbols and identities of its constituents, whether these symbols be based on traditional or rational assertion.[57] Weber explores this affinity between legitimacy and cultural configuration explicitly, guided by the thesis that it is

> not ideas but material and ideal interests that directly govern men's conduct. Yet very frequently the 'world images' that have been created by 'ideas' have, like switchmen, determined the tracks along

which action has been pushed by the dynamic of interest. 'From what' and 'for what' one wished to be redeemed and let us not forget 'could be' redeemed, depended upon one's image of the world.[58]

It is argued that Marx does the same *implicitly*. In the context of Bonapartism the state can draw upon culturally determined currents that are either explicit or subterranean. As Marx shows, the peasantry ascribes legitimacy on the basis of tradition and faith. It *enacts* the process of legitimation, whilst the state uses its institutions (particularly the army) to cultivate such a belief in its authority:

> The culminating point of the 'Napoleonic idea' is the predominance of the *army*. The army was the small peasant proprietor's *point d'honneur*, the peasant himself transformed into a hero, defending his new possessions against external enemies, glorifying his recently won nationhood, and plundering and revolutionizing the world. The uniform was the peasant's national costume, the war was his poetry, the smallholding, extended and rounded off in imagination, was his fatherland, and patriotism was the ideal form of his sense of property.[59]

In this way, legitimacy is secured for the state which is essentially despotic on the basis of the mediation of cultural symbols, as well as the ultimate sanction of force. It is the combination of these two elements that enables it to assert its own role against the sovereignty of civil society. Marx argues that 'instead of *society* conquering a new content for itself, it only seems that the *state* [in the *coup d'état* of December 1851] has returned to its most ancient form, the unashamedly simple rule of the military sabre and the clerical cowl.'[60]

However, Marx is unable to sustain the critical side of his dramaturgy indefinitely. Three elements constantly lurk in the background; his identitarian conception of class, his philosophy of history and the precepts of the paradigm of production, particularly the base–superstructure model.

Marx had identified the proletariat as the bearer of the universalistic norms of the modern age. In his Hegelian conflation of historical actors and normative principles, Marx had effectively excluded the possibility that other groups and classes could marshal under the banner of universalism. The petit bourgeoisie, specifically its party the *Montagne*, is thus a poor and partial imitation of the proletariat in its claims on behalf of sovereignty. In this sense, and in the absense of the revolutionary proletariat, Marx does not pose the question: 'Is there anything wrong with the norms that they are expressing?', but simply argues that they cannot act in any other way because of their class nature. Whilst possessing an extreme sensitivity to political modernity, Marx nonetheless lacks a sensitivity to the problematic of the institutionalization of democratic norms as well as their normative content and basis, and hence a conceptual apparatus to analyse them. He merely reshuffles the identitarian logic, and by so doing invokes his philosophy of history which posits the authentic image of politics as war, portrayed either as negative chauvinism or as positive revolution:

> In France the petty bourgeois does what the individual bourgeois would normally have to do; the worker does what would normally be the task of the petty bourgeois. Who then does the task of the worker? Nobody. It is not accomplished in France; it is only proclaimed. And it will not be accomplished within any national walls. The class war within French society will be transformed into a world war in which nation confronts nation. The worker's task will begin to be accomplished only when the world war carries the proletariat to the fore in the nation that dominates the world market, i.e. England.[61]

The interpretation of politics as war, although not Marx's only one, prepares the ground for later Jacobin interpretations and strategies that marry it with a self-legitimizing metaphysics. Although this metaphysics is derived in part from Engels, it is nonetheless part of Marx's 'materialist baggage'. In its present absence, the proletariat is teleologically imputed and transported to a later time, a different place where it will perform with due greatness and authenticity.

Marx's analysis of the state, fares no better in the long run. Again the identitarian logic of subject/object is invoked, although not in conjunction with his philosophy of history, but in conjunction with the paradigm of production. For Marx, the state, Bonaparte, *must* represent a class; it cannot hover in mid-air even though it appears to have 'attained a completely autonomous position'.[62] Bonaparte's place in history and the logic of the state are thrown back upon the identitarian model of class. Bonaparte and his state represent the small peasant proprietors.[63] With this, the base–superstructure model remains essentially intact with its imperative of production, its anthropology of labour. For Marx,

> it was the material conditions which made the feudal French peasant a small proprietor and Napoleon an emperor . . . If he [the second Bonaparte] still shares with the peasants the illusion that the cause of their ruin is to be sought, not in the smallholding itself, but outside it, in the influence of secondary influences, his experiments will burst like soap bubbles at their first contact with the relations of production.[64]

Notwithstanding the strait-jacket of Marx's own orthodoxy there is still the dynamic of cultural forms that stands outside it and is immobilized by it. This dynamic has yet to be addressed as both a problem for, and a departure from, Marx. Although constrained by the paradigm of production and its mythological components, the paradigm of class action, in conjunction with the second level of dramaturgy, draws on other components outside them to enable an unstable and untheorized analysis of class and power. Marx's second level of dramaturgy in the historico-political works draws on culturally located and articulated elements that are outside the ambit of the paradigm of production and the anthropology of labour. This is what gives the paradigm of class action its critical force and which also becomes implicitly constitutive to Marx's notion of class relations. Class formation implies as Marx shows (yet fails to follow through) the process of identity creation, memory and self-interpretation in relation to other classes. These are the unique and key features of Marx's class analysis, and when they combine to form a 'social imaginary' it is this which becomes the pivot around which the paradigm of class action revolves. This aspect is the most important part of these works. They point directly to the place of a 'hidden imaginary' in Marx's *oeuvre*, a subterranean current that resides as a suppressed moment, but which surfaces to problematize Marx's anthropology and point a direction beyond it.

7

Marx Against Marx: The 'Hidden Imaginary' – The Holzweg from the 1844 *Manuscripts*

Leitmotiv

Anti-Thesis Eleven

The practitioners have only *changed* the world in various ways; the point is to *reinterpret* it.

The spectre of the five problems that we suggested Marx addressed in his analysis of capitalism in *Capital* still haunts us. To recapitulate, these were:

1   the formal determinations of a society based on a particular social relation of production that is a relation of domination between social classes. This implies, and requires, the concept of institution, that is, the institutional arrangements by which the class form takes shape. The notion 'formal determination' denotes, according to Marx, the 'definite, specific social forms assumed by the material conditions of labour',[1] in other words, the institutionalized functional mechanisms through which a society reproduces itself. The classes do not merely 'act', they create institutional arrangements through which they impose a social (that is class) form upon society, for example, capital/wage-labour, and, as we also saw in the historico-political writings, state and civil society;

2   the logic(s) of societal reproduction and whether this also constitutes the reproduction of the social relations of domination;

3   the class struggles that may contest the social relation of domination (and/or the logic(s) of societal reproduction);

4   the ethical dimension that informs the critique of domination;
5   the other forms of domination that are not bound by either class or productive forms, but belong to societal reproduction.

Although these problems have been addressed in terms of either the paradigm of production, which resulted in competing cul-de-sacs for the development of a critical theory of capitalism in particular and modernity in general, or the paradigm of class action, which contained other anthropologically construed elements apart from labour-activity, they have yet to be formulated in terms of an anthropology that gives due consideration to the problematic of the configuration of normative complexes. This is the task ahead. They will be approached in the light of the analysis of Marx's so-called historico-political writings, in the light of the problematic of norms, values and symbols that is an integral, yet implicit and suppressed feature of those works. The presence of an imaginary in the political writings points towards the possible significance, in Marx's work as a whole, of culturally located symbols, norms and values that are invoked as co-constituting moments of human life but which lie outside the anthropological premises that help form the paradigm of production.

Moreover, their significance within Marx's paradigm of class action, and his implicit reliance upon them for explanatory force, is neither a fleeting moment, nor an idealist lapse in his work. Marx at other times draws upon them to assist either his analysis of capitalism or his conceptualization of post-capitalist society. One can argue that Marx's analysis of commodity fetishism locates a normative/value complex central to capitalism's reproduction, only to have this insight annihilated by both the anthropology of labour and the framework of totality. Post-capitalist society is conceptualized by Marx in terms that also appear to go beyond the anthropology of labour. The notions of anthropological holism, autotelic totality, and 'the free development of individualities' depend either on the subordination of humankind's metabolism with nature to a material life intrinsically tending towards all-round cultural and intellectual development (in the *Grundrisse*), or culture's separation from the necessary and constraining relation with nature through the formation of a distinct realm of freedom (*Capital*). In each case, and notwithstanding their problematic formulations, labour is linked to self-activity, variously presented and interpreted by him as a richness in needs, human wealth, or the realization of freedom as an end in itself.

The striking feature about these formulations and the aspect that unites them, is Marx's at times explicit, often implicit, reliance upon and return to, a notion of consciousness, which is transposed and incorporated into the problematic of intercourse in *The German Ideology*. It is the notion which he (ultimately) uses to establish the distinction between humankind and other species, as well as the epochal stages in human history, including post-capitalist society. It is also the criterion with which he judges the authenticity and greatness of class action.[2] Consciousness, whether it refers to freedom or the domain of norms and values, resides as the suppressed problematic in Marx's work. It is in a double sense Marx's 'hidden imaginary'.[3] On the one hand, it forms the latent background of his more explicit theorizing. It is spectral, haunting, in that the imaginary is formed by the currents that Marx unreflectively absorbs during the processes of his materialist anthropological reconceptualization of Enlightenment philosophy, especially Kant's formulation of practical reason and the structure of Hegel's ontology. However on the other hand, Marx also grasps Hegel's philosophy of consciousness as a historico-interpretative dialectic. Its impulse, in part, belongs to Marx's own anthropological reinterpretation of the Enlightenment, that is, to his claim to humanity's self-authorship and its recognition of this self-authorship. This means that within this aspect of Marx's reformulation, consciousness is not only conceptualized as humankind's self-consciousness of its utilization of nature, but also, as the 'vehicle' through which its recognition of self-creation is achieved. This depends, as we have argued, on Marx's championship of modernity's value of freedom, which he problematically transforms into autonomy and self-activity. However, it is suggested that through the presence of the interpretative dialectic, Marx implicitly recognizes the power and historical contextualization of the symbolic as a co-constituting feature of social life.[4]

It is the central concern of this chapter to follow the evolution of this aspect of the problematic of consciousness in Marx's work, notwithstanding its suppression and concealment by his notion of labour. This will be done, not so much through his notion of freedom, but rather at the level of anthropology. It is here that Marx requires consciousness as a co-constituting and co-determining element of human self-creation. Once he construes it anthropologically, consciousness sits outside the notion of labour and generates its own structures and determinations. This sets the parameters for both his analysis of the notion of freedom, and his analysis of the terrain and conflicts of his primary logic of modernity – capitalism – not in terms of its functional reproduction as a totality but in terms of labour's (necessarily incomplete) subsumption under capital, or the capitalization of social relations.

MARX'S 'HIDDEN IMAGINARY'
THE ANTHROPOLOGY OF HUMAN SELF-CREATION
AND THE PROBLEMATIC OF CONSCIOUSNESS AS AN
HISTORICO-INTERPRETATIVE DIALECTIC

In the 1844 *Manuscripts* there appears a tension within Marx's as yet
untheorized anthropology. Whilst the notion of labour sits centrally
within these works, it is counterpointed by the notion of self-creation
from which Marx generates a critique of capitalist development.
Capitalism, from this standpoint, merely replicates, but in a more
antagonistic way, the arduous task of labour which besets humankind.
On the one hand, it develops industry, 'the *open* book of the essential
powers of man';[5] but on the other, it reduces the human properties of
a person to that of worker, and in so doing, not only *dis*recognizes,
*dis*enfranchises from the community, the person who is without
work,[6] but also universalizes this 'worst possible state of privation'[7]
through the 'science of asceticism'.[8] In Marx's view, this replication
leads in both cases to a one-sided development that either occludes or
denies the worker's existence as a person with sense and sensibilities.
For Marx, these should embody the full range of not only practical, but
also emotional, aesthetic, spiritual and reasoning capacities that affirm
his or her existence as a *real* subject in an objective world.[9] In this
context, Marx's image of post-capitalist society lies beyond utilitarianism; it is portrayed as a society of cultural development that 'produces
man in all the richness of his being, the *rich* man who is *profoundly
and abundantly endowed with all the senses*'.[10]

This suggests that another image of emancipation is brought
forward by Marx. It resides outside his restrictive notion of labour;
although it contains the elements that inform his later model of
'communal and autotelic totality', it need not rely on the notion of
industry (as an early synonym of the productive forces) ultimately to
ground it. It implies a multi-dimensional (rather than either a homo-
logously structured or explicitly reductive) anthropology, which, at the
very least *includes* the problematic of consciousness, not only as an
essential human characteristic but as one that objectifies itself historically.

For Marx, consciousness embodies the self-understanding of the
species at any one time. In other words, it denotes its historically
contextualized historicity. History, according to this interpretation, is
the conscious realization of, and reflection upon, the forms that self-
creativity takes. Marx establishes this as an insight gained from Hegel's
historical dialectic when, in 1844, he states that 'man . . . has his

process of origin in *history* . . . History is the true natural history of man.' [11] This means that Marx can absorb the problematic of consciousness into the 'natural' historicity of humankind. Mind or *Geist* is no longer abstracted from the human condition but belongs irrevocably and essentially to it by virtue of a self-forming and self-reflective historical consciousness. Marx makes this clear when he says in the same breath that 'history is a conscious process, and hence one which consciously supersedes itself.' [12] This is stated in terms of objective forming processes that are both anchored in nature and history, and of which history and nature are apart. [13]

This other problematic of the anthropological status of historicity is, we suggest, translated or transposed into the notion of the 'forms of intercourse', and as such is actually given the formal status as a co-constituting moment within Marx's anthropological precepts. This transposition establishes a point of continuity between the 1844 *Manuscripts* and *The German Ideology*.

The German Ideology basically explores the idea of the object-forming and institutionalization of intersubjectively constituted human activity (praxis). It establishes systematically for the first time the phenomenology of historicity in societal terms, beginning with the family and moving on to the more comprehensive forms of social co-operation (the social forms of intercourse) that emerge through the satisfaction of needs. The transition from instinct to consciousness is made through the first historical act, which is also the first social act. Consciousness is as much part of the evolutionary threshold between ape and man as labour is. In Marx's view, society can only exist between conscious individuals: 'man's consciousness of the necessity of associating with the individuals around him is the beginning of the consciousness that he is living in a society at all.' [14] In this way, Marx does not restate human intercourse (or its constituting moments) in terms of the pure subjectivity of the Hegelian *Geist*-philosophy. Language, the practical form of consciousness, [15] is no longer the vehicle of a self-reflecting and self-positing spirit, but is itself the way through which the practical and socially configured activities of people are co-determined. Marx's anthropological reformulation of consciousness does not necessarily present it as a subordinate and superstructural moment that is derived from human existence. Rather Marx posits that human existence, as a matter of course, implies that consciousness is part of life. As Marx states:

> Men are the producers of their conceptions, ideas . . . Consciousness can never be anything else than conscious existence, and the existence of men is their actual life-process . . . Morality, religion, metaphysics,

all the rest of ideology and their corresponding forms of consciousness, thus no longer retain the semblance of independence. They have no history, no development; but men, developing their material production and their material intercourse, alter, along with their real existence, their thinking and the products of their thinking.[16]

The anthropologically conceived domain of historicity (consciousness, language and intersubjectivity) co-determines the domain of society.

This entails that society is also the context for cognition, the production of knowledge that is simultaneously both technically orientative and interpretative. These two aspects belong to the human condition. The notion of human practice implies not only humankind's production of material goods that satisfy its needs, but also of interpretations (which contain the imaginary significations) that guide and contextualize this production as a feature of humankind's historicity. In this context, consciousness embraces a continuum from myth to critique. By this time Marx's notion of species-being is a *background* notion that includes consciousness because, for him, the species becomes conscious of itself, or attains an image of itself through the cognitive forms it creates, whether they be generated through myth or reason. Historicity, then, is not merely a social product concerning the immediate sensuous environment of other human beings; it is more importantly the realm of norms and rules that embody humankind's cognitive capacity to create either mythologically or rationally constituted knowledge that denotes the subject's relation to both nature and society. This knowledge is, for Marx, mythological if it portrays nature and society as objective, alien and unassailable forces.[17] It is rational if, through it, humankind 'consciously treats all natural premises as the creations of hitherto existing men, strips them of their natural character and subjugates them to the power of the united individuals'.[18]

The introduction of the problematic of cognitive forms implicitly problematizes the categorial distinction that Marx makes between the material content which pertains to the rules of use of man-made objects or use-values and the social form which pertains not only to the types of social organization that contextualize them, but also to their restrictive norms of employment. Each side of the 'equation' is problematized. There exists in every society, on the side of the material content, constituting ways of human activity that refer to persons and not only to the use of objects. The forms of intercourse, as relations between persons, are the most obvious and important of such activities. They are constitutive through the acquisition of the rules and techniques of language. Language is the means of achieving aims *external* to the acting subjects, and as such can be referred to as what have been later termed the pragmatics of communication.[19] Alternatively, as Markus argues, there are objects the proper use of which belongs *constitutively* to the social form, and not to the technical rules. In other words, there are 'objects [for example, the flag and cross], the very *utility* of which consists in the facilitation, realisation, indication . . . of some normatively fixed social relation'.[20]

Although this expansion of the anthropological terrain to include language remains problematic and constrained by the basic separation between form and content, there is – as our reconstruction of Marx's analysis of money in the *Grundrisse* will show – at least one important pointer towards the coincidence and interpenetration of these two categories in a way that basically dissolves them. As Markus points out, the

> coincidence of 'material content' and 'economic form' means that in the objects of this type [that is money] it is impossible to separate the questions: 'How has it to be used?' and 'who may employ it, at what social occasions etc.?': these products are *objectivations* of human needs and abilities *relating to the various historical forms and modes of social communication and intercourse as such* and therefore the 'how' of their use *eo ipso* defines a given type of human contact in a definite social situation.[21]

In this formulation, then, it is not a *particular* type of rule-forming, for example purposive–technical rules, that establishes humankind as a unique species, following Marx's postulate of the difference between the architect and the bee, but rather that generalized rule-forming activity takes place as such, which *necessarily* includes as a co-constituting determinant, norm-employing interpretations. Marx anthropologically reinterprets Hegel's problematic of consciousness in a way that is suggestive of a broad notion of interpretative praxis that refers to the constitutive dimensions of meaning, of which rules and norms are part. In other words, the norms and rules do not themselves exhaust the interpretative framework, rather they are situated within it. It is this complex that both co-determines and mediates the heterogeneously structured and assembled *social* forms of intercourse. Moreover, it also generates, in the body of Marx's work, another strategy for his critique of capitalism.

ANTHROPOLOGY AND CRITIQUE
THE SUBSUMPTION MODEL AND MARX'S ANALYSIS OF MONEY

This implicit and never theorized or thematized ambivalence in Marx's anthropological background assumptions is also necessarily accompanied by a similar ambivalence in his approach to the critique of capitalism. Emerging from the gaps and unfinished pages of his work as a whole, the critique oscillates between an immanent analysis of the functional reproduction of capitalism found in *Capital*, and one concerning the historical universalization of capitalist relations, or what we prefer to term the 'capitalization of social relations'. This latter aspect characterizes Marx's model of the subsumption of labour under capital.

Although the subsumption model, too, stems from the paradigm of production, there are indications that Marx conceptualizes it, as a model for an otherwise bypassed and undeveloped critical theory of capitalism, in terms that transcend the totalizing sphere of production with its reductive anthropological determinants. The subsumption model is found in the fragmentary text of 'the Results of the Immediate Process of Production',[22] although it has a place in the *Grundrisse*, particularly in the chapter on money, where, we will argue, the 'hidden imaginary' breaks through more explicitly. Moreover, this reading back, so to speak, enables us to disconnect our interpretation from Marx's construction of the *Grundrisse* as a whole. This interpretation of Marx's chapter on money problematicizes explicitly the core anthropological precept from which the *Grundrisse* and *Capital* spring – the contradiction between the material content and social form – and occurs through Marx's own reflections on money as a symbol.

The subsumption model has its origins in *The German Ideology*. The anthropologically conceived processes of human 'metabolism' with both nature and society are the background against which Marx proceeds. The metabolic relations between humankind and nature, and the individual and society, not only indicate, for him, the emancipation of human powers, but they can also indicate relations of subordination. The distinction between pre-modern and modern societies is characterized by the typology of subsumption specific to the form of productive relation. In a society that utilizes 'the natural instrument[s] of production, individuals are subservient to [*subsumiert unter* – subsumed under] nature'.[23] All relations are established as forms that 'appear as direct natural domination'.[24] All individuals relate to property, family and tribe as they would to nature – in a direct, deferential and doxic (Bourdieu) way. In a society in which individuals find themselves as instruments of production they are analogously subsumed under a product of labour. Property appears 'as domination of labour, particularly of accumulated labour, capital'.[25] The subsumption of productive relations under the rule of capital displaces other subservient relations and presents the possibility of a (real) general capitalization of social relations. This is co-determined by, and mediated through, the universalization of the money nexus. In an argument that foreshadows, and is further developed in, the money chapter in the *Grundrisse*, Marx posits that this social subsumption presupposes independent relations which are 'only held together by exchange',[26] and that in the shape of money, form the community.

Marx, then, generates the subsumption model through, and in conjunction with, the forms of intercourse, cultural patterns, which necessarily include social relations and their historical formation. In this way, the subsumption model is suggestive for the analysis of other forms of domination (and not only the one that it mostly refers to – the subsumption of labour under capital). What becomes important, for the internal composition of this model then, is neither capitalism's functioning as such, nor the developmental and teleologically imputed impulse of the productive forces, but rather the clashes and inter-penetrations between four phenomena. First, the essentially different, and for Marx, unique pre-capitalist forms of social intercourse; secondly the constantly tension-ridden nature of the stabilization of capitalism itself through extensive expansion and renewal; thirdly, the class conflicts that are constitutive of capitalism's stabilization as a societal type; and lastly, other configurations of the modern epoch that are not constituted through capital.

To be sure the subsumption model begins, like Marx's other critical theories, with his central question: what is capitalism? Marx's definition of it in 'The Results' is, to be sure, similar to that in *Capital*. For him 'it is a process which absorbs unpaid labour, which makes the means of production into the means for extorting unpaid labour.' [27] This definition can be read in terms of an economic problem or a problem of social organization. Read as a problem of social organization, capitalism refers not only to the functional mechanisms that enable the production of surplus-value but also to the problematic of the struggles that initiate, constitute and reproduce the *organizational regime* of capital. In other words it is suggestive of a discourse concerning power and control.[28] This oscillation in Marx between a discourse concerning functional reproduction and a problematic concerning power, also involves an oscillation within the anthropological terrain itself. The problematic of power that becomes central to the subsumption model necessarily includes the processes of societal self-understanding located in the forms of intercourse, as co-constituting moments. It is through his analysis of the historical transformation of the processes of social organization that Marx momentarily undermines the theoretical principles of the paradigm of production. It is here also that he confronts the limitations of one of his most central, yet least reflected, notions – that of use-value – and the way in which it imposes a restriction on his analysis.

Marx's implicit reliance on the forms of intercourse within the model of subsumption guides his historical analysis of capitalism from the vantage point of its own evolution and subsumption of other historically contextualized value-forms and relations. In order to capture the dynamic of capitalism's historical development, he introduces the distinction between *formal* and *real* subsumption. The former is characteristic of production where the

> labour process is subsumed under capital [for the production of absolute, rather than relative, surplus value] and the capitalist intervenes in the process as its director, manager . . . [moreover] the formal subsumption can be found in the absence of the specifically capitalist mode of production.[29]

In this sense 'it is only *formally* distinct from earlier modes of production on [which] it arises.'[30] Real subsumption comes about when

> *capitalist production* . . . establishes itself as a mode of production *sui generis* and brings into being a new mode of material production . . . the latter itself forms the basis for the development of capitalist relations whose adequate form, therefore, presupposes a definite stage in the evolution of the productive forces.[31]

The distinction between them is important because it enables Marx to theorize the nature of the dynamics of societal transformation and stabilization. This transition to, and stabilization of, capitalism occurs not only in the sphere of production, but also in the broader domain of social life. In this context, the 'prehistorical' backdrop becomes an essential point of departure for the analysis of the emergence of capitalist society. The key to understanding capitalism in this particular model is the way in which the abstract principle of exchange-value formally and then really subsumes all other value-relations under its own impetus.[32] Crucially this is found in '*the takeover by capital of a mode of labour developed before the emergence of capitalist relations*'.[33] This occurs by uncoupling the traditional relations which exist within production processes in pre-capitalist societies from their values of skill, craft, deference and ritual, and replacing them with a formal relationship based solely on the condition, capacity and willingness of the productive parties to buy and sell labour-power. As Marx points out

they . . . confront each other as commodity owners and their relations
involve nothing but *money*; *within* the process of production they meet
as its components personified: the capitalist as 'capital', the immediate
producer as 'labour' and their relations are determined by labour as a
mere constituent of capital which is valorizing itself.[34]

But whilst Marx stresses that this change does not in itself imply 'a
fundamental modification in the real nature of the labour process',[35]
it does however indicate a process which not only establishes a new
relation of dependency between people who work but also transforms
the criteria of the relation, as well as the value of the work itself: work
becomes rationalizable, disciplined and surveyed.[36] The dual processes
of valorization and rationalization signify, for Marx, the fundamental
shaking loose of traditional values and the creation of a fundamentally
new value – an assumed valuelessness of the modern value-form, the
transposition of interest into indifference, of quality into quantity.[37]
This constitutes its own value. The new, dependent, social relationships
do not then evolve purely from the realm of production, they are
conditioned and structured co-determinately by the relations of
exchange. The value-ladenness of the valorization process, in shattering traditional forms of integration, asserts its domination and ethical
vacuity by being constituted through production *and* intercourse. This
is what enables the process of first formal and then real subsumption to
achieve such far-reaching effects.

To conceptualize this, though, Marx cannot but rely implicitly on
the notion of an imaginary signification for explanatory force. It is
here, if one likes, that society constructs and confronts its own
concrete historical self-definition, through which it organizes itself
and from which it cannot escape. It is (drawing on a different theoretical tradition) society's hermeneutical circle. Marx in some ways
realizes this. His opening to (and our reading of) 'The Eighteenth
Brumaire of Louis Bonaparte' is suggestive of this. He states:

Men make their own history, but not of their free will; not under
circumstances they themselves have chosen but under the given and
inherited circumstance, with which they are directly confronted. The
tradition of the dead generations weighs like a nightmare on the
minds of the living.[38]

Analogously, Marx's argument concerning the history (historicity) of
capitalism is sensitive to this problem.[39] Capitalism develops its own
self-understanding that does more than merely *describe* (as a necessary
appearance) the type of class relations. This self-understanding is a

co-constitutive process, a process which Marx implicitly analyses through labour, production and wages, not merely as forms of material organizations, but rather as constructed notions for a form of life, each variously defined in relation to value.[40] Capitalism, as Castoriadis has argued a century later, has its own central imaginary which becomes a distinct constitutive component of the multi-dimensionality of the modern epoch. Exchange-value, or price, under the regime of capital is co-constituted through its own value structure – the value-ladenness of value.[41] This ensures 'that production is not an end in itself for me, but a means'.[42] In other words, the period of formal subsumption creates and systematizes the culturally activated presuppositions that become the ground for the complex and multi-dimensional development of the period of real subsumption – advanced modernity. Its decisive features also include an increase in the continuity and intensity of labour, as well as the development of the personality structure of inner-directed, autonomous independence dictated by 'the consciousness (or better: the idea[s])' of freedom, responsibility and frugality.[43]

Marx's analysis of money plays a far more significant role in the context of this model than it does in the model of the primacy of the productive forces. It does this in two interrelated ways; by pointing to the *nature* of the historical transformation that capitalization takes and by conceptualizing this in such a way that problematicizes the foundations of historical materialism and its anthropology. Money's *value* of commensurability becomes the 'front' between pre-capitalist and capitalist social forms. The money relation between (at least) the wage-labourer and the capitalist replaces the nature-like relations of patriarchy which, for Marx, characterizes the relation between master and journeyman that exists prior to, and simultaneously in, the period of formal subsumption.[44] In this context, *money* can be seen to undermine or subsume and transform the pre-capitalist forms of intercourse and personality; it becomes a form of intercourse, *per se*. As such, and if Marx's analysis of money in the *Grundrisse* is presented in conjunction with the subsumption model contained in 'The Results', something of note occurs. The notion of money is transformed from a phenomenal expression of value (price), which in turn is the expression of abstract labour (*Capital*), to a social process of symbolic encoding that co-constitutes a new relation of power and domination. It is to this analysis that we now turn.

Like the earlier position taken in his 1843 'On the Jewish Question', money is characterized in the *Grundrisse* as a god and a despot, 'the equation of the incompatible'.[45] There is, however, quite a distance, in terms of theory construction, separating the similarly styled descriptions. Marx's analysis in the *Grundrisse*, like that in *Capital*, is ostensibly underscored by the paradigm of production. His money analysis appears to move from production relations to relations of exchange and back again to the domain of production. However despite this apparent similarity there is a substantial difference in Marx's approach to his analysis of money in the texts of the *Grundrisse* and *Capital*. The key striking feature of the difference concerns the anthropology that springs from them.

In *Capital* Marx portrays money in purely functional terms that denotes the reproduction of a deeper structure. It ultimately rests on two principles of production – the creation of man-made objects (use-values) and its organization through a class-determined division of labour. Production is the primary sphere of life. In the *Grundrisse*, though, whilst production still functions as the determining sphere, the implicit anthropology that emerges from this suggests that the social intercourse established through relations of exchange, no less than the relations of production, both mediates and co-determines the total complexity and multidimensionality of social life.

Marx's analysis of the money-form initially proceeds in a similar fashion to that in *Capital*. In both works the commodity is said to double itself into commodity and money.[46] This process of doubling appears to be analysed according to the Hegelian formulation of the unity, yet contradiction, of being and non-being. However, the outcome of Marx's formulation is not the characterization of money as the reifying concealment of the commensurability of commodities according to labour-time. Rather, Marx characterizes money in terms of its historical transformation from its imbeddedness in ancient communities as wealth, to its emergence as the autonomous representative of value through which modern intercourse is structured. To pinpoint this, Marx suggests another level of abstraction; another doubling takes place within the money-form itself. These two processes of doubling denote, for Marx, three successive historical levels in humankind's utilization and development of money. The third stage, for him, is the most crucial as it culminates in early capitalism – the period of the formal subsumption of labour under capital.

On the first level, in its first role, money 'is wealth itself . . . it is an individuated, tangible object [that] may be randomly searched for, found, stolen, discovered.'[47] On the second level, (where it is divided, *doubled* from the first) money becomes the 'general material representative of wealth',[48] symbolized in price or exchange-value. The price or exchange-value is conceptualized by Marx, as a symbol that is universally (that is socially) recognized. As Marx says, 'such a symbol presupposes a general recognition; it can only be a social symbol; it expresses, indeed, nothing more than a social relation.'[49] The important point though is that this process of symbolization, or material representation, as Marx prefers to call it, is formulated not as a phenomenology of consciousness, as he does in 1844, or a logical structure concealing a deeper reality (a necessary appearance), but as a co-constituting and determining socio-historical objectivation:

> Money only circulates commodities which have already been *ideally* transformed into money, not only in the head of the individual but in the conception held by society (directly, the conception held by the participants in the process of buying and selling). This ideal transformation into money is by no means determined by the same laws as the real transformation.[50]

Even at this level, Marx requires the notion of value to achieve symbolic representation as a necessary co-constituting act that is outside the origin of the use-value in the sphere of production. Its origin lies in the sphere of exchange. The functioning of the social system through forms of intercourse requires socially recognized symbols. It is at the third level that the notion of money as symbol takes on added force. The third function of money (of which the first two are its historical preconditions) is that it achieves a position of autonomy outside the sphere of circulation.[51] This characterizes the formation, through the structures of formal subsumption, of the early modern capitalist epoch. Its identity is structured according to a gradual universalization and abstraction from the nature-like life-world of the commodity producers. Marx's analysis of money, especially at this third level implicitly expands his anthropology. In the course of his analysis of capitalism within the parameters of the subsumption model Marx momentarily and inadvertently transcends the paradigm of production.[52] Moreover, this is done in a way that returns him to his 'critical sociology of class'.

In the *Grundrisse*, money in the modern epoch is portrayed as a social symbol that co-determines, expresses and cyphers a social relation of universalized yet isolated reciprocal dependence that is distinct from prior historical fixed forms of personal dependence. However this entails that money becomes a form of intercourse, which itself is constituted anthropologically. The key formulation is 'money as the autonomous representative of value'.[53] Marx's description of the developed autonomy of money as a symbolic objectivation in the capitalist phase of world history can be read to suggest that this later form reveals, in a completed although antinomically structured fashion, the structures and configurations of symbolic/ linguistic forms in general. Just as 'the human anatomy . . . contains a key to the anatomy of the ape',[54] the modern category of money (that is, money in its third form) can be seen to contain not only the insights into the structures and relations of pre-capitalist as well as capitalist social forms, but also insights into the determining capacities of humankind.

Money could be seen to have an existence *analogous* to that of language. Although Marx rejects comparisons between language and money on the grounds of the doubling effect,[55] their function as forms of intercourse is similar. Language/symbolism is, for Marx, the 'practical form of consciousness'. Language/symbolism can only be so concep- tualized if it is also conceived as an objectivating human universal in the same way that labour is. Hence, exchange as a form of intercourse can be conceptualized though the notion of symbolic objectivation. Marx, in his remarks on barter among certain Negroes on the West African coast, puts it thus: 'The commodities are first transformed into bars in the head and in speech before they are exchanged for one another.'[56] This is not conceptualized, by him, as an act of pure subjectivity. His comments on the world market makes this clear: it is conceptualized as a '*material and mental metabolism* which is inde- pendent of the knowing and willing of individuals'.[57] The co-deter- mining objectivation of symbolization and language is not separated from its socio-historical context. It not only underpins the nature of the processes of societal intercourse, but also, by being a historically bound objectivation, indicates the nature of society.[58] In other words the value-complex of the objectivation, that is the form of consciousness or imaginary signification which gives the objectivation meaning which is socially understood, is neither separated from its socio- historical domain, nor from the constituting moment of human life in which it is ultimately imbedded.[59]

Under capitalism, money as a symbol signifies the *value* of quanti- fication and the organizational strategies that are encased within it. Following Castoriadis[60] rather than Marx in this instance, money is a symbol of a symbol – a symbol of an imaginary that contains, co- determines and articulates the norms, values and rules of the social form of intercourse through which the societal identity of capitalism is forged. To be sure, Marx cannot analyse money in the *Grundrisse* if money's value (or imaginary) content is not assumed. Money is thus an essence of capitalism and not a 'necessary appearance'. It is an objec- tivation that is understood, that is, it has meaning. Marx puts it thus:

Exchange value as such can exist only symbolically although in order for it to be employed as a thing and not merely as a formal notion, this symbol must possess an objective existence; it is not merely an ideal notion, but is actually presented in the mind in an objective mode.[61]

In this context, the pre-capitalist processes of identity-formation become, for Marx, both the essential precondition of capitalist development, as well as the counterpoint against which the modern world is evaluated. Marx uses money as an 'analytical tool' (albeit symbol) with which he contrasts the pre-capitalist (unconscious) autotelic community with the capitalist one of mutual independence and generalized impersonality. The critique, though, obtains critical power, not merely because of Marx's *use* of 'money' as a tool, but because he realizes and presents it as a constituting feature of modern society. Money in its 'third function' smashes the ancient community to become the community itself. It is worth quoting Marx at some length on this point:

> This reciprocal dependence is expressed in the constant necessity for exchange, and in exchange value as the all sided-mediation . . . [This] reciprocal and all sided dependence of individuals who are indifferent to one another forms their social connection. This social bond is expressed in *exchange value*, by means of which alone each individual's own activity or his product becomes an activity and a product for him; he must produce a general product – *exchange value*, or, the latter isolated for itself and individualised, *money*. On the other side, the power which each individual exercises over the activity of others or over social wealth exists in him as the owner of exchange values, of money. The individual carries his social power, as well as his bond with society, in his pocket . . . This . . . is a condition very different from that in which the individual or the individual member of a family or clan (later, community) directly and naturally reproduces himself, or in which his productive activity and his share in production are bound to a specific form of labour and of product which determine his relations to others in just that specific way.[62]

These processes quicken during the period of real subsumption. The identity structure of the community, which Marx deconstructs through an analysis of the money nexus, stabilizes into an identifiable mode of life. There is a general and universal capitalization of not only social life, but also the technical/material requirements that, for Marx, underlie it.

This reading of the money process then, is suggestive of a change, or at least an ambivalence in Marx's work: should primacy be attributed to the social relations, social form, or the productive forces, the material content?

Marx's analysis of the movement from pre-capitalist societies to capitalism within the subsumption model, suggests an ambivalent 'slide' towards causal primacy of the social form, which displaces not only Marx's teleologically imputed contradiction between the material content and the social form, but also his conceptualization of the social form in terms of the relations of production. The functionalization of life for capital cuts across the divide between base and superstructure. Functionalization does not require the universalization of the money-form merely as a necessary appearance, nor the processes or redefinition and cultural reorientation towards work as a derivative ideological component. They belong as co-determining factors that stabilize a new epoch.

What we have been hinting at can now be put plainly: the sub-sumption model can be combined with the thesis that society generates its own understanding as a cultural objectivation. This objectivation, which is located in his notion of the forms of intercourse which themselves embody the forms of consciousness, is posited as a co-determining feature of any society. Under capitalism, 'the autonomously functioning mechanisms of realization of value and surplus-value through [the market]'[63] can be understood as a culturally situated law. The law of value is not only expressed through exchange-value but also as the catch-cry 'production for production's sake' and functions as a co-determining form of intercourse and establishes the dynamic for capitalism's own expansion into, and colonization of, other *spheres of production* [life] and their sub-spheres'.[64]

The destructive features of functionalization are analysed by Marx – in terms reminiscent of the analysis uncovered in his historico-political writings – as processes of totalization and redefinition. In other words, Marx notices that it is not only the totalistic and institutionalizing practices of capitalism that are important, but also the processes of redefinition and reinterpretation that are imposed upon either traditional forms of life, or those forms that are not immediately reliant upon capital for their existence. In some ways Marx also returns to the critique of capitalism evident in the 1844 *Manuscripts*. Under the regime of capital, all forms of life and activity are gradually subsumed under its institutional practices. There is also a general culturally oriented reduction of self-activity to work that enables it to be defined as either productive or unproductive. The sanction for life is located in both the activity *and* notion of productivity, and as such is 'joyously' included into the domain of capital, functionalized and quantified. As Marx states:

> An ever increasing number of types of labour are included in the immediate concept of *productive labour*, and those who perform it are

classed as *productive workers*, workers directly exploited by capital and
subordinated to its process of production and expansion.[65]

This functionalization is accompanied by a massive reorganization
and expansion within the realm of the material contents, specifically
the productive forces. It is a process that initially separates
humankind's productive metabolism with nature from the local and
traditional social limits of their development, thus establishing it as
an independent sphere of activity. Yet this results in reification. In
Marx's view, there is an inseparable and crisis-causing *fusion* of the
very technical and social determinants that capitalism initially
separated. Decisions concerning the production of material life are
subordinated to the goal of the realization of value and surplus-value
in the market-place. As Marx states:

> The more production becomes the production of commodites, the
> more each person has to and wishes to become a *dealer in commodities*,
> then the more everyone wants to make money, either from a product,
> or from his *services*, if this product only exists naturally in the form of a
> service; and this *money-making* appears as the ultimate purpose of
> activity of every kind.[66]

The productive forces, although expanded, are organized in such a
way as to bring them in line with the demands of the production of
relative surplus-value. Machinery is developed and utilized, labour
itself is organized as a use-value, and consciousness (science)
transformed; all are subsumed under the auspices of capital.[67] In other
words, 'the relations of social domination take the form of technico-
functional requirements of the labour-process itself',[68] which confront
and dominate the producer.

The processes of functionalization and reification, as outlined by
Marx in the subsumption model, tend to problematize the conceptual
structuring of his historical materialism. The origin and impetus of
reification becomes clearer than it does in *Capital* where the productive forces achieve metatheoretical primacy over the social form. In the
subsumption model, the inversion of subject and object that results
from the fusion of the materio-technical conditions with social aims, is
never presented as totally 'the material result of capitalist production'.[69]
The impetus for both the expansion and the reorganization of the
productive forces belongs, in the context of the subsumption model,
to the historically conditioned and socially objectified *desire* for
capital.

Furthermore, these constitutionally and culturally located and
determined processes of functionalization and reification are not

conceptualized by Marx purely in terms of the evolution, expansion and reproduction of a society without subjects. These processes are class relations based on typologies of power that contain the dynamics of self-interpretation.

Inherent within capitalism's expansion and renewal is the necessary reliance on the powers of 'living labour'. As Marx states further: 'the owner of labour-power confronts capital or the capitalist . . . as the *seller* of his property. He is the direct vendor of *living labour, not commodity. He is a wage-labourer.*'[70] In other words, these processes can also be analysed as a social relation based in power; it is this which confronts the worker and propels him or her to act. Marx, at least in his less one-dimensional analyses, states that the heaped-up wealth confronts the worker as '*Capital*, as wealth that controls him'.[71]

To be sure, an argument by Marx that attempts to address and include the problem-complex of power, can lead to either a circumscription of conflict within the parameters of economy and function, or to a complete submersion of conflict and the development of a one-dimensional theory as we have seen in our analysis of *Capital*. Each current belongs to Marx's 1844 critiques of Hegel and political economy. Each obscures the problematic of contestatory action. Based in an anthropological critique of Hegel that gives the totality of human powers over to the objectivating capacity of labour, Marx's critique of political economy sees this labour as alienated during work under capital. The outcome of Marx's analysis in *Capital* is either a theory of exploitation based on the buying and selling of labour-power (and evident in conflicts over wages) or a thesis that posits the complete commodification of labour. In each case, Marx's notion of labour-time, and its corollary the increasing rate of exploitation, begins as Castoriadis has shown, 'from a postulate: that the worker is completely "reified" . . . by capitalism. Marx's theory of crises starts from a basically analogous postulate: that men and classes . . . can do nothing about the functioning of the economy'.[72]

In the context of *our* reading of the subsumption model, the disjunction that Marx sees between the increases in social wealth, that are obvious under capitalism and the relative pauperization of the worker, need not be addressed by him from the standpoint of an absolutized anthropology of labour, nor from that of a one-dimensional analysis that subsequently slides into a philosophy of history. The real reason why the processes of subsumption and reification remain incomplete is that they are necessarily contested on the basis of an imposed power relation. Under capitalism, both the criteria and practices of functionality are challenged by the bearers of labour-power – the working class. And, for Marx, the battleground is the money-form – the tension-ridden repository of the modern epoch's identity, even if it is forged through a specific logic of domination.

Marx argues that 'what money circulates is not commodities but their titles of ownership.' [73] It is on this basis that capitalism is contested by the working class. Marx's analysis of wages, as it unfolds in 'The Results' (incompletely and not without the other restrictive features present) has implications for the anthropological determinations of an open-ended notion of society in which conflict is a necessary feature. The pay-packet is, for Marx, a sign-form that both determines and mediates the worker's subjugation to capital. It continually renews the 'illusion' that the contract between buyers and sellers of labour-power is both established by equals and only concerns the production of commodities. In Marx's view, it simultaneously assures and transfigures the reproduction of social relations established between unequals which is based in an organization (and imaginary) of despotic control by capital over the work-force. As he states:

> The constant renewal of the relationship of *sale and purchase* merely ensures the perpetuation of the specific relationship of dependency, endowing it with the deceptive *illusion* of a transaction, of a contract between equally free and equally matched *commodity owners*.[74]

The power-relation, which is to be sure, *functionally located*, draws on other dimensions of social life for its meaning and its reproduction, dimensions that are not reducible to its location. The logic of Marx's 'critical sociology of class' indicates that the conflicts which are immanent to capitalism and to modernity in general are informed and structured by normative complexes that belong to the total life-processes and self-understanding of the conflicting parties. The actions that take place, for example through a coin, a piece of paper (or a plastic card!), refer not only to the practical patterns of modern life, but also to a normative–interpretative complex that forms a pattern of cultural identity. It is from these value-complexes that the claims, which either enhance or challenge the dominating power-relation of capital, are generated.

The essential point of difference, for Marx, between the pre-modern and modern (movements and classes that contest the processes of modernization and capitalization), is established implicitly through the specific nature of their value-complexes. These are, for him, located in the specific identity of the community. In using the model of subsumption, Marx could be read as suggesting that the periods of formal and real subsumption are open to contestation from those who experienced alienation as a loss of communality because of either the strictures placed on the process of work itself, or of the relation of impersonal dependence between wage-labourer and capitalist. During the period of formal subsumption the precapitalist forms of intercourse, thematized by Marx as forms of property, become the primary point of reference for conflict. However, in Marx's view the communitarian unity can be of a more or less despotic character, and more or less dependent on other-worldly references.[75] In a reconstruction that problematically minimizes and historicizes the role of tradition, Marx views the working class in the period of established capitalism as marshalling under the banner of autonomy and freedom, interpreted by him as an opposition to all forms of authority. Once the money-form is seen as embodying an organizational imaginary of despotism by those embroiled in it during their daily working lives, it can be challenged by another imaginary, that of freedom which Marx posits (at his most Kantian) as a participatory democracy.[76] It is from this perspective that he enthusiastically supports the Paris Commune.

In this way, the subsumption model could have been enlarged to encompass other aspects of domination and conflict. The *social* forms of intercourse, with which the subsumption model is concerned, provide Marx with an opening through which he could have analysed other configurations of domination and conflict that are both older and broader than the class-form. These are, for example, conquest, the relation between town and country, patriarchy, medieval corporatism (guilds and estates) and the state.[77] In this context Marx never explicitly refers to struggles concerning either the emancipation of civil society from, or its subsumption under, the state. However, both processes of pluralization and subsumption can be seen to be implicit in this reconstruction of his historico-political writings through the paradigm of class action; in certain letters on the so-called Eastern Question; as well as in his 'Secret Diplomatic History of the Century'.[78].

In *The German Ideology* Marx argues that he locates the process of societal stabilization and conflict in the contradiction between the productive forces and the forms of intercourse.[79] But as we have argued, the message of the hidden imaginary is that the forms of intercourse also have their own internal logic and dynamic that is not reducible to their interaction with the productive forces. This suggests a shift towards the primacy of the social form over the material content.

The shift, though, alters both sides of Marx's conceptual 'equation' that constitutes his materialist conception of history. The alteration occurs not only by Marx outlining implicitly another anthropological determinant apart from labour, that is, consciousness, but also by analysing it both historiographically and sociologically, that is, by contextualizing it. In other words, Marx's anthropology of the hidden imaginary works implicitly with a conception of cognitive structures that denote a general and universal human capacity for self-interpretation and self-representation. Moreover, the organization of all social activity, including the metabolism with nature, cannot but be referred to as an interpretative complex. It is this interpretative complex, and not only human practices, that also determine and stabilize the socio-historical organization of society; and yet it can only exist within a socio-historical context.

Our reading of *The German Ideology,* the *Grundrisse* and 'The Results' brings Marx to a specific point where his problematic of the anthropological self-constitution of the species meets later problematics that are concerned with the dimensions of norms and values. The common element among these contemporary approaches is a concern that intersects Marx's competing yet suppressed and only barely theorized anthropologically located presuppositions detailed above. It (the common element) involves the notion of human self-expression, or more specifically an historico-interpretative dialectic that, it is argued, is embodied in language, once language is conceptualized as self-reflective in a way similar to that in which Marx generates the notion of self-activity, at least under the auspices of 'the hidden imaginary'.[80] This contemporary historico-interpretative current is already indicative of a major and significant paradigm shift, in both the human and natural sciences, which accepts the interpretative constraints of the hermeneutical circle (notwithstanding different approaches within this problematic, as well as Habermas' own attempt to construct a two-fold *Aufhebung* of it). In the light of our construction of 'the hidden imaginary', we can say that Marx joins hands (so to speak) with the interpretavists, and gives the construction of the social world back to society and social actors, thus side-stepping his own tendency to break out of the hermeneutical circle. Together they suggest that the key processes of societal structuration or institutionalization take place through interpretative value-relations that can now be defined provisionally as normatively constituted cultural objectivations or interpretative spheres that carry the historico-social function of communicative self-understanding. These are, in modernity, both ideological, self-reflective and structurally differentiated (although of course, there are tendencies and strategies of retotalization). In other words, we can interpret Marx's 'hidden imaginary' as implying that the transitions between historical epochs, the relations between systems of material production and their natural environment, social actors and classes, are constituted and mediated by the development of interpretative complexes, at the heart of which lie imaginary significations. These penetrate the rules and institutions of society.

But we have reached the absolute limitations (the 'outer limits') of our (over)-interpretation of Marx.

8
Running on Time

The critical theory that emanates implicitly yet logically from the subsumption model never gains theoretical ground nor legitimacy in Marx's *oeuvre* and the tradition which is to follow him. The subsumption model fails to be generated into a general interpretative framework and instead remains suppressed and paralysed. Why is this current, and the insights contained within it, lost? Marx is fundamentally a modernist. Or more specifically, he renders a particular view of modernity absolute, and conceptualizes this in two specific ways. On the one hand, Marx's reductive strategy that gives primacy to the productive forces, is expanded into a philosophy of history. This, moreover, connects him to one strand of the traditions of the Enlightenment – the strand that later leads to the primacy of instrumental reason. On the other hand, the reductive strategy also provides Marx with the explanatory device with which he analyses modernity – capitalism – in *Capital*, (and which is lacking in the *Grundrisse* and 'The Results') – the theory of value. Each is underpinned and governed by a strict notion of material life: the technical mastery of nature by purposive rules.

The fundamental wrench from metaphysics that Marx thinks he achieves is not without its price (to use an unfortunate metaphor). It homogenizes the multidimensional and heterogeneous processes of human self-creation that Kant and Hegel variously and problematically formulated in their respective returns to politics. These returns occurred after the Enlightenment's one-sided exploration of human rationality, and Rousseau's invocation of virtue and absolutization of freedom. They took the shape of either the formulation of the public sphere and the use of critical judgement (Kant), or the formulation of *Sittlichkeit* through corporatist integration (Hegel). In discovering a historically new type of domination in the sphere of economy Marx attempts to connect the problematic of political freedom to the problematic of the general reproduction of society. However, precisely because of the *specific nature* of Marx's connection of these two problematics, the differences between Kant, Hegel and Marx are not fundamental in all respects. Whilst there are glimpses of multi-dimensionality in Kant's and Hegel's respective philosophies of cognition (which can be located anthropologically in the use of language), they both lapsed into one-dimensionality when they formulated their philosophies in transcendental and ontological terms respectively. In drawing implicitly and unreflectively on these holisitic (metaphysical) traditions (particularly their Hegelian aspects) Marx also effects a series of reductions and occlusions revolving around the notion of labour.

The 'causalties' are both the problematic of consciousness and the political dimension which (at least within the Kant–Hegel tradition that utilizes an Aristotelean conception of politics) necessarily and explicitly draws on the problematic of consciousness with its reference to norms and values. Marx reduces the political dimension primarily to a discourse concerning class interest. This means that Marx's potentially fruitful political anthropology of the universalization of freedom and autonomy in all spheres of life is paralysed and suppressed, and so is the problematic of the cultural orientation and location of the configurations of social domination and emancipation. Marx's homo-genization of self-activity through the notion of labour which is simultaneously an abstraction from, and a reduction of, the human condition, sets the scene for his further theoretical interrogations and interpretation. The result is the dogmatic self-assuredness and yet perplexing complexity of the paradigm of production with its internal distinction between the material contents and the social form, which unreflectively absorbs more from its precursors than it can acknowledge.

In other words, there are two parallel processes involved in Marx's self-suppression and paralysis of the 'hidden imaginary': his unique redefinition of freedom and concomitant philosophy of history, and his anthropological reconceptualization that accompanies it and furnishes the key explanatory device for his analysis of capitalism. The paradigm of production underlies Marx's redefinition of freedom as well as his analysis of capitalism through the idea of abstract labour *sui generis* (which appears only in *Capital*). We shall look at each in turn, beginning with Marx's notion of freedom.

Marx, to be sure, never gives up the basic notion of freedom that belongs to the modern age. However, the problematic of freedom and its criteria is transformed from the domain of norms (Kant and Hegel) to an explicitly materio-anthropological redefinition that places it centrally within the self-production of human life. Under this anthropologically informed redefinition, the problematic of freedom is transferred, by Marx, to the domain of necessity and abundance. This means that Marx conflates the Enlightenment's own reading of rationality with his own notion of freedom. In this way, it not only loses the capacity to confront its own normative foundations, but also in more general terms has the capacity to thematize norms only in a negative way. The progressive feature of the modern world is, for Marx, that it both liberates humankind from its necessary dependence on nature, as well as strips all pre-capitalist societal types of the normative powers in which they are 'doxically' entrenched. For Marx freedom simply means the extension of the modern world's *rational* organization of its technical mastery of nature (against *irrational* practices imbedded in capitalism), so that abundance is assured. This sets the parameters for all other freedoms.

For Marx, then, the 'all rounded development of the individual' is simultaneously and co-extensively conceptualized as including the general and universal 'liberation of humankind'. Marx's notion of freedom does not, from the end of 1843, specifically address the problematics of political freedom, voluntary action, independence or the 'recognition of necessity'. Rather, for him, there is a basic contradiction between freedom and necessity. Marx's distinctively new formulation of freedom has been summarized by Agnes Heller as: 'Where there is necessity there is no real (essential) freedom, and where there is real (essential) freedom, there is no necessity . . . It is constraint (necessity) rather than authority that figures as the opposite of freedom.' [1] This basic contradiction absorbs and neutralizes each of the other dimensions of freedom.

The project of emancipation, in Marx's view, belongs axiomatically to the sphere of production and historically to the capitalist epoch. This is the converse of Marx's sensible critique of Jacobinism's crude Communism and anti-industrialization. For him, capitalism (more emphatically in the *Grundrisse* and more cautiously in *Capital*) sets the scene for 'the many-sided development of the individual' through the socialization of the process of production. In his view, there is a link between collective organization and the development of the individual, because socialization not only brings individuals together, but by so doing also sets in motion an ever-increasing social wealth that is situated in the material fact of production without any of the exterior trappings that typify pre-capitalist societies. New needs emerge from both the production process and the universalizing nature of capital.

This entails though, that capitalism acquires a privileged status that is predicated on, and yet conceals, a residual finalism and teleology which is built into Marx's conflation of rationality and freedom. The contradiction that Marx posits between bourgeois political economy and proletarian class-consciousness is formulated in terms of the *necessary* organization of social production and consumption that 'replaces the indirect, irrational and reifying operations of market mechanisms with the conscious and direct computation of socially necessary labour expenditures . . . Capitalism can be apprehended in its "essence" only if it is seen as inherently transient to socialism.'[2] This means that Marx, like Hegel before him, can break out of the hermeneutical circle in which lesser mortals are either comfortably or uncomfortably entwined. He not only totalizes society by presenting the truth of modern society as a functionally integrated cell-form determined by wage-labour and capital and analysed with the 'tools' of dialectical–empirical science, but also totalizes history. The relationship between epochs, and the evolution from one to another, is prescribed by successive movements away from the realm of necessity. Marx's formulation of freedom not only turns on the developmental rationalizing impulse of capitalism, but also conflates the complex and multi-dimensional features of unique socio-historical types and periods with the presumed general capacities of humankind that push it beyond necessity and towards freedom.

Moreover, capitalism's elevation to a privileged historical position is the necessary corollary and converse of Marx's depiction of conflict in terms of the two-class model. Taken together, they determine the location of conflict, its philosophical construction and interpretation. The conflicts which subsumption generates are, for Marx, locatable *only* within capitalism itself. The social movements of peasants, vagabonds, the crowd, *le peuple*, cannot, in his view, constitute the real (true) ground of social conflict because they do not belong to the progressive dimension of capitalism (that is, its progressive expansion of social productivity), only to its prehistory because they are not the functionally located working class. Marx invariably and inevitably (given the dominant logic of his theory and his interpretation and subsequent conflation of the modern notions of freedom and rationality) mythologizes the conflicts that *do* occur within mature capitalism, by characterizing them in terms of the two-class model. As we have seen, his analysis of the struggles over the length of the working day (notwithstanding the rare introduction of conflict into his analysis of capitalism in *Capital* vol. I) also contained this mythological component. Moreover, this component is heightened when the conflicts over an imposed and reified power-relation are reduced to a philosophy of history in which the Paris Commune for example, is seen by Marx as a world-historical drama, in which his *real* addressee and revolutionary subject, the working class, 'manifests' itself as 'the glorious harbinger of a new society'.[3]

Whilst Marx's redefinition of freedom, with its teleology and finalism, is formulated as early as the 1844 *Manuscripts*, it only gains full flight as a 'proletarian Gallic cock' under the auspices of the paradigm of production. This is the conceptual 'scaffolding' (notwithstanding its internal complexity) through which Marx conceptualizes the determining features of humankind's self-creation. The creation of an expanding realm of use-values (or human-made objects) guarantees for him, not only the satisfaction of human needs, but also the self-affirmation of human autonomy. All of this is conceptualized in Marx's 'mature' formulation of historical materialism, where he finally awards primacy to the material contents. These, as an extension of human powers, push humankind beyond the boundaries of mere necessity and thus raise the possibility and eventuality of its complete liberation from both the tutelage of nature and the socially determined forms of domination. In this context, Marx's *theory of history*, which is already grounded in technics, is transformed into a *philosophy of history*. The evolution of human societies is not only guided by technical development, but this development is also posited teleogically. Despite Marx's claims that he distances himself from the Hegelian movement, he subordinates his own analyses of historical periods and conflicts to the teleology of Hegel's *Geist*-philosophy. In other words, despite the lucid critique of Hegel's teleology in the 'Introduction' to the *Grundrisse*, Marx falls behind Hegel's *The Philosophy of History*. Marx's reconstruction of the patterns of sociohistorical development is reminiscent of the developmental logic that Hegel imputes to the Absolute Spirit. Hence, he can work with a series of oppositions:

mythology vs rationality/freedom
imagination vs practical mastery
subjectivity vs objectivity
unconsciousness vs consciousness
childhood vs adulthood

These oppositions manifest themselves as Marx's criteria, of which rationality/freedom is the primary value, for assessing stages in human history as successively progressive. Marx's philosophy of history gets the better of him. His response to reification is to posit either a vast expansion of the productive forces in a type of scientific Utopia or a social reorganization of them according to the principles of instrumental rationality. Once so expanded, and/or reorganized, the unlimited production of use-values which are the outward sign, for Marx, of a progressive epoch is no longer problematic for him.

Gone is his sensibility towards the specific socio-historic contextualization of human self-creation and self-interpretation in all its
complexity and multidimensionality. Pre-capitalist forms are no
longer conceptualized as societies in their own right which structure
and manifest their forms of intercourse in conscious processes of self-
definition and self-organization. Vulcan, Jupiter and Hermes are
summarily dispatched to the underworld, their places taken by the
engine, the lightning-rod and the production line.[4] Humankind
belongs to the future.

Marx's philosophy of history has an internal relation to his anthropology through his notion of use-value. We must stress, though,
that Marx does not reduce his anthropology to a philosophy of history.
The former is also drawn upon to construct the theory of value that
furnishes the key to the analysis of capitalism. This is, as indicated
above, the other current that paralyses and suppresses 'the hidden
imaginary'. This returns us to the loose threads left after our analysis of
Capital.

Labour, for Marx, is the concrete activity that is objectified in each
use-value or 'man'-made object. This point, established in the 1844
'Critique of Hegel's Dialectic and General Philosophy' (a critique
already foreshadowed in 'On the Jewish Question', and reiterated as a
philosophy of praxis in the 'Theses on Feuerbach') remains the core
anthropological presupposition of the paradigm of production.
Concrete labour is the common denominator of all use-values, and by
extension, of all human societies and histories.

The reduction of human self-creation to labour, once superimposed
on the social form, steers Marx's analysis of the modern epoch in a
specific direction, that is, to the analysis of capitalism. This entails a
dual process of identification; on the one hand, that capitalism is
co-extensive with modernity, and on the other that the composition
of civil society is ultimately exhausted by an analysis of this social
complex. Marx takes over, but in an inverted (and ultimately no less
problematic way), Hegel's world of Objective Spirit.

Marx's analysis of capitalism in *Capital* follows this logic, although it
also completes the reductive–abstractive procedure that successfully
short-circuits the critical potential of the subsumption model. Beginning with the world of Objective Spirit, he analyses capitalism as a
functional, reproductive totality through the Hegelianized categories
of wage-labour and capital. Moreover, Marx also takes over political
economy's *own* definitions of time and value under the guise of his
anthropology of labour as the paradigmatic human activity. Smith and
Ricardo calculate the commensurability of exchangeable products in
terms of time spent in their manufacture. Marx takes this specific

process, which he calls valorization, and transforms it into something more than it really is.

All products are man-made objects. As such, for Marx, they are united by the human labour embodied in them, no matter what their phenomenal form. Under capitalism, once use-values become commodities, they are united by something else that leaves this physical world (that is the physical property of both the concrete labour and the material of the use-value) behind. This something else according to Marx is 'human labour in the abstract'.[5] As such, it forms the interconnected 'web of life' between each and every commodity. This common social substance is the 'crystal' that unites them. It is internal to the structure and nature of the commodity. This 'social substance' is what makes them values. Thus the notion of abstract labour is absorbed into his anthropology. This anthropology is now formulated in terms of a labour-power (as reproduced, even if indirectly, by human labour) that has value *in* it, rather than imposed upon it from the outside.

Moreover, Marx argues, in an effort to empirically ground his social chemistry with its dialectical structure, that the measurement (criterion, judgement!) of this abstract labour is established through time:

> A use-value, or useful article . . . has value only because abstract human labour is objectified or materialized in it. How, then, is the magnitude of this value to be measured? By means of the quantity of the 'value-forming substance', the labour, contained in the article. This quantity is measured by its duration, and the labour-time is itself measured on the particular scale of hours, days etc.[6]

Socially necessary labour-time is the homogeneous labour that Marx finds 'underneath' each exchange-value, as 'quantitatively determined exchange, presupposes an "equalisation", an equality/identity of essence . . . of the objects exchanged – an essential homogeneity.'[7]

However, this means that Marx, by arguing that he has 'deciphered' the truth behind the appearance of exchange-value, completes the interrelated homogenizing and reductive tendencies that are already present in his anthropology. As Castoriadis notes: 'This chemistry is clearly alchemy – an alchemy which . . . allows [s] the social-historical to be transformed into the physiological and vice versa.'[8] Following from political economy, and with a coquettish deference that contains Hegelian undertones, to nineteenth-century chemism, Marx transforms his critique of capitalism into metaphysics. Internal to his argument that capital abstracts labour from concrete labour and changes it into units of time to generate surplus-value, is the assumption that labour *has* value. Unlike the subsumption model, which recognizes the specific nature and power of capitalism's redefinition and restructuring of a hetereogeneous life-world, Marx's analysis of capitalism in *Capital* takes one side of this insight (restructuration) and transforms it, obliterating the critical force of the subsumption model. This critical force lay in the realization that value is imposed externally *on* labour by capital and that the latter also alters the overall orientation of social activity. Together, they constitute a new nexus of power-relations, which is co-constituted and challenged by a subordinate class that is not a commodity.

The critique in *Capital*, though, cannot in the final analysis be disconnected from Marx's homogenizing and reductionist metaphysics. For him, the heterogeneous and mutually irreducible types of activities that constitute modern society (including aesthetic creation, politics, language and 'spiritual reflection') are subsumed under the paradigm of production, and the problematic of the latter is then reduced to the notion of abstract labour. What matters, in his view, is that once abstract labour is identified as an indeterminate activity that gives birth to a 'crystalline' substance, all these other activities (from production to intercourse), in the final analysis count only 'as one homogeneous mass of human labour-power'.[9] Moreover, this identification/abstraction of labour-power is not only formulated as a reduction of labour-activity to instrumental rationality. Behind this also lurks a physiological reduction, or a 'double abstraction'. Marx affects a naturalistic slide to enable him to locate the expenditure of labour-powers. In other words, the exclusion of forms of co-operation and intercourse from the domain of the technical mastery of nature through the application of purposive rules is accompanied by another shift; the process is seen by Marx as entirely natural, that is, 'as a process of purely "physical interaction"'.[10] This he locates in the domain of physiology,[11] which can be assessed quantitatively through units of time that calculate how the labour is expended under different societies, different histories and different conditions. Time becomes the criterion through which the activity of human life is judged. Use-values are not only utilities, they are utilities that have an efficient, that is, instrumental, quality ascribed to them through the notion of time. Time, for Marx, may not be money, but it is the criterion of judgement that also hides the residual finalism built into his conflation of freedom and rationality.

This ensures that neither time nor rationality can be questioned immanently because Marx has immunized them by ascribing to them a naturalistic status through the notion of labour. It also means that his notion of use-value is in fact not neutral as he assumes. Rather, it embodies a double-sided abstraction: on the one hand, the abstraction/reduction of all human activity to labour and, on the other, the subsumption of all human products under the abstract criteria of utility and rationality. In shattering the myth of *homo economicus*, 'the myth which sums up the whole process of the naturalization of the system of exchange-value, the market and surplus value and its forms',[12] Marx replicates it on another level. Labour, in its double capacity, dominates all spheres of life. The notion of the material content (to which the use-value belongs) is an abstraction, an expression of a utilitarian rationalism that has been absorbed unreflectively as the 'providential code that watches over the correlation of the object with the needs of the subject'.[13] The meaning of labour as at least one *objectivation* of the multidimensionality of human needs, is removed further from the domain of the social. The notion of purposiveness (to which he ascribes the general intellect) is further anchored in a more restricted interpretation of material life.

This precludes a reflection, by Marx, concerning the role of cultural orientations and processes of interpretation that are imbedded within the life-activity of humankind. The fourth and fifth problems that we located in Marx's analysis of *Capital*[14] cannot be addressed by Marx from within the constraints of the paradigm of production. When, in late 1843, Marx recognized the link between an economic form based on formally free functional relations that in fact concealed a new form of domination (unfreedom), he opted for a notion of anthropological holism that is developed into either a reconcilable or fixed contradiction between the material content and social form. This basic distinction, which informs the paradigm of production and its two predominant models, entails Marx's acceptance of not only a utilitarian rationalism, but also of a notion of private property which itself belongs to the criterion of use. This notion of property also shores up the homogenizing and reductive anthropology. It helps also to account for Marx's ultimate insensitivity to the problematic of culturally located normative complexes in general, and those of democratic politics in particular, as we saw in his model of 'communal and autotelic totality'.

However, the anthropological holism itself belongs to Marx's fundamental and uncritical acceptance of both political economy's self-definition of civil society and of Hegel's absorption and description of it as primarily a sphere of needs (to be sure, informed by negative freedoms), and not as an enlightened public sphere that includes potentially the extension of democracy into all spheres of life. This means that the more open-ended and heterogeneous element that is given to it not unproblematically by Kant, is jettisoned. Both Hegel and Marx construct totalizing images of society, despite Marx's critical intention, that undermine the problematic of detotalization and pluralization. As has been implied in the 'hidden imaginary', this problematic is located not only at the level of society's institutional reproduction. It is also located and co-determined through its self-definitions and self-interpretations, in other words, through its social imaginaries. This means that the normative complex of democracy and its own competing formulations is itself a culturally located imaginary that confronts and challenges other imaginaries.[15]

Marx's ultimately one-sided critical confrontation with the anthropological heritage of his own age entailed that any theoretical reflections concerning the foundations for a publicly orientated and pluralized – that is, democratically organized – society, were subsumed under the notion of an integrated social system which was seen to be coextensive with the capitalization of social relations. Marx assumed, in developing a critical theory of the whole of modern society, that capitalism's development of the productive forces was essentially unproblematic and through mechanization and rationalization would create the conditions for the classless society. As we have argued, each of these sides of Marx's theory construction is finally interpreted through an objectivistically construed notion of labour which is reliant on a naturalistic slide for explanatory force. In other words, there is an internal limit to Marx's own theorizing, and it can also be seen – even if remotely – as the intellectual–historical origin for the technocratic corruption of socialism and the levelling of the historical diversity of modernity.

Notes

INTRODUCTION

1 Castoriadis in his 'On the History of the Workers' Movement' and 'Socialism and autonomous society' argues that the modern world revolves around two competing imaginaries (rather than logics): that of the market and that of the autonomous society. He posits a third which, for him, typifies and constitutes another 'version of modernity and is the central imaginary of Soviet-type societies – the strato-bureaucratic imaginary'. See C. Castoriadis, 'On the History of the Workers' Movement'; 'Socialism and Autonomous Society'; 'Facing the War'; 'Reflections on "Rationality" and "Development"'. For The Budapest School the modern world is conceptualized as a series of separate developmental logics that appear simultaneously in modernity, thus none is coextensive with it. These logics are democracy, capitalism and industrialization. More specifically the logics refer to constantly competing patterns of institutional complexes which form relational patterns in conjunction with the other logic(s) that are themselves guided by 'value-ideas', the main two in modernity being freedom and life. See Ferenc Fehér and Agnes Heller, 'Class, Modernity, Democracy'; Ferenc Fehér, Agnes Heller and Gyorgy Markus, *Dictatorship over Needs*. Habermas' approach is somewhat different from the previous two. According to him, whilst modernity is a specific historical complex, it represents the outcome of a specific evolutionary trajectory as a rationalization of two quasi-transcendental cognitive resources or competences. These, undergoing a massive expansion and reorientation during the Enlightenment, give rise to a systemic reorganization or a cultural differentiation pertaining either to cognitive-instrumental (scientific), moral-practical or aesthetic-expressive (artistic) types of rationality. See J. Habermas, 'Modernity versus Postmodernity'; 'The Entwinement of Myth and Modernity', *New German Critique*, 26, 1982, pp. 13-30.

2 Charles Taylor, *Hegel*, p. 6.

3 Ibid., pp. 30-11.
Taylor, *Hegel*, gives a useful summary of this current. The self-defining subject dispenses with the projection of meaning onto things and instead concentrates on the cognitive processes of observation and correlation of natural and external phenomena, a mapping of regularities. This results in a series of contingent correlations that do not conform to an a priori pattern. The world is no longer seen as a unified whole nor as the embodiment of meaning – it is demagified. The important point of this change, according to Taylor, is that the meaning and purpose of the correlations that are posited 'apply exclusively to the thought

and actions of subjects' (p. 9). Moreover, the categories of correlation are set aside and 'objectified'. They are presented by the new interrogators of reality as sufficient categories through which a series of efficient causal relations between constituents can be explained without recourse to an immanently construed purpose.

4 Taylor, *Hegel*, pp. 11–29. See also J. G. Herder, 'Essay on the Origin of Language', *On the Origins of Language*, pp. 87–166.

5 Taylor, *Hegel.*, p. 16.

6 Ibid., p. 22

7 As his title suggests Markus identifies Marx's project as the formation of a critical theory. The notion of critical theory means, for Markus, that Marx's work can be identified from two inter-related perspectives. Critical theory, generally, denotes the constant theme that functions as the guide for social transformation against the recognition of the crisis-complex of modern society. In other words, critical theory is the attempt to link the perspective of theoretical interpretation to that of practical intervention. In all of Marx's works reality is not merely described by a social theory which creates an objective body of knowledge, rather the theory also identifies immanent tendencies for social transformation. More specifically, according to Markus, Marx simultaneously and 'actively' pursues his insight that society is constituted of dominant and subordinate classes, and addresses his theory to the subordinate class of proletarians. They, as a collective subject, are invited to 'reach through' the theory (and their own self-consciousness), and recognize and articulate the consciousness of their radical needs which remain undeveloped under the impact and weight of existing social relations.

In addressing the problematic of Marx's theoretical development in this way, Markus identifies both the broader notion of critical theory (or theories) which provides the unifying element throughout Marx's work as well as the key element around which the theoretical shifts occur – that is, the procedure of critique within the critical theory itself. But in drawing attention to what is felt to be an implicit distinction between critical theory and critique, we have already diverged from Markus' own intent. There is good reason for this. The notion of critical theory (as Markus uses it) requires an internal differentiation in the sense that some strategies of critique both remain at a lower level of theorizing than others and subordinated to the problematic of practical interventions. The notion of critique operates simultaneously on a number of levels. Critique, in the first instance is motivated by Marx's desire to find a solution to the social problems of his epoch, and in this sense it is immanently related to the tradition of practical reason – to the problematic of 'What is society?'. As Habermas points out, 'critique is set in motion by the practical interest in deciding the process of crisis toward a favourable issue, the good' (Habermas, *Theory and Practice*, p. 214). But for Marx critique cannot be, as the earlier Kantian and Hegelian versions of practical reason were, grounded in transcendental or ontological principles. Rather, the critical insight of a world of class domination propels Marx to establish the grounds for its critique and its overcoming within the world of the living subjects who experience the domination. Practical reason, with its emphasis on 'the good', is grounded, for Marx, in both people's material life activities as well as the material conditions of society. These are 'posited by it first of all not as explanatory principles of a theory of social structure and change, but as the terrain of the decisive social struggles for a coming radical-practical transformation of society' (Markus, 'The Human Use of Man-made Objects', pp. 9–12).

This means that the struggles that occur over the notion of 'the good' concern two problem complexes which inform the whole of Marx's work. He instills into the 'activity' of critique itself the recognition of conflict grounded in the notion of social production and class conflict, both of which become pivots around a materialist grounding of the project of practical reason.

Against the backdrop of the above remarks, Markus' main point in 'The Four Forms of Critical Theory' stands in starker and more poignant relief – that Marx's project of constructing a critical theory of society cannot be seen as a homogeneous one. The typological classifications of the four possible forms are important because they give a clear indication of the nature of each of the stages of Marx's development, and the way in which a core project undergoes conceptual and theoretical re-formulation. It is on this latter point, that is the problem of theory construction, that I will concentrate. Embedded in the critical enterprise itself are heterogeneous and alternative formulations which denote four basic concerns. The first concern of critique, because of its practical component, is the identification of an empirical-practical addressee – the working class. The theory raises different arguments concerning the working class's revolutionary role and the alternative socio-political strategies which it can use to enact this role. This is related to the second and third concerns: the definition of the goal of emancipation which is formulated in terms of a future socialist society in response to the critique of capitalism, and the identification of the mechanisms of the self-transcendence of capitalism, respectively. The fourth concern (and certainly for our purposes the most crucial, because it both draws in and subsumes the other two) is the method of the theory construction. Markus points to the vicissitudes that occur in the inter-relation between the analytico-theoretical and critico-practical moments of the project, that is, the alternative understandings of the relation between philosophy and so-called material reality and its reproduction. Jean Cohen, in her book, *Class and Civil Society*, also draws our attention to the same underlying principle of critique that propels each of the four forms of critical theory. She argues that within their broader framework, five versions of critique can be isolated. However, using Markus' own typology we will argue that there is a sixth version of critique that can be isolated. This is found in the *Grundrisse*, a text that Cohen largely and systematically ignores.

The first one is an immanent critique which propels Marx's specifically political critique of Hegel in 1843. The operation of critique functions in the recognition of the distorted relation between the real and the ideal. The second and third versions are found within the 1844 *Manuscripts* and are characterized as either an unmasking critique or a transcendental critique. The critical function of unmasking locates the foundations of modern society within the economics of capitalism, that is within the wage-labour/capital nexus, whilst the transcendental critique grounds this within an anthropological core that now becomes stabilized through the notion of labour. The fourth version, which is specifically an ideological one, locates the unmasking critique within the functional reproduction of a class society. Here, in the *German Ideology*, critique is placed within the paradigm of production for the first time. The fifth version, which is not included in Cohen's typology but which Markus rightly includes as a specific form within the topographies of critical theory, is located in the *Grundrisse*. Here critique functions in a more historically contextualized form than in any other works within a model of a self-transcending capitalist development which itself dictates the way in which the process of critique is organized – that is, 'according to the principle of ascendence *from the abstract to the concrete*' (Markus, 'Far Forms . . .' p. 91). The final version of critique departs significantly from the previous forms. It is the defetishizing critique found in *Capital* (exemplified in the theory of value-form), in which the movement of thought is from essence to appearance. Both the *Grundrisse* and *Capital* belong to Marx's 'rediscovery' of Hegel, particularly *The Logic*. The Hegelian *ontological dialectic* with its emphasis on categorial and systemic holism informs the very core of *Capital*. It is, as one may say, its *idée fixe*.

These six forms of critique, then, indicate the heterogeneous complexity of Marx's project and the way in which problematic formulations internal to the theory itself - as well as Marx's attempts to formulate a coherent theoretical and practical alternative to both capitalist society and the tradition that he intersects - propel him to generate alternative and, we shall argue, competing critical theories.

There is, then, an internal distinction between critique and theory. We have isolated six moments of critique, but (following Markus) only four forms of *critical theory*. The disjuncture between the number of critiques and the number of critical theories is solved once the question as to the status of the 1843 works is raised. These, as we have already noted, include Marx's most immediate and direct response to Hegel. It is interesting to note that Markus does not rate these works a mention. They too, however, have a programmatic status because of the way in which they meet the challenge of the Enlightenment's notions of freedom and rationality through the specific method of immanent critique. In this sense, we suggest that the works of this period constitute the *first form of critical theory*. However, in contradistinction to Cohen, we will argue that although the 1843-44 works *overall* contain three forms of critique, these are less cohesive and more fluid than the later ones in which the process of critique internally stabilizes. Hegel's immanentism and a Kantian transcendentalism are both found in the 1843 works. The unmasking critique takes over and subsumes the immanent critique of *The Philosophy of Right*, whilst the transcendental form which helps to ground the immanent critique is transposed into a materialist phenomenology that is transcendentally deduced from the concept of labour. This, from 1844 onwards, provides the *anthropological core* from which all of the subsequent critical theories take their cue. The concept of labour enables Marx to establish the materio-anthropological grounding of the project of practical reason. In other words, Marx generates his images of humankind, society and emancipation from the anthropology of labour and thus establishes the relation between theory and critique which brings together (or at least to the foreground) the two problem complexes which inform the whole of his work: the notions of social production and class conflict.

There are, then, five forms of critical theory. These are structured according to the following works:

1 The works of 1843 (especially "A critique of Hegel's doctrine of the State")
2 *The Economic and Philosophical Manuscripts* of 1844
3 *The German Ideology*, "Wages", and "The poverty of Philosophy" (1845-1847)
4 The *Grundrisse* (1857-1858)
5 *Capital* (1867)

The last three critical theories denote the formation and systematization of the paradigm of production, as well as changes and tensions within it. However, there is a different body of work, to which Markus does not refer, that establishes the other recognizably coherent current. The politico-historical writings of the 1850s have a special place *outside* the forms of critical theory and constitute Marx's paradigm of class action. The recognition of an autonomous, yet supposedly interdependent paradigm does not undermine the validity of the periodizations of Marx's thought which we have already accepted, with some modification. This is because, although Marx's political works or commentaries in which the paradigm of class action is explicitly utilized cover some 25 years from 1848 to 1871, they develop alongside the paradigm of production.

However, Marx's attempts to come to terms with the processes of social transformation and the dynamics of class conflict result in a series of conceptual residues and overloads. This means that these typological and paradigmatic classifications of Marx's work do not exhaust an interpretation of it. This is the important point. What I have termed Marx's 'hidden imaginary', which points towards and explores a possible residual philosophical anthropology neither derived from nor reliant upon the notions of labour and production for critical force or conceptual robustness, indicates that textual interpretation and criticism are never wholly bound to the formal parameters and structures of an author-imputed (or tradition-imputed) meaning.

8 This claim is not Marx's privileged possession. Rather, as we have been arguing, it has a long history which, in drawing on the various anthropological images in specific ways, forms other currents and cultural traditions, including instrumentalized rationalism, romanticism and Jacobinism

9 Markus, 'Four Forms of Critical Theory', pp. 80–81.

10 See, for example, Habermas, *Legitimation Crisis*; Castoriadis, 'On the History of the Workers' Movement'

11 This is a specific use of A. Touraine's notion of class struggle. See his *The Self-Production of Society*; and *The Voice and the Eye*. Marx's works that point directly to another coherent paradigm of class action are his other political works: 'The Class Stuggles in France' (1850), 'The Eighteenth Brumaire of Louis Bonaparte' (1852), 'The Civil War in France' (1871).

12 These theoretical projects constitute both the implicit reference points for this work and the horizon beyond its immediate path. However, it is beyond the scope of this work to refer explicitly to these theoretical enterprises as projects in their own right with their own logics and metatheories; we can only mention the barest outlines of each of their metatheories.

1 Habermas' communication theory of society (which is a result of his interpretation of Marx's notion of social labour as well as his dialogue with systems theory and linguistic philosophy) develops two anthropological and cognitive deep (or quasi-transcendental) structures that are imbedded in language. One pertains to humankind's control over external nature (instrumental action), and the other pertains to the intersubjectively constituted life-world and the identity of the speaking subject (communicative action). These cognitive competences are the mechanisms around which processes of systemic integration and social integration develop, and through which societies evolve. Social change occurs, in Habermas' view, when first the underlying cognitive competences are utilized to generate new cognitive resources (knowledge) that can then solve problems pertaining to either the social system or the dynamics of social integration. The process of mediation and point of intersection between the two occurs in the cognitive and ideological structures of the life-world itself. For Habermas, 'the historical materialist approach is directed to a structural analysis of the development of world views.' See 'Toward a Reconstruction of Historical Materialism', in his *Communication and the Evolution of Society*, (Boston, Beacon Press, 1979), p 169.

2 Cornelius Castoriadis develops a notion of the imaginary significations of society. According to Castoriadis socio-historical formations organize themselves through an imaginary signification which is a complex of terms and referents for which there is no sufficient real or rational basis, yet are socially constraining for all societal members.

3   Alain Touraine's theory of social movements ruptures the notion of society as a functional totality through his notion of historicity and its relation to class conflict. Historicity is the 'field' of social action, that is, the activity exerted by society (constituted through classes) upon itself. It is composed of a combination of three components; the model of knowledge, accumulation and cultural model. According to him, the field of historicity is at the centre of class conflict; it is appropriated by social movements that bring into play a double dialectic of domination and contestation. In this sense, conflict is both open-ended and only partly concealed under the demands of function.

4   The paradigm of objectivation which stems from Lukács is developed further in the work of The Budapest School, in particular that of Agnes Heller. In her model the paradigm of objectivation is internally differentiated into three spheres; the sphere of objectivation 'in itself' (the sphere of basic anthropolgical determinants and norms and rules which are given and must be mastered by all social members), the sphere of objectivation 'for itself' (the sphere through which societies and human beings develop meaning), and the sphere of objectivation 'in and for itself' (the realm of institutions that create either together or separately the identity of a particular socio-economic structure). She orientates her conception of each sphere to her underlying problematic – the nature of ethical conduct generally; and in the modern world in particular.

See, in respect of each:

J. Habermas, *Knowledge and Human Interests*; *Communication and the Evolution of Society; The Theory of Communicative Action*; C. Castoriadis, *Crossroads in the Labyrinth*, Kate Soper and Martin H. Ryle (Sussex, Harvester Press, 1984); 'The Imaginary Institution of Society', *The Structural Allegory*. A. Touraine, *The Self-Production of Society*. Agnes Heller, *Everyday Life, Rationality of Reason, Rationality of Intellect*, (unpublished manuscript, 1982); *A Theory of History*.

These four theoretical enterprises do not in any way foreclose a recognition of the importance of other thinkers and their projects, such as Antonio Gramsci, the first generation of the Frankfurt School (in particular Adorno and Horkheimer) and Michael Foucault.

1   CIVIL SOCIETY AS THE PUBLIC

1   I. Kant, 'Conjectural Beginning of Human History', 'The End of All Things', 'Idea for a Universal History from a Cosmopolitan Point of View'; 'What is Orientation in Thinking?', *Critique of Practical Reason and Other Writings in Moral Philosophy*, especially Kant's endnote, p.305. For an interesting analysis of Kant's other Copernican Revolution see W. J. Booth, 'Reason and History: Kant's Other Copernican Revolution'.

2   Kant, *Immanuel Kant's Critique of Pure Reason*, (hereafter referred to as *Critique of Pure Reason*) p. 635, see also pp. 629–52. The questions are: 'What can I know?'; 'What ought I do?' and 'What may I hope?'

3   This is the question with which Lucien Goldman, in his book *Immanuel Kant*, begins his critical appraisal of Kant's critical philosophy. See pp. 101–130. We more consciously, though, follow van de Pitte's analysis by recognizing that, in presenting not only a rational justification and systematic presentation of the inter-relation of physical and moral reality through the organization of the higher faculty of cognition, but also a teleological philosophy of history, Kant provides a

philosophical system which is centred on the problematic 'What is humankind?'.
See: Frederick van de Pitte, *Kant as Philosophical Anthropologist*.

4 Kant, 'What is Enlightenment?', p. 3.

5 Kant, 'Idea for a Universal History', p. 14. See also *Anthropology From a Pragmatic Point of View*, tr. M. J. Gregor (The Hague, Martinus Nijhoff, 1974), especially 'On the Character of the Species', pp. 182-93, and the First Thesis in his 'Idea for a Universal History', pp. 12-13 where he states: 'In man (as the only rational creature on earth) those natural capacities which are directed to the use of his reason are to be fully developed only in the race, not in the individual.'

6 Put this way, the evolution of reason, in Kant's view, transforms humankind's relation and attitude to nature. Technique embodies a certain rationality principle, that is a rational utilization of available skills: *Anthropology*, pp. 184-85. To be sure, Kant places 'technical reason' first on a scale of the ascending priorities of reason, but it is the ethical constitution of reason that concerns him the most, and which emerges as the primary formation of reason's capacity, as we shall see.

7 Kant, 'Idea for Universal History', p. 13.

8 See Kant 'Conjectural Beginning of Human History', pp. 57-58.

9 Booth, 'Reason and History', p. 57.

10 Taylor, *Hegel*, p. 31.

11 Kant, 'What is Orientation in Thinking?' p. 296.

12 Kant, *Critique of Practical Reason*, p. 258.

13 Van de Pitte, *Kant as Philosophical Anthropologist*

14 See Kant, *The Critique of Judgement*, pp. 21-35.

15 Ibid., p. 38.

16 Ibid., pp. 37-8.

17 Kant, *Anthropology*, p. 183.

18 Van de Pitte, *Kant*, p. 48.

19 Kant, *Anthropology*, p. 191.

20 Kant, 'Idea for a Universal History' especially Theses Four and Seven (pp. 15-16, 18-21); 'Perpetual Peace' and 'An Old Question Raised Again: Is the Human Race Constantly Progressing?', in Beck (ed.) *Kant on History*, pp. 85-154.

21 See footnote 6.

22 Kant, 'Idea for a Universal History', Thesis Five, p. 17; see also Manfred Riedel, 'Transcendental Politics? Political Legitimacy and the Concept of Civil Society in Kant'.

23 Kant, 'Idea for a Universal History' Thesis Six, p. 16.

24 Ibid., p. 17.

25 Kant, 'Idea for a Universal History', p. 17

26 Kant, *Critique of Practical Reason*, p. 130.

27 Kant, 'On the Common Saying: "This May be True in Theory, but it does not Apply in Practice"', (hereafter footnoted as 'Theory and Practice', p. 73).

28 Kant, 'Conjectural Beginning of Human History', p. 59.

29 Kant, *Critique of Practical Reason*, pp. 143-47.

30 Ibid., pp. 193-94

31 Susan Meld Shell, *The Rights of Reason: A Study of Kant's Philosophy and Politics*, p. 117, [my emphasis].

32 For an analysis of these competing directions see: Thomas Auxter, 'Kant's Conception of the Private Sphere'; Dick Howard, 'Kant's Political Theory: The Virtue of his Vices'; Hannah Arendt, *Lectures on Kant's Political Philosophy*, edited and with an interpretative essay by Ronald Beiner, esp. pp. 58-65

33 Kant, 'Idea for a Universal History', p. 16.

34 This problematic of the social constitution of social conflict is essentially what attracts Kant to Rousseau. According to Kant, Rousseau was the first thinker to pose the distinction between 'natural man' and 'cultural man' within a socially constituted definition of freedom. Rousseau, in viewing the civilizing process as one which adds many dimensions to human experience, sees it as creating an artificiality which is, in many ways, inimical to morality and virtue. For Kant, this constitutes Rousseau's fundamental insight:

> In his *On the Influence of the Sciences* and *On the Inequality of Man* he shows quite correctly that there is an inevitable conflict between culture and the human species, considered as a natural species of which every member ought wholly to attain his natural end. But in his *Emile* and *Social Contract*, and other writings he tries to solve this much harder problem: how culture was to move forward, in order to bring about such a development of the dispositions of mankind, considered as *moral* species, as to end the conflict between the natural and moral species. Now here it must be seen that all evils which express human life, and all vices which dishonour it, spring from this unresolved conflict. ('Conjectural Beginning of Human History', pp. 60–61.)

In realizing this, Kant takes up the idea of 'cultural man', not as Rousseau had done in its historical sense but in an ethical and teleological one. So while accepting the ethical insight imbedded in the Rousseauesque anthropology, Kant rejects the confusion between the historical and normative assumptions which lead Rousseau to the position of a 'general will' that is ultimately based on the background assumption of a social contract between people as citizens (as political actors). Kant recognized that the Rousseauesque general will cannot address the question of how it itself is to gain legitimate recognition of a *power* over citizens. In other words, in accepting a distinction between the natural and the social, Rousseau also generates a distinction between domination and communication (or discourse based on the constituent nature of society), and between compulsion and freedom, which drives his own notion of the social contract to paradoxical conclusions concerning the institutional realization of the general will. Kant thinks he avoids this modern problem of the complexity of the inter-subjectively established relations of society. He conceives the social contract, not as a fact, but rather as a norm based on an a priori principle of practical reason which becomes the standard by which society is judged as an appearance. Kant proceeds analytically, presupposing that civilization, in both its social and political formations, constitutes the context which alone reveals the essential and permanent aspect of humankind. For two competing views concerning Kant's relation to Rousseau see Ernst Cassirer, *Rousseau, Kant, Goethe*; and S. Axinn, 'Rousseau versus Kant on the Concept of Man'. Reidel, in his article 'Transcendental Politics?' problematizes both Rousseau's and Kant's conceptions and formulations of political man and freedom.

35 Kant, 'The Metaphysics of Morals', para 46, p. 139; see also 'An Old Question Raised Again', p. 144.

36 Kant, 'The Metaphysics of Morals'.

37 Kant, 'What is Enlightenment?', p. 5.

38 Arendt, *Lectures*, p. 60.

39 Hannah Arendt and Jürgen Habermas are two contemporary theorists who address this problem centrally. For Arendt the public is the space which resides outside the institutional realm of political life as such, and entails the use of critical judgement concerning normatively grounded notions of politics. See her *The Human Condition*, and *Lectures*. Habermas takes as his departure point the

formal criterion of participation in political life and structures this according to
the 'ideal speech situation'. See Habermas, 'What is Universal Pragmatics?', in
his *Communication and the Evolution of Society*, pp. 1–68; 'Hannah Arendt's
Communication Concept of Power'; 'The Gauss Lectures'.

40 Kant, 'What is Enlightenment?', p. 5.
41 Ibid.
42 Kant, 'What is Orientation in Thinking?', p. 303.
43 Ibid.
44 See Kant's endnote to 'What is Orientation in Thinking?', p. 305
45 Kant, Appendix II ('Of the Harmony which the Transcendental Concept of
Public Right Establishes between Morality and Politics'), 'Perpetual Peace', in
Beck (ed.) *Kant on History*, p. 134.
46 Kant, 'Theory and Practice', p. 79.
47 Ibid., p. 80.
48 Ibid., p. 76.
49 Ibid.
50 The important point concerning civil society and the constitution, for Kant, (in
terms of a theory of ethical progress) is that in subjecting themselves to constraint,
social actors become bound to laws which they themselves have created even if
they misunderstand their origin and inhibit their development.

It is *only from Providence* that man anticipates the education of the human race,
taking the species as a *whole* – that is *collectively* and not in terms of its individual
members, where the multitude does not form a system, but only an aggregate gathered
together. Only from Providence does he expect his species to tend towards the constitution
it envisages, which is to be based on the principle of freedom but at the same time on the
principle of constraint in accordance with law. That is he expects it from a wisdom which is
not *his*, but is yet the Idea of his own reason, an Idea that is impotent (by his own fault).
(Kant, *Anthropology*, pp. 188–89).

In other words, the resolution of conflict takes place in ways which *represent*
reason in all its possibilities, reason as an idea, which, although it may lie buried
under the weight of superfluous action, remains the pre-eminent signification of
the ethical status of people's actions as a species. In this way, they should 'feel
ennobled by the consciousness of it: namely by their awareness of belonging to a
species that lives up to a man's vocation as reason represents it to him in the
Ideal', ibid., p. 190 ('The Conjectural Beginning of Human History' can be seen
as an earlier version of this thesis). Moreover, this ideal, which represents the
content of a practical reason, is not conceived as a Utopia; it is utilized in the
praxis-orientation of people's lives. As Kant notes: 'this Idea is in itself un-
attainable; it is not a constitutive principle (the principle of everlasting peace
amid the most vigorous actions and reactions of men). It is only a regulative principle, [directing us] to pursue this diligently as the destiny of the human race, not
without solid grounds for supposing that man has a natural tendency towards it.'
Anthropology, p. 191.
51 Kant, *Anthropology*, p. 185. See also 'Conjectural Beginning of Human History',
p. 68.
52 Arendt, *Lectures*, p. 63. I have, through the background intercession of
Habermas' communication ethics, changed her notion of the public to include
generalized participation in the institutional life of society.
53 Kant, 'The Metaphysics of Morals', para 49.
54 Kant, 'Theory and Practice', p. 74.

55 See Riedel, 'Transcendental Politics?'.
56 Kant, 'Theory and Practice', p. 74.
57 Ibid., p. 77 [my emphasis].
58 Ibid., p. 78.
59 Ibid.
60 Ibid.
61 Riedel, 'Transcendental Politics?' p. 605.
62 This suggests that, according to the criterion laid down in Kant's own 'Metaphysics of Morals', esp. para 49, the vision of the state that emerges from this is a *paternalistic* one at the very least. Accordingly, Kant can be viewed as an early social democrat.
63 P. Gay, *The Enlightenment. An Interpretation* especially 'A Faith for the Canaille', pp. 517–28.
64 Kant, 'An Old Question Raised Again', pp. 152–3.
65 See Kant in Gay, *The Age of Enlightenment*, p. 519.
66 Riedel, 'Transcendental Politics?' p. 611.
67 Ibid., pp. 611–12. See also D. Howard, *From Marx to Kant*. It was not possible to consider Howard's analysis of Kant in his recently published book in this chapter, particularly as it bears on the Kantian structuring of reason in transcendental terms.

2   THE DIALECTICAL ANTHROPOLOGY OF FREEDOM

1 G. W. F. Hegel, *Hegel's Philosophy of Right*, para. 260.
2 Charles Taylor, *Hegel*, pp. 131–3 and chapter VIII, '*The Phenomenology* as Interpretive Dialectic', pp. 214–21.
3 Hegel, *Hegel's Science of Logic*.
4 Hegel, *Philosophy of Right*, para. 269 addition.
5 Hegel in the preface to *The Phenomenology of Spirit* states: 'The True is the whole. But the whole is nothing other than the essence consummating itself through its development. Of the Absolute it must be said that it is essentially a *result*, that only in the *end* is it what is truly is', para. 20.
6 Taylor, *Hegel*, p. 218.
7 See Heller, *A Theory of History*, p. 114 in which the notion of a value-idea is linked to the basic premissing of historical interpretation in terms of universal ideas.
8 Hegel, *Philosophy of Right*, para. 1.
9 Hegel, *Philosophy of History*, pp. 17–18.
10 Hegel, *Phenomenology*, para. 184.
11 Ibid, para. 179
12 A. Kojève, *Introduction to the Reading of Hegel*, p. 222. See especially chapter 7: 'The Dialectic of the Real and the Phenomenological Method in Hegel'. As Vincent Descombes points out (in *Modern French Philosophy*), Kojève interprets Hegel through an almost Feuerbachian juxtaposition of Marx. However, we should ask, which Marx? In my view it is a phenomenological reading of the 1959 'Preface' in which Kojève uses the notions of work and history in their evolutionary guise without asking whether these notions themselves are at all problematic. While this raises problems for Kojève (as Descombes indicates), it is the anthropological interpretation which is of interest here.
13 Hegel, *The Philosophy of History*, p. 19.

14 These remain implicit anthropological currents in Hegel. Following Habermas' discussion of Hegel's Jena *Philosophy of Mind* which can be used as a corrective to Kojève's 'materialist' analysis (Habermas, 'Labour and Interaction: Remarks on Hegel's Jena *Philosophy of Mind*', in his *Theory and Practice*, pp. 142-169) these are reformulated through the categories of Absolute Spirit from *The Phenomenology* onwards. Work and politics belong to (or actualize) the realm of Objective Spirit, whilst language remains the central yet subliminal and thus unthematicized, anthropological medium through which reason is articulated. Moreover, it (language) only comes to full fruition as *the* constitutive and reflective medium in the doctrine of Absolute Spirit.

15 Hegel, *The Phenomenology*, para. 187.

16 See Kojève, *Introduction*, pp. 224-7.

17 Hegel, *The Phenomenology*, para. 190-1.

18 Ibid., para. 192-3.

19 Ibid., para. 196.

20 Ibid., para. 195.

21 Ibid., para. 196.

22 Ibid., para. 20.

23 Ibid., para. 30.

24 Habermas, 'Labour and Interaction', p. 153.

25 Hegel, *The Phenomenology*, op. cit., para. 33.

26 Ibid., para. 197.

27 Hegel posits history as that which 'unites the objective with the subjective side, and denotes quite as much the *historian revuum gestarum*, as the *res gestare* themselves; on the one hand, it comprehends not less what has *happened*, than the narration of what has happened. This union of the two meanings we must regard as of a higher order than mere outward accident'. (*The Philosophy of History*, p. 60; see also 61.)

28 Ibid., p. 63. See also *Hegel's Philosophy of Right*, op. cit., para. 57.

29 See *The Philosophy of History*, p. 61, where Hegel argues that it is the state that first presents subject matter that is not only *adapted* to the prose of history, but involves the production of such history in the very process of its becoming self-identity.

30 Hegel, *Philosophy of Right*, para. 258.

31 Ibid., para. 135 addition; see also para. 106.

32 Ibid., para. 28.

33 Ibid., para. 29.

34 Ibid., para. 135.

35 Ibid., para. 29.

36 See: Joachim Ritter, *Hegel and the French Revolution*, esp. pp. 45-7. See also J. Habermas, 'Hegel's Critique of the French Revolution', in his *Theory and Practice*, pp. 121-42.

37 Ritter, *Hegel and the French Revolution*, p. 47.

38 While Hegel, to be sure, points to the absolutization of freedom (following directly from Rousseau) as the second component of the Jacobin consciousness, he is aware that this absolutization transforms freedom into *absolute equality*, which then becomes the central virtue of Jacobinism. See Hegel, *Philosophy of Right*, para. 5 addition.

39 Hegel, *Philosophy of Right*, para. 139. [my emphasis].

40 See *Philosophy of Right*, para. 138. In the *Phenomenology of Spirit*, this is analysed as the 'law of the heart', para. 367ff.

41 *Philosophy of Right*, para. 140.

42 Ibid., 5.

43 Hegel, *Phenomenology*, para. 584.

44 'The universal will goes *into itself* and is a *single*, *individual* will do which universal law and work stand opposed. But this *individual* consciousness is no less directly conscious of itself as universal will; it is aware that its object is a law given by that will and work accomplished by it; therefore in passing over into action and in creating objectivity, it is doing nothing individual but carrying out the laws and functions of the State.' Ibid., para. 587.

45 Ibid., para. 594.

46 Ibid., para. 592, also para. 575.

47 Hegel, *Philosophy of Right*, para. 5. In the *Phenomenology* Hegel also states: '[They] cannot achieve anything positive, either universal works of language or of reality, either of laws and general institutions of *conscious* freedom, or of deeds and works of a freedom that *wills* them', para. 588.

48 Hegel, *Philosophy of Right*, para. 5 addition.

49 Ibid., para. 29.

50 *Phenomenology*, para. 588.

51 *Philosophy of Right*, op. cit., para. 7. The text reads: 'The will is the unity of . . . particularity reflected into itself and so brought back to universality, i.e. it is universality. It is the self-determination of the ego, which means that at one and at the same time the ego posits itself as its own negative, i.e. it is restricted and determinate, and yet remains by itself, i.e. in its self-identity and universality.'

52 This analysis acknowledges T. E. Wartenburg's 'Poverty and Class Theory in Hegel', although in Hegelian terms as I interpret it, it should be 'class relation', not 'class structure'. See also S. Avineri, 'Labour, Alienation and Social Classes in Hegel's *Realphilosophie*', pp. 196–215; Taylor, *Hegel*, chapter XIV, 'Ethical Substance', pp. 365–88.

53 *Philosophy of Right*, para. 182 addition.

54 Ibid., para. 182.

55 Ibid., para. 189. See also Joachim Ritter, 'Person and Property', in his *Hegel and the French Revolution*, especially pp. 68–82 and 137–43 respectively. Also Raymond Plant, 'Hegel and Political Economy', parts I and II.

56 *Philosophy of Right*, para. 170: 'It is not merely property which a family possesses; as a universal and enduring person, it requires possessions specifically determined as permanent and secure, i.e. it requires wealth. The arbitrariness of a single owner's particular needs is one moment in property taken abstractly, but this moment, together with the selfishness of desire, is here transformed into something ethical, into labour and care for a common possession.'

57 Ibid., para. 189 addition.

58 See ibid., paras. 40, 45–46, 50. In this way, possession and appropriation are necessary but not sufficient conditions for property ownership. Property *as a right* has to be recognized, which presupposes a mutually recognized normative order (ibid., para. 71, 182, 187, 190; see also Ritter, 'Person and Property', p. 138) that mediates all objects of the will. This mediation, which takes the form of a codified legal system, the administration of justice and the resolution of disputation through civil law, becomes the positive side of civil society, liberated from the prerogatives of the pre-modern state.

59 Ibid., para. 189 addition.

60 Ibid., para. 199.

61 Ibid.

62 Ibid., para. 199.

63 Ibid., para. 241.

64 Ibid., see paras 245-8.
65 Ibid., see paras 44, 130, 242.
66 Ibid., para. 120.
67 Ibid., para. 244 addition.
68 Ibid., para. 243. [my emphasis].
69 As paragraph 243 intimates.
70 Ibid., see addition para. 244.

3   THE SCIENCE OF SOCIETY

1 Hegel, *Philosophy of Right*, p. 10. This is reiterated in the 1831 'Preface' to the second edition of Hegel's *Science of Logic*, esp. p. 39.
2 *Philosophy of Right*, para. 145.
3 Ibid.
4 Ibid., para. 144.
5 Ibid., para. 243.
6 Ibid., para. 267.
7 Hegel, *Logic*, p. 490.
8 Ibid., p. 584.
9 Ibid., p. 593.
10 See J. Habermas, *Knowledge and Human Interests*, pp. 13-19; see also Kant, 'Preface' to the Second Edition of the *Critique of Pure Reason*, p. 18.
11 Hegel, *Phenomenology*, op. cit., para. 76.
12 See ibid., para. 76.
13 Ibid.
14 Ibid., para. 41-6.
15 Ibid., para. 47.
16 Habermas, *Knowledge and Human Interests*, p. 20.
17 See chapter two above, especially 'Reason through an active history'.
18 Hegel, *The Logic*, p. 594.
19 Habermas, *Knowledge and Human Interests*, op. cit. p. 11 [my emphasis].
20 Hegel makes this clear at the end of the Introduction to *The Phenomenology*, para. 89.
21 Hegel, *The Logic*, p. 49.
22 Ibid., p. 58.
23 Ibid; see also pp. 28, 48, 50.
24 Ibid., p. 53.
25 Ibid., p. 35.
26 Ibid., p. 546.
27 Hegel, *Phenomenology*, para. 84.
28 Hegel, *Logic*, op. cit., p. 32.
29 Ibid., p. 35.
30 Ibid., p. 37.
31 Hegel, *Phenomenology*, paras 36-7.
32 Hegel, *Logic*, p. 28; see also p. 59.
33 Hegel, *The Logic of Hegel: Translated from the 'Encyclopaedia of the Philosophical Sciences'*, hereafter referred to by the short title *Encyclopaedia*, para. 166-9.
34 Hegel, *The Phenomenology*, para. 84.
35 This is Hegel's own self-understanding of these works. See Introduction to *The Logic*, p. 50. See also Taylor, *Hegel*, for his excellent analysis of the 'dialectic of

categories' and their movement from indeterminancy to absolute knowledge. It is also one of the conceptions which is taken or absorbed into the Marxian tradition, especially through Engels' intermediation. Our task, however, is not to engage in a repetitious analysis of this movement, but to concentrate on the 'dialectical method' as it informs Hegel's main concern – the actualization of freedom. It is in this that the secret of his sublimated/benign social theory lives.

36 Taylor, *Hegel*, p. 106.
37 See Hegel, *The Phenomenology*, para. 87.
38 Hegel, *The Logic*, p. 827.
39 Ibid., p. 842.
40 See Taylor, *Hegel*, pp. 98–100, see also pp. 225–6.
41 G. Lukács, *Hegel's False and His Genuine Ontology*, p. 96.
42 Hegel, *The Logic*, p. 101.
43 See Taylor, *Hegel*, p. 104.
44 The positing of a dual movement, i.e. of negativity and positivity, as Marcuse does (*Reason and Revolution*, pp. 123–128) is a little misleading. Hegel in fact, speaks about a dialectical *triplicity*: the first negation of immediate opposition posits unity within the difference, which becomes the second negation. This yields a *positive* self-identity *for* Reason (the third element or movement). Hegel states: 'The Notion itself is *for us*, the first instance, *alike* the universal that is in itself, *and* the negative that is for itself, *and* also the third, that which is both in and for itself; the *universal* that runs through all the moments of the syllogism; but the third is the conclusion in which the Notion through its negativity is mediated with itself and thereby posited for *itself* as the *universal* and the *identity of its moments*.' (Hegel, *Logic*, p. 837–8).
45 Hegel, *Logic*, p. 830.
46 Ibid.
47 Ibid., p. 105.
48 Ibid., p. 106.
49 Marcuse, *Reason and Revolution*, p. 124.
50 Hegel, *Logic*, p. 545.
51 Ibid. See also pp. 551–2 and p. 842.
52 Ibid. See p. 837.
53 Ibid., p. 28.
54 Ibid., p. 579, 578.
55 Hegel, *Phenomenology*, para. 21.
56 Hegel, *Logic*, p. 64.
57 Hegel, *Encyclopaedia*, para. 225. For Hegel, the teleological dynamic of civilization is quite distinct from that of nature. Nature's development is unproblematic – it moves from potentiality to realization in conformity with an organic principle that is outside the domain of time. Reason, though, uses the human world as its theatre, as its true stage for realization. Civilization is mediated by consciousness and will. As such, the distinction between theoretical and practical reason, which is dissolved under the aegis of Absolute Spirit, is reconstituted, not epistemologically, but teleo-ontologically. Judgements, proper, belong to the world of Notions – to self-conscious freedom and refer to ethical norms and aesthetics. The efficacy of perception still belongs to the domain of the natural. See Hegel, *Encyclopaedia*, para. 171.
58 See chapter one above 'Kant's critical anthropology and civil society'.
59 See Hegel, *Encyclopaedia*, op. cit., para. 162.
60 See chapter two above, especially 'Reason in Action – the Formation of *Sittlichkeit*'.

61 *Encyclopaedia*, para. 213.
62 Ibid., para. 160, [my emphasis].
63 See chapter two above esp. 'Reason in Action'.
64 Hegel, *Logic*, p. 515.
65 Ibid., pp. 515-16.
66 Hegel, *Encyclopaedia*, para. 160.
67 Hegel, *Logic*, pp. 755-74 and *Encyclopaedia*, para. 214.
68 Lukács, *Hegel's False and his Genuine Ontology*, p. 68. See also Hegel, *Logic*, p. 842.
69 Lukács, p. 71.
70 Hegel, *Philosophy of Right*, para. 257.
71 Ibid., para. 258.
72 Ibid., 272, see also para. 270 addition.
73 Hegel, *Logic*, p. 838.
74 Ibid., p. 840.
75 Ibid.
76 See *Philosophy of Right*, para. 258, and p. 43 above.
77 Hegel, *Philosophy of Right*, para. 258.
78 Ibid., para. 269 addition and para. 276 addition.
79 See N. Luhmann, *The Differentiation of Society*, esp. p. 79.
80 Hegel, *Philosophy of Right*, 276 addition.
81 Ibid., para. 188.
82 Ibid., para. 202-5.
83 Ibid., para. 201. See para. 201 addition.
84 Ibid., para. 207.
85 Ibid., para. 207 addition.
86 Ibid., para. 250.
87 Ibid., para. 205.
88 Ibid., para. 252.
89 Ibid., para. 253 and para. 152.
90 See Hegel, *Philosophy of Right*, para. 206-7, 258, 301, 302. The sovereign power, as representative of the expression of the free will of the state and as the embodiment of reasoned subjectivity, is mediated by the objective consideration of the state as a whole through the appointment of ministers and the public service, which in turn is mediated by the estates general which are grounded in the organic composition of the estates of society. Thus the estates are composed of two houses, one which is the 'family home' of the landed class, the other which is the home of the rational interests of civil society. The two houses function precisely in the syllogistic fashion of the intermediation – the upper house mediates the lower house with the crown whilst the lower house mediates the sovereign with civil society. Public affairs are brought into actual existence, particularly mediated by universality.
91 Taylor, *Hegel*, p. 444.
92 See Hegel, *Philosophy of Right*, paras 300-11. Hegel turns his back on direct suffrage, the cornerstone of the modern liberal-democratic state. For him, the membership of the modern Parliaments represent no one but themselves, removed from their multifaceted constituencies. They reduce politics to a game of self-interest, self-satisfaction and party power blocs. The obverse of this is the atomization and potential indifference of the electorate itself. Representatives too because of the complex nature of constituent life, cannot represent everybody; politics then becomes the strategy of access and lobby and electoral neutralization. Hegel's theory of the organic state, then, is not only a response

to the Jacobinization of politics, but also an answer to English utilitarianism, in which he uses the force of private interest dissolving the bonds of society by fracturing and segmenting the political identity which coheres, and is articulated, in the state.

93 Ibid., para. 301.
94 Ibid., para. 265.
95 Ibid., para. 261.
96 Ibid., para. 318.
97 Ibid., para. 257.
98 Hegel, *The Philosophy of History*, pp. 29–33.
99 Hegel, *Philosophy of Right*, para. 258.
100 Th. W. Adorno, *Negative Dialectics*, p. 309.

4 FROM THE POLITICS OF STRANGERS TO THE WORLD OF ESTRANGED NEEDS

1 K. Marx, 'On the Jewish Question', *Early Writings*, p. 220.
2 Marx, 'Critique of Hegel's Doctrine of the State', pp. 138–9.
3 Ibid., pp. 160–1.
4 Marx, 'Letter to Arnold Ruge' (Sept. 1843), p. 207. This is also somewhat phlegmatically reiterated in his 'A Contribution to the Critique of Hegel's Philosophy of Right. Introduction', pp. 245–7.
5 Ibid., p. 208.
6 Marx, 'Critique of Hegel's Doctrine of the State', pp. 125–6, 134 and 186.
7 Ibid., p.87.
8 Ibid., p. 143.
9 Ibid., p. 194, 192.
10 Ibid., p. 107.
11 Ibid., pp. 107–8.
12 See ibid., pp. 141, 158.
13 Ibid., pp. 185–6.
14 Ibid., p. 186.
15 Hegel, *Philosophy of Right*, para. 308. For consistency Knox's translation has been used, although it differs from the Livingstone and Benton translation which is given in the *Early Writings*.
16 Marx, 'Critique of Hegel's Doctrine of the State', p. 187.
17 See chapter one. In this work 'Civil Society as the Public: Kant's conception of modern political man'.
18 Marx, 'Critique of Hegel's Doctrine of the State', p. 191.
19 Ibid.
20 Ibid., p. 141.
21 Ibid, p. 188. See R. N. Hunt, *The Political Ideas of Marx and Engels*, pp. 83–84 for an interesting and illuminating, although brief discussion of Marx's emulation of democracy in the ancient world, particularly Periclean democracy. Here he analyses the democratization of the functional/administrative organization of society.
22 Marx, 'Critique of Hegel's Doctrine of the State', pp. 157–8.
23 See analysis to follow.
24 Marx comments that: 'If by the constitution we mean the universal, fundamental determinants of the rational will, it follows that every people (State) must have

this as its premise and that this premise must constitute its political credo.'
'Critique of Hegel's Doctrine of the State', p. 120.

25 Ibid., p. 148.

26 Ibid.

27 Ibid., p. 187.

28 Fehér points out that *overall* Marx views the period from 1789 to 1815 as a
bourgeois drama. 'On the Jewish Question' and *The Holy Family*, though, so
Fehér argues, stand out as non-mythological although unsystematic analyses
precisely because the French revolutionary period is not seen as homogeneous and
unambiguous. See Fehér, 'The French Revolutions as Models for Marx's
Conception of Politics'; François Furet, *Interpreting the French Revolution*, pp.
180 and 201. Whilst our analysis treats 'On Jewish Question' and *The Holy
Family* as a unit, it is important to note the difference of critical grounding that
separates them, that is the movement from a politically centred anthropology to
an historico-economically centred one that takes place after 1844. The analysis of
the French Revolution in *The Holy Family* is a minor part of it. As we shall see,
Marx's Kantian critique of the French revolutionary period overlaps into his more
mature writings. It again enters to inform his analysis of the 1848 Revolution and
its aftermath, the rise and fall of Louis Bonaparte. See below, chapter 6, 'The
Paradigm of Class Action'.

29 Marx and F. Engels, *The Holy Family*, p. 151.

30 Marx, 'On the Jewish Question', p. 234; see also Marx and Engels *The Holy
Family*, p. 148.

31 Marx and Engels, *The Holy Family* pp. 148-54; see also 'On the Jewish
Question', p. 222.

32 Marx and Engels, *The Holy Family*, p. 153. It is worth quoting the major part of
Marx's analysis:

> [Napoleon] was no terrorist with his head in the clouds. Yet at the same time he still
> regarded *state* as an *end in itself* and civil life only as a treasurer and his *subordinate* which
> must have no *will of its own*. He *perfected the Terror by substituting permanent war* for
> *permanent revolution* . . . If he despotically suppressed the liberalism of bourgeois society –
> the political idealism of its daily practice – he showed no more consideration for its essential
> *material* interests, trade and industry, whenever they conflicted with his political interests
> . . . In his home policy, too, he combated bourgeois society as the opponent of *the state
> which in his own person he still held to be an absolute aim in itself*. [Final emphasis mine]

33 See D. Howard, *The Development of the Marxian Dialectic*; Murray Wolfson,
Marx: Economist, Philosopher, Jew. Steps in the Development of a Doctrine;
Hunt, *The Political Ideas of Marx and Engels*.

34 Marx, 'On the Jewish Question', p. 239.

35 Ibid., p. 239.

36 Ibid., p. 218.

37 Ibid., p. 234.

38 Marx, 'A Contribution to the Critique of Hegel's *Philosophy of Right*.
Introduction', p. 256.

39 See Fehér and Heller, 'Class, Modernity, Democracy'.

40 This strategy then becomes the *raison d'être* for a part of the Marxian tradition
from Plekhanov to Kautsky and Althusser.

41 Marx, 'A Contribution to the Critique of Hegel's *Philosophy of Right*.
Introduction' p. 257. The imputation of both workerist and masculinist images is
deliberate on my part. The 'materialization' of social conflict de-emphasizes the
crucial component of a 'social imaginary' in mediating conflict, whilst the precise

location of conflict denies either theoretical or practical significance to other struggles such as the nineteenth-century women's movement. The *process of recognition* of social conflict by Marx results in a loss of politics (as a discourse concerning a radicalized conception of democracy) and a simultaneous conflation of the constituent features of society, a conflation that results (from late 1843 onwards) in a functionalization of society. The origin of the base-superstructure model belongs here, at the end of 1843.

42 Wellmer, *Critical Theory of Society*, p. 81. In the introductory note to the 'Economic and Philosophic Manuscripts 1844' Marx reflects on his earlier interpretation of Hegel. This work will be referred to as the 1844 *Manuscripts* hereafter.

43 Wellmer, *Critical Theory of Society*.

44 Marx now explicitly begins 'from the premises of political economy', 1844 *Manuscripts*, p. 322.

45 Markus, 'Four Forms of Critical Theory', p. 82.

46 Marx, 1844 *Manuscripts*, pp. 288 and 293.

47 Cohen, *Class and Civil Society*, esp. pp. 36-40.

48 Ibid., p. 38.

49 Markus, 'Four Forms of Critical Theory', pp. 82-3.

50 Marx, 1844 *Manuscripts*, p. 355.

51 The first manuscript, which covers wages of labour, profit of capital, rent of land and estranged labour, details Marx's first systematic analysis of political economy, especially that of Smith and Ricardo. The second manuscript, on the relationship of private property, continues this in an attempt to uncover the pure form of capitalist relations through a reading of the dialectic of recognition. The third manuscript is, in some ways, the most important and far-reaching. It deals with private property and labour, private property and Communism, need, production and the division of labour, money and a critical reflection on Hegel's dialectic and general philosophy, against the background of Feuerbach's generic self-affirmative anthropology.

52 See Marx, ibid., p. 389.

53 Marx, 1844 *Manuscripts*, p. 328.

54 Ibid., p. 352.

55 See Istan Mészáros, *Marx's Theory of Alienation*, esp. chapter 6.

56 Marx and Engels, *The Holy Family*, p. 149.

57 Marx, 1844 *Manuscripts*, p. 295.

58 Ibid., p. 287.

59 Ibid., p. 377.

60 Ibid., p. 378.

61 Ibid., p. 336.

62 Ibid., p. 341.

63 See 'Wages', *Collected Works*, esp. p. 426.

64 Marx and Engels, *The Communist Manifesto*, p. 82. See also p. 83 for Marx's argument that surrounds the famous phrase - 'all that is solid melts into air.'

65 Marx, 1844 *Manuscripts*, p. 348.

66 Ibid., p. 354.

67 Ibid., p. 356.

68 Marx, 'Critique of the Gotha Programme', p. 388.

69 Ibid., p. 331.

70 Marx, 1844 *Manuscripts*, p. 333.

71 Habermas, 'Between Philosophy and Science: Marxism as Critique', *Theory and Practice*, p. 218. This is the essence of Marx's commentary on the Silesian weavers

rising in 'Critical Notes on the Article "The King of Prussia and Social Reform by a Prussian"', pp. 402–20.
72 Ibid., p. 395.
73 Markus, 'Four Forms of Critical Theory', p. 84.

5   *THE GERMAN IDEOLOGY* AND THE PARADIGM OF PRODUCTION

1 Markus, 'Four Forms of Critical Theory', p. 85.
2 Marx, Preface to *A Contribution to a Critique of Political Economy*, p. 22.
3 Marx and F. Engels, *The German Ideology*, pp. 57–60.
4 Markus, 'Four Forms of Critical Theory', p. 92.
5 Ibid.
6 Marx and Engels, *The Communist Manifesto*, p. 79.
7 See C. Castoriadis, 'Value, Equality, Justice, Politics: From Marx to Aristotle, and from Aristotle to Ourselves', 260–339.
8 Marx and Engels, *The German Ideology*, p. 50
9 Ibid., see pp. 42, 50, 59.
10 Ibid., see pp. 59.
11 Ibid., p. 47.
12 Ibid., p. 48.
13 Ibid.
14 Ibid., p. 63.
15 Ibid., see also pp. 64, 122.
16 Ibid., pp. 51, 62.
17 Ibid., p. 54.
18 Ibid., pp. 43–6, 68–72.
19 Markus, 'Four Forms of Critical Theory', p. 85.
20 Marx, *Grundrisse*, 1973, pp. 85–88.
21 Ibid., p. 83.
22 Marx, *Capital*, vol. I, p. 90.
23 Marx, *Grundrisse*, p. 86.
24 Ibid., pp. 89, 91.
25 Ibid., pp. 99–100.
26 Ibid., p. 97.
27 Marx and Engels, *The German Ideology*, p. 57.
28 Ibid., p. 43.
29 The works of Alain Touraine, Jürgen Habermas, Anthony Giddens, and Pierre Bourdieu represent theoretical legacies that address this major legacy in Marx's work. Michel Foucault, through an interpretation of Nietzsche's notion of genealogy, provides another point of contact.
30 Marx and Engels, *The German Ideology*, p. 51.
31 Ibid.
32 Ibid., see pp. 51–4, pp. 68–9.
33 Ibid., p. 54.
34 Marx, *Grundrisse*, pp. 83–5, 103–5, 322.
35 Ibid., p. 706.
36 Ibid., p. 409.
37 Ibid., p. 325.
38 Marx and Engels, *The German Ideology*, p. 93.
39 Marx, *Grundrisse*, p. 101.

40 Marx's epistemological or metatheoretical reflections belong to the earlier 1843–4 period, although the much later (1897) 'Notes of Wagner' has elements of this, although from a completely different vantage point. Like a good Hegelian, Marx was aware that *method* was a misnomer – the construction of a theory and its relation to the world was itself a theoretical and practical enterprise. However, he rarely subjected his theorizing to epistemological metacritique in the same way that Hegel does in the *Logic*. The structure of his particular praxistic anthropology insulates the theory from such efforts. It is for this reason that he absorbs more Hegel than he bargained for.

41 Marx, *Grundrisse*, pp. 100–1.

42 Ibid., p. 101.

43 Ibid.

44 Ibid., p. 102.

45 Ibid., p. 103.

46 Ibid., p. 104.

47 The notion of autotelic labour activity refers to Marx's appropriation and redefinition of Aristotle's concept of praxis as an activity that has its end in itself, as distinct from *poiesis* which assumes some form of purposive teleology of externalizing ends. The Aristotelean notion of praxis in the most general form refers to the heterogeneous array of activities that constitute the well-lived life. In this sense, Marx uses it as a counterpoint against political economy's utilitarian devaluation of human activity to *work*, which itself denotes a certain type of devalued series of social relations. As we shall see, though, the critical intent of Marx's use of this Aristotelean based formulation is undercut by his own anthropology.

48 Marx, *Grundrisse*, p. 476.

49 Ibid., p. 831.

50 Arnason, 'Contemporary Approaches to Marx: Reconstruction and Deconstruction' p.65. See also Marx, *Grundrisse* pp. 489–490.

51 Marx, *Grundrisse*, p. 471.

52 Ibid., pp. 484–5.

53 Ibid., p. 491. See also, p. 182 where Marx talks about the social character of production.

54 Ibid., pp. 484–5.

55 Ibid., p. 483.

56 Ibid., p. 486.

57 Ibid., p. 498.

58 Ibid., p. 496.

59 Ibid., see pp. 153–9, 409–10, 473. These two things, freedom and the holistic anthropology, give Marx only a tangential relation to nineteenth-century Romanticism. His earlier arguments against the Jacobins join hands with those against the Romantic movement. Marx says, in relation to Romanticism, that 'it is as ridiculous to yearn for a return to that original fullness as it is to believe that with this complete emptiness history has come to a standstill. The bourgeois viewpoint has never advanced beyond this antithesis between itself and this romantic [and jacobin] viewpoint, and therefore the latter will accompany it as its legitimate antithesis up to its blessed end.' Ibid., p. 162.

60 Ibid., p. 105.

61 Ibid., p. 156.

62 Markus, 'Alienation and Reification in Marx and Lukács', p. 147. See Marx, *Grundrisse*, esp. pp. 153–9.

63 Marx, *Grundrisse*., p. 701. See Notebooks VI and VIII esp. p. 604 (pauperization), pp. 690-712 (the development of free time) and pp. 831-2 (the objectification of alienation).
64 Marx and Engels, *The German Ideology*, p. 93.
65 Marx, *Grundrisse*, p. 706.
66 Ibid., p. 704.
67 Marx, *Capital* vol. I, p. 102.
68 G. A. Cohen, *Karl Marx's Theory of History: A Defense*, esp. chapter 2.
69 Marx, the 1859 'Preface', pp. 20-1.
70 Marx, *Capital* vol. I, p. 290; see also p. 133.
71 Habermas, *Knowledge and Human Interests*, esp. 'The Idea of the Theory of Knowledge as Social Theory', pp. 46-63.
72 Marx, 1859 'Preface', p. 121.
73 Marx, 'The Results of the Immediate Progress of Production', p. 1053.
74 Wellmer, 'Communication and Emancipation', p. 234. See also his 'The Latent Positivism of Marx's Philosophy of History', in his *Critical Theory of Society*, pp. 67-119.
75 Habermas, *Knowledge and Human Interests*, chapter 2, esp. pp. 31-7.
76 Ibid. and p. 43-53.
77 Marx, *Early Writings*, p. 355.
78 The technical mastery of nature through the application of purposive rules entails that the productive metabolism between nature and humankind and society and the individual is neither instinctive nor merely physiological, it is planned and purposeful, either through direct labour-activity or through the development of instruments of labour (technologies). The latter are merely

    thing[s] or a complex of things, which the worker interposes between himself and the object of his labour and which serves as a conductor, directing his activity onto that object. He makes use of the mechanical, physical and chemical properties of some substances in order to set them to work on other substances as instruments of his power, and in accordance with his purposes. (*Capital* vol. I, p. 285).

    Marx makes this clear in his famous distinction between the bee and the architect in the chapter on the 'Labour Process', in *Capital* vol. I, p. 284.
    As indicated by Heller ('Paradigm of Production: Paradigm of Work' and Castoriadis ('Technique', in Soper and Ryle (tr.) *Crossroads in the Labyrinth*, this is also related to Marx's reformulation of Aristotle's conceptualization of human activity in terms of *poiesis* (self-creation), *techné* (technical manipulation) and *logos* (the truth reason).
79 G. Markus, 'The Human Use of Man-made Objects', p. 25; see also pp. 16-22 and 27-9.
80 Marx, *Capital* vol. I, p. 289.
81 Ibid., pp. 289-301.
82 Ibid., p. 124.
84 Ibid., p. 286.
85 Marx, 1859 'Preface', p. 21. This is reiterated in almost the same way in *Capital* vol. III; 'Distribution Relations and Production Relations', especially pp. 883-4.
86 See Marx, 1858 'Preface', p. 20 and *Capital* vol. I, p. 286. See also *Capital* vol. III, chapters 48 and 51.
87 Marx, *Capital*, vol. I, p. 135.
88 Markus, 'Four Forms of Critical Theory', p. 92.
89 Marx, *Capital*, vol. I, chapters 25-31, especially 'The General Law of Capitalist

Accumulation', pp. 775-7 and 'The Historical Tendency of Capitalist Accumulation', pp. 928-9.

90 See for example Marx's discussion of Money, ibid., pp. 227-32 and p. 769.

91 Ibid., p. 344.

92 Ibid., pp. 274, 874.

93 Kant, 'Conjectural Beginning of Human History', p. 59.

94 Marx, *Capital*, vol. I, p. 548; see also p. 280.

95 Ibid., p. 450.

96 See *Capital*, vol. I, p. 280.

97 Cohen, *Class and Civil Society*, p. 153.

98 H. G. Backhaus, 'On the Dialectics of the Value Form'.

99 Markus, 'Alienation and Reification in Marx and Lukács', p. 142. See also his 'Four Forms of Critical Theory', esp. pp. 88-9.

100 See Hegel, *The Logic*, p. 575. The phrase 'friend of science' comes from Hegel's coy recognition of his supporters in the 1816 'Foreword' to 'The Doctrine of the Notion' in the *Logic*. He calls them 'those friends of this science'. Marx is a self-stated detractor of Hegel's metaphysics, but this, as our interpretation suggests, is only half the story. However, the importance of Marx's second encounter with Hegel should not be *over*-emphasized. There are those who place this Hegelian influence at the centre of Marx's *Capital* and view it as the secret methodology behind the categories of wage-labour/capital. (They also see *Capital* itself as the pivot, core and *magnum opus* of Marx's works as a whole.) See, for example, Winfield, 'The Logic of Marx's *Capital*'; Zeleny, *The Logic of Marx*; Levine, *Dialogue within the Dialectic*; the 'Value-Form Analysis' of Backhaus, Eldred, Roth, et al., *Thesis Eleven*, 1, 4, 7 1980, 1982, 1983; and the series of papers by Meikle, Ruben, Arthur, Fisk and Mepham contained in J. Mepham and D. H. Ruben (eds) *Issues in Marxist Philosophy*, vol. I. I argue, though, that several things are occurring simultaneously. Marx's 'return' to Hegel is contextualized by a systematic development of an independent although internally tension-ridden theory of society that predates the 'return'. This theory development also intersects, criticizes and absorbs three other currents – nineteenth-century socialist thought, the tradition of political economy and positivism. These currents remain largely unexamined in this work. However, Marx's earlier encounter with Hegel functions as the more important, formative and lasting legacy that helps to structure the critique of capitalism that he wishes to generate. All of these elements combine and coalesce in *Capital* in an incomplete synthesis. My basic argument is that the legacy of the early encounter with Hegel and the methodological concerns which determine the later return (and is itself influenced by the first) together combine to undermine and deflect Marx's critique of capitalism and his construction of a critical theory and anthropology of modernity. The first and second encounters constitute Marx's own 'negative dialectic'. However there is another residual reliance on Hegel which is neither dependent on an ontologizing metatheory, nor on the anthropological reduction inherent in the problematic of the productive forces. This is found in the subsumption model and has its positive place as an 'interpretative dialectic' in Marx's 'hidden imaginary'.

101 Cohen, *Class and Civil Society*, p. 150.

102 Ibid.

103 Ibid., p. 154.

104 Backhaus, 'On the Dialectic of the Value-Form', p. 101. Here he quotes in part from R. Banfi, 'Problem und *Scheinprobleme ben Marx und im Marxismus*' in: *Folgen eines theorie*, Frankfurt/M 1967 S.172

105 Marx, 'Preface' to the first edition of *Capital* vol. I, p. 90.
106 Ibid., p. 92.
107 Markus, 'Four Forms of Critical Theory', p. 91.
108 To be sure, the more accurate word here is 'constitutes', given language theory from Wittgenstein to Habermas, but my point in using 'reflect' is to show the internal logic of Marx's paradigm.
109 The movement of the dialectic of categories in Hegel's *The Logic* is from the essence's unfolding of the categories through appearance to the essential relation of the Absolute to itself. In some way Marx mimics this, but begins with appearance as *schein*, as illusion (which comes before Essence in *The Logic*) and thus 'moves' from illusory being to actuality.
110 Backhaus, 'On the Dialectic of the Value-Form', op. cit., p. 104, paraphrasing Marx.
111 Marx, *Capital*, vol. I, p. 169.
112 Ibid., pp. 88, 221.
113 Ibid., p. 137; pp. 141–56. See also Marx on the representation/self-understanding of political economy (capitalism as law), ibid., p. 174, footnote 34; p. 771; (labour) p. 142, footnote 18; and pp. 172–75 including footnote 33. Marx repeats an insight stated in the 'Introduction' to *Grundrisse* concerning the redefinition of labour as universal value (wealth) creating activity, together with its utilitarian and protestant component (pp. 104–6). This last point is left underdeveloped by Marx because of conceptual constraints, but is analysed in its own right, as is well known, from a different theoretical standpoint (that is, the cultural rationalization of patterns of rational action) by Max Weber in his 1904 *The Protestant Ethic and the Spirit of Capitalism*.
114 Marx, *Capital*, vol. I, p. 165.
115 Ibid., p. 99; see also note 25, p. 161. Backhaus' comment here is useful. As he points out:

> The commodity becomes a 'thing-like' other, but nevertheless remains itself in its other non-being . . . [It] is itself and at the same time its other: money. It is therefore the identity of and non-identity. The commodity is equal in essence to money and at the same time different from it. ('On the Dialectic of the Value-Form', pp 110–9.)

116 Marx, *Capital*, vol. I, p. 148.
117 Ibid., p. 150.
118 Ibid., p. 132. See also p. 150 and pp. 293–5 'The Valorisation Process'. The use-value is, for Marx 'a piece of natural material adapted to human needs by means of a change in its form' (p. 287). Labour is objectified through the use-value as purposeful activity; as the universal human element that is expressed in each use-value and connects them as heterogeneous objects. Through this labour the use-value, so Marx argues, has both qualitative and quantitative aspects. It is determined by both the type of need that is being satisfied as well as the (socio-historically conditioned) level of technical sophistication of the concrete labouring activity that is required for its production. Marx terms this, logically yet disastrously, 'socially necessary labour-time'. (See ibid., p. 129; and 'The Dual Character of the Labour Embodied in Commodities', pp. 131–7; and p. 293.) It is logical in two senses; first, as a critical notion it enables Marx to conceptualize the rationalization of time under capitalism and secondly, it is merely an extension of the redefined anthropology of labour that appears from 1859 onward. This is what is disastrous about it. It is precisely the technicist reduction of labour to a positivist interpretation concerning units of time. As we

shall see, this has dire consequences for the *political* nature of his critique of capitalism.

119 Ibid., p. 128:

> If we disregard the use-values of commodities, only one property remains, that of being the products of labour . . . If we make abstraction from its use-value, we abstract also from the material constituents and forms which make it a use-value . . . All its sensuous characteristics are extinguished . . . With the disappearance of the useful character of the products of labour the useful character of the kinds of labour embodied in them also disappears; this in turn entails the disappearance of the different concrete forms of labour. They can no longer be distinguished, but are all together reduced to the same kind of labour, human labour in the abstract . . . There is nothing left of [the products of labour] but the same phantom-like objectivity; they are merely congealed quantities of homogeneous human labour, i.e. of human labour-power expended without regard to its form of expenditure. All these things now tell us is that human labour-power has been expended to produce them, human labour is accumulated in them. As crystals of this *social* substance, which is common to them all, they are values – commodity values.

120 See Marx's analysis of Aristotle's *Nichomachean Ethics*, in *Capital* vol. I, pp. 151-2. Castoriadis' reading of Marx in 'Value, Equality, Justice, Politics'.

121 Capital, vol. I p. 168; see also pp. 173–174.

122 Ibid., p. 167.

123 Backhaus, 'The Dialectic of the Value-form', p. 107.

124 Marx, *Capital* vol. I, p. 151.

125 Ibid., p. 175.

126 Marx, Sixth Thesis in 'Theses on Feuerbach', p. 122, [my emphasis].

127 We argue, in contradistinction to Jean Cohen in *Class and Civil Society*, that there are two processes rather than one occurring which short-circuit Marx's critical theory of class. In Marx, class conflict is not absorbed under the auspices of the systemic reproduction of capital, as such. It is either *circumscribed* by the functional analysis (which belongs to the social form), or it is *annihilated* altogether from the vantage point of the material content. Cohen fails to take seriously Marx's conceptual distinction between material content and social form, as well as the significant changes in his arrangement of the concepts, particularly between *Grundrisse* and *Capital*. In her effort to trace the systemic absorption of the parameters and nature of class conflict she collapses them into one another, and by so doing fails to account for the emergence of a *limited* notion of conflict in *Capital* itself, that is, trade unionism. Her problem can be traced back to her interpretation of Marx's value-form. She interprets it as a representation only and not as a socially constitutive class relation (p. 157). This is not only a problem of formalism, but also a problem of Marx's reliance on Hegel's metaphysics and his own construction of a reductive anthropology. For Cohen the distinction between exchange-value and value

> need not imply an essence/appearance dialectic. Nor does the discussion of forms of value refer to a substance that appears through these forms. Instead the dynamic relation between the forms of exchange and production categories comprises a dynamic moving from abstract to concrete determinations of a system logic that forms a totality of significations requiring no external substance as referent. (p. 158).

The movement of thought from the abstract to the concrete, however, pertains more accurately to the logic of *Grundrisse*, a text that ought not, as Markus argues correctly, to be collapsed into *Capital*. The defetishizing critique uncovers both a totality of social relations and an anthropologically construed substance, through the movement of thought from necessary appearances to the realm of the essence (the sphere of production). It is here that the notion of totality not only conditions Marx's formalism (as Cohen herself intimates), but also enters in an emphatic sense to guide the structure and logic of Marx's argumentation in *one* specific direction. Moreover, it relies on an external referent (substance) for explanatory force which propels his analysis in the direction that Cohen suggests. Each interpretation minimizes the role of representational forms, even if these both inform and are situated at the core of Marx's analysis in *Capital*. Value, understood as a self-constituting social relation, is also constituted representationally, but this is already restricted by a reductive and utilitarian interpretation of the anthropology of labour.

128 Marx, *Capital* vol. I, p. 344.
129 Ibid., pp. 388–9. Marx's analysis of surplus-value is guided by the notion of time. This problem-complex is explored in later literature by E. P. Thompson, 'Time, Work-Discipline and Industrial Capitalism'; J. Le Goff, *Time, Work and Culture in the Middle Ages*; Z. Bauman, *Memories of Class*, esp. chapters 2 and 3.
130 Marx, *Capital* vol. I, pp. 412–13.
131 Ibid., p. 408.
132 Ibid.
133 Ibid., p. 413.
134 Ibid., p. 416.
135 Ibid., p. 339.
136 Ibid., p. 270.
137 Ibid., pp. 549–50.
138 It is not surprising that if this devaluation were taken seriously, Marx's notion of socialism would amount to no more than the working class's right to participate in the social wealth that it produced through the form of increased wages. Yet this is the extent of social conflict, inherent in Marx's notion of society as a functional whole located in the sphere of production, constituted by two classes. Wages are in this both the necessary forms of *appearance* and the necessary forms of *struggle* under his construction of the labour theory of value. See the isolated fragment 'The Sale and Purchase of Labour-Power and the Trade unions', published as an appendix to the Penguin edition of *Capital* vol. I, pp. 1066–75.
139 Ibid., p. 165; [my emphasis].
140 Ibid., p. 171.
141 Ibid., p. 172.
142 The similarity between the definition of alienation in the 1844 *Manuscripts* and the analysis of fetishism in *Capital* belongs to the sense of disconnection of the producers from the product of their labour. In *Capital* vol. I Marx argues:

> The mysterious character of the commodity-form consists . . . simply in the fact that the commodity reflects the social characteristics of men's own labour as objective characteristics of the products of labour themselves, as the socio-natural properties of these things. Hence it also reflects the social relation of the producers to the sum total of labour as a social relation between objects, a relation which exists apart from and outside the producers. (pp. 164–65)

143 Ibid., p. 165.
144 Ibid., 'The Valorisation Process', pp. 293–306.

145 Ibid., p. 209, [my emphasis]. I have altered the last phrase of the quotation in accordance with the translator's own note. The main text reads 'between the conversion of things into persons and the conversion of persons into things'. See also 'The Trinity Formula', in *Capital* vol. III, esp. p. 815. For an analysis of the genesis and meaning of reification in Marx, see Markus, 'Alienation and Reification in Marx and Lukács', esp. pp. 149–54.

146 See Marx, *Capital*, vol. I, chapters 13, 14 and 15 on 'Co-operation', 'The Division of Labour and Manufacture', and 'Machinery and Large-Scale Industry', pp. 439–639.

147 Marx, *Capital*, vol. III, p. 820 [my emphasis].

148 See *Capital* vol. I, pp. 602, 637–8 and *Capital* vol. III, pp. 878 and 884.

149 L. Colletti, 'Bernstein and the Marxism of the Second International', pp. 45–108; J. Habermas, 'Introduction: Some Difficulties in the Attempt to Link Theory and Praxis', in the *Theory and Practice*, pp. 1–40; A. Heller, 'The Legacy of Marxian Ethics Today'.

6   THE PARADIGM OF CLASS ACTION

1 Marx, *Capital*, vol. III, pp. 885–6.

2 Cohen, *Class and Civil Society*, pp. 177–183. See also 'Why Class' by Jean Cohen and Dick Howard in *Between Labour and Capital*, ed. P. Walker, (Boston, South End Press 1979), pp. 67–95.

3 Marx, *Capital*, vol. III, p. 886.

4 There are two separate and competing approaches in contemporary historiography and social theory that explicitly merge from this paradigm and which address this question. They are represented respectively in the works of E. P. Thompson and Alain Touraine.

5 Marx and Engels, *The Communist Manifesto*, p. 79.

6 Both Habermas and Castoriadis point to a competing paradigm of class action in Marx's work. See Habermas, *Knowledge and Human Interest*, esp. chapter 3; and Castoriadis, 'On The History of the Workers' Movement', esp. p. 14.

7 Marx and Engels, *The German Ideology*, p. 94.

8 Ibid., p. 64.

9 Ibid., pp. 65–6.

10 See not only the historical writings, but also *The German Ideology*, *The Communist Manifesto* and the aforementioned *Capital*. Marx's interpretation of class belongs initially to the 1843 'Introduction'.

11 Cohen, *Class and Civil Society*, pp. 89–90.

12 Marx and Engels, *The German Ideology*, p. 43.

13 Cohen, *Class and Civil Society*, p. 122.

14 Ibid., p. 116.

15 Marx, 'The Eighteenth Brumaire of Louis Bonaparte', p. 214.

16 Marx, 'The Class Struggles in France', p. 76. For the notions of dramaturgy in Marx see H. Redner, 'Character, Action and Representation in Marx', (unpublished manuscript 1984); S. S. Prawer, *Karl Marx and World Literature*, esp. chapter 8 and 9; J. P. Riquelme, '*The Eighteenth Brumaire of Karl Marx* as Symbolic Action'. A decade later Marx invokes the dramaturgical notion of politics when writing about the Crimean War. See his *The Eastern Question*: *A Reprint of Letters Written 1853–1856 Dealing with the Events of the Crimean War*, especially Letter 58. 'War with Russia', p. 324.

17 The proletariat throughout these works is viewed by Marx as a homogeneous group united by the conditions of wage-labourers. In this, he does not depart from his position in his early works, which includes the subject/object universalism. The caste of state officials, according to Marx constitutes its existence under the auspices of the state. It includes, foremostly, the 'artificial' caste of bureaucrats, who exist alongside the army, the police, the judiciary, ministers and, in the context of French Catholic society, priests. See 'The Class Struggles in France', p. 113, and 'The Eighteenth Brumaire of Louis Bonaparte', p. 245.

18 The petty bourgeoisie is constituted of small proprietors, shop keepers, traders and crafts people. See 'The Class Struggles in France', p. 65.

19 The bourgeoisie, according to Marx, is constituted of two fractions – the financial aristocracy and the industrial bourgeoisie. The *financial aristocracy* is composed of bankers, stockbrokers, owners of mass transport, of extractive industries and landed property. They constitute the period of early capitalist accumulation in which the countryside predominated over the city. The *industrial bourgeoisie* is made up of manufacturers and commercial traders and constitutes contemporary capitalism with its predominance of the city. See Marx, 'The Class Struggles in France', pp. 36–9, 88; 'The Eighteenth Brumaire', pp. 173–4, 215–24.

I will allow Marx's description of the lumpenproletariat to speak for itself, even though it is in the context of his analysis of the class basis of Bonaparte's rule.

> Alongside decayed *roués* of doubtful origin and uncertain means of subsistence, alongside ruined and adventurous scions of the bourgeoisie, there were vagabonds, discharged soldiers, discharged criminals, escaped galley slaves, swindlers, confidence tricksters, *lazzaroni*, pickpockets, sleight-of-hand experts, gamblers, *macquereaux*, brothel-keepers, porters, pen-pushers, organ-grinders, rag and bone merchants, knife- grinders, tinkers and beggars: in short the whole indeterminate fragmented mass, tossed backwards and forwards which the French call *la bohème* . . . [The lumpenproletariat is] the scum, the leavings, the refuse of all classes. ('The Eighteenth Brumaire of Louis Bonaparte, p. 197).

See also 'The Class Struggles', pp. 52–3. They are a class, unlike the peasantry which is only a 'pseudo-class', because they act in their own right. They are no longer presented as the 'passive scum', mere tools for intrigue (*The Communist Manifesto*) but are capable of an instrumentalist volition. The Bonapartist experience caused Marx to have a more subtle view.

20 Marx, 'The Eighteenth Brumaire', pp. 238–9.

21 See also S. Aronowiz, 'The Professional-managerial Class or Middle Strata', pp. 215–17.

22 See Marx, 'The Class Struggles in France', p. 72.

23 G. Lukács, *History and Class Consciousness*.

24 See A. O. Hirschman, *The Passions and the Interests: Political Arguments for Capitalism before its Triumph*, (New Jersey, Princeton University Press, 1977).

25 See chapter four of this work, especially 'The Tensions and Directions of the 1843 Works'.

26 Fehér, 'The French Revolutions as Models for Marx's Politics', p. 61.

27 See Prawer, *Karl Marx and the World of Literature*.

28 Malvolio is Olivia's steward in Shakespeare's *Twelfth Night; or What you Will*. A puritan by heart and nature he is the object of a farcical ruse in which he is left bewildered and looking ridiculous. For Marx's commentary on 'the bourgeois farce' see 'The Class Struggles in France', p. 56 and 'The Eighteenth Brumaire', pp. 169–70.

29 For Marx, the Bonapartist regime is a monster: 'The work of art the bourgeois

republic, has not been distorted into a monstrous shape by the black magic of Circe. It has lost nothing but the appearance of respectibility. The parliamentary republic contained present day France in finished form. It only required a bayonet thrust for the abscess to burst and the monster to spring forth before our eyes.' ('The Eighteenth Brumaire', p. 235).

30 See 'The Civil War in France', pp. 228, 232.
31 See 'The Class Struggles in France', p. 43, and 'The Eighteenth Brumaire', p. 157.
32 See 'The Class Struggles in France', p. 72, and 'The Eighteenth Brumaire', p. 244.
33 See 'The Class Struggles in France', pp. 43-6, 58-9, and 'The Eighteenth Brumaire', p. 171.
34 Marx, 'The Eighteenth Brumaire', pp. 197-8.
35 Ibid., pp. 234-5.
36 Marx, 'The Class Struggles in France', pp. 121-8.
37 Ibid., p. 71.
38 Ibid., p. 127.
39 Ibid., pp. 56, 134-5; and 'The Eighteenth Brumaire', p. 193; see also 'The Chartists', esp. p. 264; 'The Civil War in France', section III.
40 Marx, 'The Class Struggles in France', pp. 65, 84 and 104: 'The Civil War in France', section III, especially pp. 209-17.
41 Marx, 'The Civil War in France', pp. 207-17.
42 Ibid., p. 213. Marx's commitment to the pedagogical self-enlightenment of the actors involved also becomes the basis for his critique of the Jacobins who intruded into the heady days of the Commune, See ibid., p. 219.
43 Marx, 'The Eighteenth Brumaire', pp. 186, 237-43.
44 Ibid., pp. 199, 247.
45 Ibid., pp. 235, 193-5; 'The Class Struggles in France', pp. 101, 127-34.
46 Marx, 'The Eighteenth Brumaire', p. 236.
47 Ibid., see pp. 243-5 where Marx states:

an enormous bureaucracy with gold braid and fat belly is the 'Napoleonic idea' which is the most congenial of all to the second Bonaparte . . . The political centralization that modern society requires can arise only on the debris of the military and bureaucratic government machinery . . . *still burdened with its opposite feudalism.'* (Addition from footnote 53 emphasized).

49 Cohen, *Class and Civil Society*, p. 118. See also Marx, 'The Class Struggles in France'.
50 Marx, 'The Eighteenth Brumaire', pp. 176-7.
51 Marx, 'The Class Struggles in France', p. 96.
52 Marx, 'The Eighteenth Brumaire', p. 96.
53 Marx, 'The Class Struggles in France', p. 128.
54 Marx, 'The Eighteenth Brumaire', pp. 238-44. See also 'The Class Struggles in France', pp. 72-4 (the peasant's vote) and 115-19 (materialist interpretation of their actions).
55 Marx, 'The Eighteenth Brumaire', p. 239. See also 'The Class Struggles in France', pp. 85-6.
56 Cohen, *Class and Civil Society*, p. 122.
57 See Max Weber, *Economy and Society*, vol. I. pp. 31-8, 212-16.
58 Max Weber, 'The Social Psychology of the World's Religions', p. 280.
59 Marx, 'The Eighteenth Brumaire', p. 244.

60 Ibid., p. 149.
61 Marx, 'The Class Struggles in France', pp. 111–12.
62 Marx, 'The Eighteenth Brumaire', p. 238.
63 Ibid.
64 Ibid., p. 241.

7   MARX AGAINST MARX

1 Marx, *Capital* vol. III, p. 824.
2 Marx and Engels, *The German Ideology*, p. 93.
3 Castoriadis, 'The Imaginary Institution of Society', pp. 6–45.
4 Marx's contextualization of the problematic of consciousness is the aspect that Castoriadis takes over and transforms into the imaginary significations.
5 Marx, 1844 *Manuscripts*, p. 354.
6 Ibid., p. 335.
7 Ibid., p. 360.
8 Ibid., p. 361.
9 Ibid., pp. 353–4.
10 Ibid., p. 354.
11 Ibid., p. 391.
12 Ibid.
13 Ibid., p. 390.
14 Marx and Engels, *The German Ideology*, p. 51.
15 Ibid.
16 Ibid., p. 47.
17 Ibid., p. 51. Marx's attitude towards mythological knowledge is presented a little more cautiously in the 1857 'Introduction' to *Grundrisse* (pp. 110–11). In that work it is seen as evidence of an unfettered ability of humankind for imagination. Marx argues that the mythologically construed patterns of artistic and cultural creation count as norms and models of beauty to a modern world encased in technological consciousness. As technological consciousness advances it demolishes the creative nature of mythology which becomes only the memory of a world to which humankind cannot return. All of this does not diminish Marx's own tendency to positively attribute a maturation process to technological consciousness itself, and by so doing, view the world of antiquity as the precocious childhood of humanity.
18 Marx and Engels, *The German Ideology*, p. 86.
19 Habermas represents one current that develops this in his quasi-transcendentally constituted paradigm of communication. See his 'What is Universal Pragmatics?' and 'Historical Materialism and the Development of Normative Structures', in his *Communication and the Evolution of Society*, pp. 1–68, and 95–129 respectively.
20 Markus, 'The Human Use of Man-made Objects', p. 34.
21 Ibid., p. 35.
22 The subsumption model, elucidated in the so-called missing sixth chapter of *Capital* vol. I, 'The Results of the Immediate Process of Production' was written it seems between June 1863 and December 1866. Originally listed for inclusion in vol. I, Marx subsequently put it aside for reasons that are still unknown. We can only surmise that he recognized the aforementioned difference between it and the *project of Capital*, vol. I (as a critique of capitalism presented as a functional totality). For a theoretically stilted interpretation of this piece see E. Mandel's

'Introduction' to the Penguin edition of *Capital* vol. I, pp. 943–7, in which edition 'The Results' also appears as an appendix.

23 Marx and Engels, *The German Ideology*, p. 68.
24 Ibid. This aspect is in part taken up later, as we have seen, in Marx's analysis of pre-capitalist societal formations (1857–8).
25 Ibid.
26 Ibid.
27 Marx, 'The Results', p. 1044.
28 The social configuration of functions and the reduction of labour to time, which denotes 'the very necessity of first transforming individual products or activities into exchange-values, into *money*', confronts the producers, so Marx argues in 'The Results', 'as a *capitalist* arrangement that is *imposed* on them'. See Marx, *Grundrisse*, p. 158 and 'The Results', p. 1052.
29 Ibid., p. 1019.
30 Ibid., p. 1025.
31 Ibid., p. 1035.
32 This is the unexpected result of Marx's formulation. He is, however, unable to explore this nexus fully because he has absorbed political economy's definitions of use-value and property. Through these he homogenizes the heterogeneity of needs, activities and cultural orientations. We shall return to this in the final section.
33 Marx, 'The Results', p. 1021 [my emphasis]. This is also stated by Marx in *Grundrisse*:

> This pulling away of the natural ground from the foundations of every industry and this transfer of its conditions of production outside itself, into a general context – hence the transformation of what was previously superfluous into what is necessary, as an historically created necessity – it is the tendency of capital. (p. 528, see also p. 532)

34 Marx, 'The Results', p. 1020 (see also pp. 1025–31).
35 Ibid., p. 1021.
36 Ibid., see also pp. 1010–12.
37 Ibid., pp. 1012–14.
38 Marx, 'The Eighteenth Brumaire', p. 146.
39 This is recognized in the 1844 *Manuscripts*, particularly the first, and is developed as late as the *The Theories of Surplus Value*.
40 See for example 'The Results', particularly Marx's analysis of the relation between productive and unproductive labour, pp. 1039, 1046–9, and wages pp. 1062–4.
41 This problematic of the socially created hermeneutical circle is the aspect that Castoriadis later transforms, via Aristotle, into the notion of the proto-value, and traces back as the core problem in Marx's critique of capitalism in his essay 'Value, Equality, Justice, Politics: From Marx to Aristotle and from Aristotle to Ourselves'. He argues that:

> we find ourselves trapped in the same circle: what is the worth of this worth, the value of this value? What is the merit of this merit, and the dignity of this dignity? Or, to put it another way: why is *this* value value? This circle is the circle of Proto-value, which is to say of the institution of a nuclear imaginary social signification; and it is impossible to account for it, to give reasons for it. (pp. 296–7)

Weberian sociology also confronts this problem and addresses it through the notion of the meaning of social action. For other contemporary approaches see

Heller, *A Theory of History*, and Habermas' formulation of the paradigm of communicative action in 'What is Universal Pragmatics?', *Communication and the Evolution of Society*.

42 Marx, *Grundrisse*, p. 196.

43 Ibid., p. 1031. See also pp. 1028-34 and the *Grundrisse*, p. 106 and p. 232. Here, once again, Marx notices the phenomenon of Protestantism and its 'alliance' with capitalism. However, he fails to take it seriously. Following Weber (*The Protestant Ethic and the Spirit of Capitalism*) and N. Elias (*The Civilising Process* esp. vol. II), the emergence of Protestantism in the Occident is a major point of reference for the analysis of the transition to the period of real subsumption.

44 See Marx, *Grundrisse*, p. 191. See also 'The Results', p. 1020.

45 Marx, *Grundrisse*, p. 163 and pp. 199, 221-3; 'On the Jewish Question', p. 239.

46 Marx, *Grundrisse*, p. 145 and p. 168.

47 Ibid., p. 221.

48 Ibid.

49 Ibid., p. 144, see also p. 167.

50 Ibid., p. 187. Marx adds, 'Their interrelation is to be examined.' The point of our argument is that it is *never* really examined by him.

51 Ibid., pp. 216, 226. The movement from the second to the third levels introduces Marx's confusion between a socially rational mechanism for distribution, the market, and the reification of social relations which appears under capitalism. The confusion leads him to conflate the dimensions of symmetrically structured mechanisms of exchange (which include the market) and emancipation from reified forms of power. This conflation offers only one solution for Marx's notion of post-capitalist society – the abolition of the market. This solution, though, is problematic, to say the least. It means that Marx was unable to address the question of the *nature* of distribution in complex societies, a failure which eventually led some of his interpreters to try to replace the market with authoritarian structures and institutions. I have discussed this aspect of Marx (and of the Leninist appropriation of socialism) in my review of Radaslav Selucky *Marxism, Socialism, Freedom: Towards a General Democratic Theory of Labour-Managed Systems'*. See also Fehér, Heller, Markus, *Dictatorship over Needs*.

52 In the course of Marx's analysis of the formation of the capitalist epoch, he momentarily and only inadvertently transcends the paradigm of production. As Arnason argues, Marx's analysis of the pre-capitalist community points to this feature in his work. See J. P. Arnason, 'Contemporary Approaches to Marx, Reconstruction and Deconstruction', esp. pp. 61-67.

53 Marx, *Grundrisse*, p. 236.

54 Ibid., p. 105.

55 Ibid., pp. 162-3.

56 Ibid., p. 142.

57 Ibid., p. 161 [my emphasis].

58 Marx's comments on barter are suggestive of this interpretation. On the level of exchanges he notes that:

In the crudest barter when two commodities are exchanged for one another, each is first equated with a symbol which expresses their exchange value, e.g. among certain Negroes on the West African coast, = x bars . . . (The bar has a merely imaginary existence, just as in general, a relation can obtain a particular embodiment and become individualised only by means of abstraction). (Ibid., p. 142).

This partial and incomplete form of exchange indicates, for Marx, that exchange does not

> yet dominate production as a whole, but concerns only its superfluity and is hence more or less *superfluous* (like exchange itself); an accidental enlargement of the sphere of satisfactions, enjoyments (relations to new objects). It therefore takes place at only a few points (originally at the borders of the natural communities, in their contact with strangers), is restricted to a narrow sphere, and forms something which passes production by, is auxiliary to it; dies out just as much by chance as it arises. The form of barter in which the overflow of one's own production is exchanged by chance for that of others' is only the *first* occurrence of the product as exchange value in general, and is determined by accidental needs, whims etc. (Ibid., pp. 204–5).

59 Ibid., p. 222–4, esp. Marx's analysis of greed and money.
60 Castoriadis, 'The Imaginary Institution of Society'.
61 Marx, *Grundrisse*, p. 154.
62 Marx, *Grundrisse*, pp. 156–7, see also 225–6.
63 Markus, 'Alienation and Reification in Marx and Lukács', p. 152.
64 See Marx, 'The Results', pp. 1037–8.
65 Ibid., p. 1040. See also pp. 1041 and 1044.
66 Ibid., p. 1041.
67 Ibid., pp. 1024, 1035–8, 1052–6.
68 Markus, 'Alienation and Reification', p. 152.
69 Marx, 'The Results', p. 1037.
70 Ibid., p. 1040.
71 Ibid., p. 1062.
73 Ibid., p. 194.
74 Ibid., p. 1064, see also p. 1063.
75 See Marx, *The Eastern Question*, especially, pp. 277–8, 315–23, 453, 483–8. See also *Grundrisse*, pp. 409–10.
76 See, for example, Marx, *The Eastern Question*, p. 189.
77 Despite the sketchy and brief remarks addressed to them in *The German Ideology* where these non-class forms are found in the main (although some are developed more fully in later works), each is mediated by a notion of property, which, to be sure, foreshadows its critical centrality in 'Communal and autotelic totality', but in a way that moves it in an opposite direction from that model derived from the paradigm of production.
78 Marx, *The Eastern Question*, esp. pp. 29, 78, 80–1, 356, 452, 482–91, 525. See also, 'The Secret Diplomatic History of the Century', esp. sections V and VI. Both of these works deal with aspects of the Crimean War, either from a historical point of view ('The Secret Diplomatic History') or from a 'day-by-day' account and reflection upon it. The interesting aspect of the letters that constitute the *Eastern Question* as well as 'The Secret Diplomatic History of the Century' is that Marx's disdain for Russia is conceptualized in normative terms that point towards a positive assessment of the West's development of a political civil society with formalized rights, and a negative assessment of Russia's reliance upon the state to achieve both a limited and bureaucratized modernization and unification.
79 Marx and Engels, *The German Ideology*, p. 89.
80 See our discussion of Habermas, Castoriadis and The Budapest School, particularly Agnes Heller, in the Introduction to this work. See also Markus, '"Ideology" and its ideologies: Lukacs and Goldmann on Kant'. For a history

and analysis of this expressivist current see Taylor, *Hegel*, pp. 3–50; 'Interpretation and the Sciences of Man'; 'Theories of Meaning'; pp. 281–302. For a slightly more epistemological vantage point see his 'Understanding in Social Science' and the reply by Richard Rorty and discussion between Taylor, Rorty and Dreyfuss in *Review of Metaphysics*, Sept. 1980, pp. 3–55. See also Ricoeur, *Hermeneutics and the Human Sciences*; Habermas, *Knowledge and Human Interests*, including the postscript in *Philosophy of the Social Sciences*, 3, 1973, pp. 157–89; H. G. Gadamer, *Philosophical Hermeneutics*. Richard Rorty, *Philosophy and the Mirror of Nature*.

8   RUNNING ON TIME

1 Agnes Heller, 'Marx and the Liberation of Humankind', pp. 358–62.
2 Markus, 'The Human Use of Man-made Objects', p. 53.
3 Marx, 'The Civil War in France', p. 233.
4 Marx, *Grundrisse*, p. 110.
5 Marx, *Capital* vol. I, p. 128.
6 Ibid., p. 129.
7 Castoriadis, 'Value, Equality, Justice, Politics', p. 262.
8 Ibid., p. 266.
9 Marx, *Capital*, vol. I, p. 129.
10 Markus, 'The Human Use of Man-made Objects', p. 54.
11 Marx, *Capital*, vol. I, pp. 134, and 137. This current is expressed most explicitly in Marx's 'Notes on Wagner'.
12 Mark Poster, 'Introduction', in Baudrillard *Mirror of Production*, pp. 18–19.
13 J. Baudrillard, *For a Critique of the Political Economy of the Sign*, p. 133. Baudrillard's critique of Marx in both this work and in *The Mirror of Production*, pinpoints the 'fetish' of production in Marx's work, yet mimics the worst features of this. He simply turns the tables and invokes the sign-form as the 'independent variable', and by so doing, ends with a similar 'one-dimensionality' thesis to that of Marcuse in *One-Dimensional Man*.
14 See Chapter 7.
15 This, it seems, is the logic of Castoriadis' position, and the converse of Heller's notion of a democratic ethics that structures all types of social action, and Fehér's critiques of the 'barbarous' side of modernity. See: Castoriadis: 'Socialism and Autonomous Society'; 'From Ecology to Autonomy'; 'The Crisis of Western Societies'; 'Reflections on "Rationality" and "Development"'. The thread that connects these articles is Castoriadis' notion of imaginary significations, the rational/non-rational self-conceptions of a society that lie at the heart of its various institutional practices, and are rooted in its (society's) cultural and intellectual history.

Heller: *A Theory of History*; *The Power of Shame*, an anthology containing three essays that address the problem of the relation between socio-cultural formation, values and ethics. The main essays in this context are 'The Power of Shame' and 'Everyday Life, Rationality of Reason, Rationality of Intellect'. These add a culturalist reading to her more 'formal' formulations of democratic politics contained in her other writings, for example 'The Moral Maxims of Democratic Politics'; F. Fehér: 'In the Bestiarium (A Contribution to the Cultural Anthropology of "Real Socialism"'; 'Review of Pin Yathay *L'Utopie Meurtrière*'. Fehér analyses one of the 'bestiarium' of modernity, 'real existing socialism' or the dictatorship over needs (the other two are traditional liberal capitalism and Nazism). He traces it back to the Enlightenment's unresolved tensions between politics, ethics, epistemology and anthropology, through which filter a specific Jacobin image of modern man. See also 'The Frozen Revolution'.

Bibliography

Adorno, Th. W., *Negative Dialectics*, tr. E. B. Ashton, (London, Routledge and Kegan Paul, 1973).

Althusser, L., *For Marx*, (Harmondworth, Penguin, 1969).

Arendt, H., *The Human Condition*, (Chicago, University of Chicago Press, 1958).
Lectures on Kant's Political Philosophy, ed. R. Beiner, (Chicago, University of Chicago Press, 1982).

Arnason, J. P., 'Contemporary Approaches to Marx, Reconstruction and Deconstruction', *Thesis Eleven*, 9, 1984, pp. 52-73.
'Review of *Zur Rekonstruktion des Historischen Materialismus*', *Telos*, 39, Spring 1979, pp. 201-18.

Aronowitz, S., 'The Professional-managerial Class or Middle Strata', in *Between Labour and Capital*, ed. Pat Walker, (Boston, South End Press, 1979).

Auxter, T., 'Kant's conception of the private sphere', *The Philosophical Forum*, XII, 4, Summer 1981, pp. 295-310.

Avineri, S., 'Labour, Alienation and Social Classes in Hegel's *Realphilosophie*', in *The Legacy of Hegel*, ed. J. J. O'Mally, (The Hague, Martinus Nijhoff, 1973).

Axinn, S., 'Rousseau versus Kant on the Concept of Man', *The Philosophical Forum*, XII, 4, Summer 1981, pp. 348-55.

Backhaus, H. G., 'On the Dialectics of the Value-Form', *Thesis Eleven*, 1, 1980, pp. 99-120.

Baudrillard, J., *For a Critique of the Political Economy of the Sign*, (St Louis, Telos Press, 1981),
The Mirror of Production, (St Louis, Telos Press, 1975).

Bauman, Z., *Memories of Class*, (London, Routledge and Kegan Paul, 1982).

Benhabib, S., 'The Development of Marx's Thought and the Hermeneutics of Critique: Comments on George Markus' "Four Forms of Critical Theory - Some Theses on Marx's Development"', *Thesis Eleven*, 5/6, 1982, pp. 289-97.
'The "Logic" of Civil Society: A Reconsideration of Hegel and Marx', *Philosophy and Social Criticism*, 8, 2, Summer 1981, pp. 149-66.
'Modernity and the Aporias of Critical Theory', *Telos*, 49, Fall 1981, pp. 38-59.

Booth, W. J., 'Reason and History: Kant's other Copernican Revolution', *Kant Studien*, 74, 1, 1983, pp. 56–71.

Cassirer, E., *Rousseau, Kant, Goethe*, J. Gutmann, P.O. Kristeller and J. H. Randell, (Princeton, Princeton University Press, 1970).

Castoriadis, C., 'The Crisis of Western Societies', *Telos*, 53, Fall 1982, pp. 17–28.

'Facing the War', *Telos*, 46, Winter 1980–81, pp. 43–61.

'From Ecology to Autonomy', *Thesis Eleven*, 3, 1981, pp. 7–22.

'From Marx to Aristotle, from Aristotle to Us', *Social Research*, 1978, pp. 667–738.

'The Imaginary Institution of Society', in *The Structural Allegory*, ed. J. Fekete (Minneapolis, University of Minnesota Press, 1984).

Modern Capitalism and Revolution, (London, Solidarity pamphlet, 1974).

'On the History of the Workers' Movement', *Telos*, 30, Winter 1976–7, pp. 3–42.

'Reflections on "Rationality" and "Development"', *Thesis Eleven*, 10/11, 1985, pp. 18–36.

'Socialism and Autonomous Society', *Telos*, 43, Spring 1980, pp. 91–105.

'Value, Equality, Justice, Politics: From Marx to Aristotle and from Aristotle to Ourselves', in *Crossroads in the Labyrinth*, tr. Kate Soper and Martin H. Ryle, (Brighton, The Harvester Press, 1984), pp. 260–337.

Cohen, G. A., *Karl Marx's Theory of History: A Defense*, (Oxford, Clarendon Press, 1978).

Cohen, J. L., *Class and Civil Society: The Limits of Marxian Critical Theory*, (Amherst, The University of Massachusetts Press, 1982).

Cohen, J. L. and Howard, D., 'Why Class?', *Between Labour and Capital*, ed. P. Walker (Boston, Southend Press, 1979), pp. 67–95.

Colletti, L., 'Bernstein and the Marxism of the Second International', in *From Rousseau to Lenin*, (London, New Left Books, 1972).

Marxism and Hegel, (London, New Left Books, 1973).

Descombes, V., *Modern French Philosophy*, (London, Cambridge University Press, 1980).

Elias, N., *The Civilising Process*, (London, Basil Blackwell, 1978–1983); vol. I: *The History of Manners*; vol. II: *State Formation and Civilization*.

Engels, F., 'On social relations in Russia', in Marx-Engels Reader, ed. R. C. Tucker (New York, Norton and Co., 1972).

Fehér, F., 'The French Revolutions as Models for Marx's Conception of Politics', *Thesis Eleven*, 8, 1984, pp. 59–76.

'The Frozen Revolution', (unpublished manuscript, 1978).

'In the Bestiarium (A Contribution to the Cultural Anthropology of "Real Socialism")', *Praxis International*, 2, 3, Oct. 1982, pp. 268–83.

'Review of Pin Yathay, *L'Utopie Meurtrière*', *Telos*, 56, Summer 1983, pp. 193–205.

Fehér, F. and Heller, A., 'Class, Modernity, Democracy', *Theory and Society*, 12, 2, 1983, pp. 211–44.

Fehér, F., Heller, A. and Markus, G., *Dictatorship over Needs*, (Oxford, Basil Blackwell, 1983).

Furet, F., *Interpreting the French Revolution*, (Cambridge, Cambridge University Press, 1981).

Gadamer, H. G., *Philosophical Hermeneutics*, tr. D. E. Linge (Berkeley, University of California Press, 1976).

Gay, P., The Enlightenment. *An Interpretation* vol. II, (London, Weidenfeld and Nicholson, 1969).

Geraets, Th. F., *Rationality Today*, (University of Ottawa Press, 1979).

Giddens, A. (ed.), *Positivism and Sociology*, (London, Heinemann Educational Books, 1974).

Goldman, L., *Immanuel Kant*, (London, New Left Books, 1967).

Habermas, J., *Communication and the Evolution of Society*, tr. Thomas McCarthy, (Boston, Beacon Press, 1979).
'The Gauss Lectures' (Series of six lectures given at Princeton University, 1971; unpublished manuscripts).
'Hannah Arendt's Communication Concept of Power', *Social Research*, 44, 1, 1977, pp. 3–24.
'History and Evolution', *Telos*, 39, Spring 1979, pp. 5–44.
The Theory of Communicative Action, vol. I, tr. Thomas McCarthy, (Boston, Beacon Press, 1984).
Knowledge and Human Interests, tr. J. J. Shapiro (London, Heineman Educational Books, 1972).
Legitimation Crisis, tr. Thomas McCarthy, (Boston, Beacon Books, 1975).
'Modernity versus Postmodernity', *New German Critique*, 22, Winter 1981, pp. 3–14.
'A Postscript to *Knowledge and Human Interests*', *Philosophy of the Social Sciences*, 3, 1973, pp. 157–89.
Theory and Practice, tr. J. Viertel, (London) Heineman Educational Books, 1974).

Hegel, G. W. F., *Hegel's Philosophy of Right*, tr. T. M. Knox (London, Oxford University Press, 1979).
Hegel's Science of Logic, tr. A. V. Miller (London, George Allen and Unwin Ltd., 1969).
The Logic of Hegel: Translated from the Encyclopaedia of the Philosophical Sciences tr. William Wallace, (Oxford, Clarendon Press, 1892).
Phenomenology of Spirit, tr. A. V. Miller, (Oxford, Clarendon Press, 1979).
The Philosophy of History, tr. J. Sibree (New York, Dover Publications, 1956).

Heiman, G., 'The Sources and Significance of Hegel's Corporatist Doctrine', in *Hegel's Political Philosophy: Problems and Perspectives*, ed. Z. A. Pelcjynski, (Cambridge, Cambridge University Press, 1971), pp. 111–35.

Heller, A., 'The Emotional Division of Labour Between the Sexes: Perspectives on Feminism and Socialism', Part I: *Social Praxis*, 7, 3/4, pp. 205–18; Part III: *Thesis Eleven*, 5/6, 1982, pp. 59–73.
'The Legacy of Marxian Ethics Today', *Praxis International*, 1, 4, January 1982, pp. 346–64.

'Marx and the Liberation of Humankind', *Philosophy and Social Criticism*, 3/4, 1982, pp. 358-62.

'The Moral Maxims of Democratic Politics', *Praxis International*, I, 1, April 1981, pp. 39-48.

'Paradigm of Production: Paradigm of Work': *Dialectical Anthropology*, 6, 1, August 1981, pp. 71-9.

The Power of Shame, (London, Routledge and Kegan Paul, 1985).

A Theory of History, (London, Routledge and Kegan Paul, 1982).

Herder, J. G. in *On The Origins of Language*, (New York, Frederick Unger Publishing Co., 1966).

Hirschman, A. O., *The Passions and the Interests*: *Political Arguments for Capitalism Before its Triumph*, (Princeton, Princeton University Press, 1981).

Honneth, A., 'Work and Instrumental Action: On the Normative Basis of Critical Theory', *Thesis Eleven*, 5/6, 1982, pp. 162-84.

Howard, D., *The Development of the Marxian Dialectic*, (Carbondale Southern Illinois University Press, 1972).

'From Marx to Kant: The Return of the Political', *Thesis Eleven*, 8, 1984, pp. 77-91.

'Kant's Political Theory: The Virtue of his Vices', *Review of Metaphysics*, 34, 2, December 1980, pp. 325-350.

Hunt, R. N., *The Political Ideas of Marx and Engels*, (London, Macmillan, 1975), vol. I: *Marxism and Totalitarian Democracy 1818-1850*.

Kant, I., 'Conjectural Beginning of Human History', in *Kant on History*, ed. Lewis White Beck (Indianapolis, Bobbs-Merrill Publishing Co., 1983).

Anthropology From a Pragmatic Point of View, tr. M. J. Gregor, (The Hague, Martinus Nijhoff, 1974).

The Critique of Judgement, tr. James Creed Meredith (Oxford, Clarendon Press, 1964).

Critique of Practical Reason and Other Writings in Moral Philosophy, tr. Lewis White Beck (Chicago, University of Chicago Press, 1949).

'The End of all Things', in Beck (ed.) *Kant on History*.

'Idea for a Universal History from a Cosmopolitan Point of View', in (ed.) *Kant on History*.

Immanuel Kant's Critique of Pure Reason, tr. Norman Kemp Smith (London, Macmillan, 1978).

'The Metaphysics of Morals', *Kant's Political Writings*, (ed.) Hans Reiss tr. N. B. Nisbet (Cambridge, Cambridge University Press, 1970).

'On the Common Saying: "This May be True in Theory, but it does not Apply in Practice"', in Reiss (ed.) *Kant's Political Writings*.

'What is Enlightenment?', in Beck (ed.) *Kant on History*.

'What is Orientation in Thinking?', in Kant *Critique of Practical Reason and Other Writings on Moral Philosophy*.

Kojève, A., *Introduction to the Reading of Hegel*, (Ithaca, Cornell University Press, 1980).

Le Goff, J., *Time, Work and Culture in the Middle Ages*, (Chicago, University of Chicago Press, 1980).

Levine, N., *Dialogue within the Dialectic*, (London, George Allen and Unwin, 1984).

Luhmann, N., *The Differentiation of Society*, (New York, Columbia University Press, 1982).

Lukács, G., *Hegel's False and his Genuine Ontology*, tr. David Fernbach (London, Merlin Press, 1978).

History and Class Consciousness, (London, Merlin Press, 1971).

Mandel, E., 'Introduction', in Marx *Capital*, vol. I, (Harmondsworth, Penguin, 1979).

Marcuse, H., *One Dimensional Man*, (London, Abacus, 1972).

Reason and Revolution: *Hegel and the Rise of Social Theory*, (London, Routledge and Kegan Paul, 1973).

Markus, G., 'Alienation and Reification in Marx and Lukács', *Thesis Eleven*, 5/6, 1982, pp. 139-61.

'Four Forms of Critical Theory – some Theses on Marx's Development', *Thesis Eleven*, 1, 1980, pp. 78-93.

'The Human Use of Man-made Objects: Marxian Materialism and the Problem of Constitution' (unpublished MS), now published as 'Practical-social Rationality in Marx – A Dialectical Critique', parts I and II, *Dialectical Anthropology*, part I: 4, 1979, pp. 255-88; part II: 5, 1980, pp. 1-31.

'"Ideology" and its ideologies: Lukács and Goldmann on Kant, *Philosophy and Social Criticism*', 8, 2, Summer 1981, pp. 125-47.

Marx, K., *Capital*, vol. I, tr. Ben Fowkes (Harmondsworth, Penguin, 1979).

Capital, vol. III, (Moscow, Progress Publishers, 1971).

'The Chartists', in *Surveys from Exile*, ed. David Fernbach (London, Pelican, 1973).

'The Civil War in France', in *The First International and After*, ed. David Fernbach (Harmondsworth, Penguin, 1974).

'The Class Struggles in France', in Fernbach (ed.) *Surveys from Exile*.

'A Contribution to the Critique of Hegel's *Philosophy of Right*. *Introduction*', in Marx *Early Writings*, tr. Rodney Livingstone and Gregor Benton (London, Penguin, 1981).

'Critical Notes on the Article "The King of Prussia and Social Reform by a Prussian"', in *Early Writings*.

'Critique of Hegel's Doctrine of the State', in Marx *Early Writings*.

'Critique of the Gotha Programme', in *The Marx-Engels Reader*, ed. R. C. Tucker (New York, Norton and Co., 1972).

Early Writings, tr. Rodney Livingstone and Gregor Benton (London, Penguin, 1981).

The Eastern Question: *A Reprint of Letters Written 1853-1856 Dealing with the Events of the Crimean War*, eds. Eleanor Marx Aveling and Edward Aveling, (London, Frank Cass and Co. Ltd., 1969).

'Economic and Philosophical Manuscripts (1844)', in Marx *Early Writings*.

'The Eighteenth Brumaire of Louis Bonaparte', in Fernbach (ed.) *Surveys from Exile*.

Grundrisse, tr. Martin Nicolaus, (Harmondsworth, Penguin, 1973).

'Letter to Arnold Ruge', in Marx *Early Writings*, p. 207.

'Notes on Wagner', in *Karl Marx: Texts on Method*, ed. and tr. Terrrell Carver (Oxford, Basil Blackwell, 1975), pp. 179-219.

'On the Jewish Question', in Marx *Early Writings*.

'The Poverty of Philosophy', in *Collected Works*, vol. 6 (London, Lawrence and Wishart, 1976).

Preface to *A Contribution to the Critique of Political Economy*, (Moscow, Progress Publishers, 1970).

'The Results of the Immediate Process of Production', Appendix to Marx, *Capital*, vol. I.

'The Sale and Purchase of Labour-power and the Trade unions', Appendix to Marx, *Capital*, vol. I, pp. 1066-1075.

'Secret Diplomatic History of the Century', in *The Unknown Karl Marx*, ed. Robert Payne, (New York, New York University, 1972).

The Theories of Surplus Value, vol. I-III, (London, Lawrence and Wishart, 1967-72).

'Theses on Feuerbach', in Marx and Engels *The German Ideology*.

'Wages', *Collected Works*, (London, Lawrence and Wishart, 1976), vol. 6: 1845-48, pp. 415-37.

Marx, K. and Engels, F., *The Communist Manifesto*, (Harmondsworth, Penquin, 1967).

The German Ideology, ed. C. J. Arthur (New York, International Publishers, 1974).

The Holy Family or Critique of Critical Criticism, (Moscow, Progress Publishers, 1980).

Mepham, J. and Ruben, D. H. (eds), *Issues in Marxist Philosophy*, (Brighton, Harvester Press, 1979), vol. I: *Dialectics and Method*.

Mészáros, I., *Marx's theory of Alienation*, (London, Merlin Press, 1970).

Ollman, B., *Alienation: Marx's Conception of Man in Capitalist Society*, (Cambridge, Cambridge University Press, 1971).

Pitte, F. P. van de, *Kant as Philosophical Anthropologist*, (The Hague, Martinus Nijhoff, 1971).

Plant, R., 'Hegel and Political Economy - I', *New Left Review*, 103, 1977, pp. 79-9.

'Hegel and Political Economy - II', *New Left Review*, 104, 1977, pp. 103-13.

The Positivist Dispute in German Sociology, tr. and ed., G. Adey, and D. Frisby, (London, Heinemann Educational Books, 1976).

Poster, M., 'Introduction', in Baudrillard *The Mirror of Production*.

Prawer, S. S., *Karl Marx and World Literature*, (Oxford, Clarendon Press, 1976).

Rader, M., *Marx's Interpretation of History*, (New York, Oxford University Press, 1979).

Redner, H., 'Character, Action and Representation in Marx', (unpublished manuscript, 1984).

Riedel, M., 'Nature and Freedom in Hegel's *Philosophy of Right*', *Hegel's*

Political Philosophy: Problems and Perspectives, ed. Z. A. Pelczynski, (Cambridge, Cambridge University Press, 1971), pp. 136-51.

'Transcendental Politics? Political Legitimacy and the Concept of Civil Society in Kant', *Social Research*, 48, 3, Autumn 1981, pp. 588-613.

Ricoeur, P., *Hermeneutics and the Human Sciences*, (Cambridge, Cambridge University Press, 1981).

Riquelme, J. P., 'The *Eighteenth Brumaire* of Karl Marx as Symbolic Action', *History and Theory*, 19, 1, 1980, pp. 58-72.

Ritter, J., *Hegel and the French Revolution*, tr. Richard Dien (Winfield, Cambridge, Mass. The MIT Press, 1982).

Rorty, R., *Philosophy and the Mirror of Nature*, (Princeton, Princeton University Press, 1980).

Rousseau, J. J., *The Social Contract*, (Harmondsworth, Penguin, 1974).

Rundell, J., 'Radaslav Selucky, *Marxism, Socialism, Freedom: Towards a General Democratic Theory of Labour-Managed Systems*', *Te•₊s*, 50, Winter 1981-2, pp. 228-34.

Shell, S. Meld, *The Rights of Reason: A Study of Kant's Philosophy and Politics*, (Toronto, University of Toronto Press, 1980).

Taylor, C., *Hegel*, (Cambridge, Cambridge University Press, 1975).

'Interpretation and the Sciences of Man', *Review of Metaphysics*, 25, 1, 77, Sept. 1971, pp. 3-51.

'Theories of Meaning', *Man and World*, 13, 1980, pp. 281-302.

'Understanding in Social Science', *Review of Metaphysics*, 34, 1, Sept. 1980, pp. 25-38.

Thompson, E. P., 'Time Work-Discipline and Industrial Capitalism', *Past and Present*, 38, December 1967, pp. 56-97.

Thompson, J. B. and Held, D. (eds), *Habermas: Critical Debates*, (London, The Macmillan Press Ltd, 1982).

Touraine, A., *The Self-Production of Society*, tr. Derek Coltman (Chicago, University of Chicago Press, 1977).

The Voice and the Eye, tr. Allan Duff (Cambridge, Cambridge University Press, 1981).

Wartenburg, T. E., 'Poverty and Class Theory in Hegel', *Philosophy and Social Criticism*, 8, 2, Summer 1981, pp. 167-82.

Weber, M., *Economy and Society*, vol. I, ed. G. Roth and C. Wittich, (Berkeley, University of California Press, 1978).

The Protestant Ethic and the Spirit of Capitalism, tr. Talcott Parsons (London, Unwin University Books, 1971).

'The Social Psychology of the World's Religions', in *From Max Weber*, ed. H. H. Gerth and C. Wright Mills (London, Routledge and Kegan Paul, 1970).

Weil, E., 'The Hegelian Dialectic', in *'The Legacy of Hegel': The Marquette Hegel Symposium, 1970*, ed. J. J. O'Malley (The Hague, Nijhoff, 1973), pp. 49-64.

Wellmer, A., 'Communication and Emancipation: Reflections on the Linguistic Turn in Critical Theory', in *On Critical Theory* ed. John O'Neill

(London, Heineman, 1971).

Critical Theory of Society, tr. J. Cumming (New York, Seabury Press, 1974).

'Reason, Utopia and the Dialectic of Enlightenment', *Praxis International*, 3, 2, July 1983.

Winfield, R., 'The Logic of Marx's Capital', *Telos*, 27, Spring 1976, pp. 111–39.

Wolfson, M., *Marx: Economist, Philosopher, Jew. Steps in the Development of a Doctrine*, (New York, St Martin's Press, 1982).

Zeleny, J., *The Logic of Marx*, (Oxford, Basil Blackwell, 1980).

Index